D0154435

Bloom's Modern Critical Interpretations

The Adventures of
  Huckleberry Finn
The Age of Innocence
Alice's Adventures in
  Wonderland
All Quiet on the
  Western Front
Animal Farm
The Ballad of the Sad
  Café
Beloved
Beowulf
Black Boy
The Bluest Eye
The Canterbury Tales
Cat on a Hot Tin
  Roof
Catch-22
The Catcher in the
  Rye
The Chronicles of
  Narnia
The Color Purple
Crime and
  Punishment
The Crucible
Cry, the Beloved
  Country
Darkness at Noon
Death of a Salesman
The Death of Artemio
  Cruz
The Diary of Anne
  Frank
Don Quixote
Emerson's Essays
Emma
Fahrenheit 451
A Farewell to Arms
Frankenstein
The Glass Menagerie
The Grapes of Wrath

Great Expectations
The Great Gatsby
Gulliver's Travels
Hamlet
Heart of Darkness
The House on Mango
  Street
I Know Why the
  Caged Bird Sings
The Iliad
Invisible Man
Jane Eyre
The Joy Luck Club
Julius Caesar
The Jungle
King Lear
Long Day's Journey
  into Night
Lord of the Flies
The Lord of the
  Rings
Love in the Time of
  Cholera
Macbeth
The Man Without
  Qualities
The Merchant of
  Venice
The Metamorphosis
A Midsummer Night's
  Dream
Miss Lonelyhearts
Moby-Dick
My Ántonia
Native Son
Night
1984
The Odyssey
Oedipus Rex
The Old Man and the
  Sea
On the Road

One Flew Over the
  Cuckoo's Nest
One Hundred Years of
  Solitude
Othello
Persuasion
Portnoy's Complaint
Pride and Prejudice
Ragtime
The Red Badge of
  Courage
Romeo and Juliet
The Rubáiyát of Omar
  Khayyám
The Scarlet Letter
A Separate Peace
Silas Marner
Slaughterhouse-Five
Song of Solomon
The Sound and the
  Fury
The Stranger
A Streetcar Named
  Desire
Sula
The Sun Also Rises
The Tale of Genji
A Tale of Two Cities
"The Tell-Tale Heart"
  and Other Stories
Their Eyes Were
  Watching God
Things Fall Apart
The Things They
  Carried
To Kill a Mockingbird
Ulysses
Waiting for Godot
The Waste Land
Wuthering Heights
Young Goodman
  Brown

Bloom's Modern Critical Interpretations

Anne Frank's
The Diary of Anne Frank
New Edition

Edited and with an introduction by
Harold Bloom
Sterling Professor of the Humanities
Yale University

BLOOM'S
LITERARY CRITICISM
An imprint of Infobase Publishing

Bloom's Modern Critical Interpretations:
Anne Frank's *The Diary of Anne Frank*—New Edition
Copyright © 2010 by Infobase Publishing
Introduction © 2010 by Harold Bloom

All rights reserved. No part of this publication may be reproduced or utilized in any form
or by any means, electronic or mechanical, including photocopying, recording, or by any
information storage or retrieval systems, without permission in writing from the publisher.
For more information contact:

Bloom's Literary Criticism
An imprint of Infobase Publishing
132 West 31st Street
New York NY 10001

Library of Congress Cataloging-in-Publication Data

Scholarly Look at *The Diary of Anne Frank*
Anne Frank's the *Diary of Anne Frank* / edited and with an introduction by Harold
Bloom. — New ed.
    p. cm. — (Bloom's Modern Critical Interpretations)
  Includes bibliographical references and index.
  ISBN 978-1-60413-868-9 ((hardcover : alk paper) : alk. paper) 1. Frank, Anne,
1929–1945. Achterhuis. 2. Holocaust, Jewish (1939–1945)—Psychological aspects.
  3. Holocaust, Jewish (1939–1945)—Influence. I. Bloom, Harold. II. Title.
DS135.N6F7356 2010
940.53'18092—dc22   2010003472

Bloom's Literary Criticism books are available at special discounts when purchased in
bulk quantities for businesses, associations, institutions, or sales promotions. Please call
our Special Sales Department in New York at (212) 967-8800 or (800) 322-8755.

You can find Bloom's Literary Criticism on the World Wide Web at
http://www.chelseahouse.com.

Contributing editor: Pamela Loos
Cover design by Alicia Post
Composition by Bruccoli Clark Layman
Cover printed by IBT Global, Troy NY
Book printed and bound by IBT Global, Troy NY
Date printed: May 2010
Printed in the United States of America

10 9 8 7 6 5 4 3 2 1

This book is printed on acid-free paper.

All links and Web addresses were checked and verified to be correct at the time of
publication. Because of the dynamic nature of the Web, some addresses and links may
have changed since publication and may no longer be valid.

Contents

Editor's Note   vii

Introduction   1
   Harold Bloom

The Authenticity of the Diary   5
   David Barnouw

Twisting the Truth: *The Diary of Anne Frank*   29
   Deborah E. Lipstadt

Postmarked from Amsterdam:
   Anne Frank and Her Iowa Pen Pal   37
   Shelby Myers-Verhage

Writing Herself Against History:
   Anne Frank's Self-Portrait as a Young Artist   45
   Rachel Feldhay Brenner

Anne Frank: The Redemptive Myth   75
   Judith Goldstein

Revisiting the *Diary:* Rereading Anne Frank's Rewriting   83
   Nigel A. Caplan

Reconsidering Anne Frank: Teaching the Diary
   in Its Historical and Cultural Context   101
   Pascale Bos

How to Tell a True Ghost Story:
     The Ghost Writer and the Case of Anne Frank   111
     Aimee Pozorski

Finding Meaning in the Diaries of Anne Frank   125
     Wayne Howkins

The Child Victim as Witness
     to the Holocaust: An American Story?   143
     Mark M. Anderson

Chronology   163

Contributors   167

Bibliography   169

Acknowledgments   173

Index   175

Editor's Note

My Introduction centers upon a remarkable fantasy of Nathan Zuckerman's, in Philip Roth's *The Ghost Writer*, where a young woman, Amy Bellette, suffers the delusion of believing that *she* is Anne Frank.

Since *The Diary of Anne Frank* is more of an historical emblem than a literary work, many of the essays in this volume are necessarily exercises in morality and history. Others examine attacks on the diary's authenticity.

HAROLD BLOOM

Introduction

ANNE FRANK's *THE DIARY OF ANNE FRANK*

In Philip Roth's accomplished novel, *The Ghost Writer*, there is a remarkable fantasy that could be called "The Return of Anne Frank." Nathan Zuckerman, the portrait of the artist Philip Roth as a young man, stays overnight at the home of the Jewish novelist Lonoff (taken by some as a version of Bernard Malamud, but actually a composite figure). Also in the house is a mysterious young woman, Amy Bellette. In Nathan's imagination she is the actual Anne Frank, who somehow survived the death camp and now lives incognito as Lonoff's assistant. Amy denies having read Anne Frank's *Diary*, which inspires Nathan to an eloquent description of the book:

> She was a marvelous young writer. She was something for thirteen.
> It's like watching an accelerated film of a fetus sprouting a face,
> watching her mastering things . . . Suddenly, she's discovering
> reflection, suddenly there's portraiture, character sketches,
> suddenly there's long intricate eventful happening so beautifully
> recounted it seems to have gone through a dozen drafts. And no
> poisonous notion of being *interesting* or *serious*. She just is.

This remains the most accurate tribute to the *Diary*, at least that I've encountered. A child's diary, even when she was *so* natural a writer, rarely could sustain literary criticism. Since *this* diary is emblematic of hundreds of thousands of murdered children, criticism is irrelevant. I myself have no special qualifications except as a literary critic. One cannot write about Anne Frank's *Diary* as if Shakespeare, or Philip Roth, is the subject. Jewish cultural survival is a complex problem, involving as it does issues of memory,

1

discontinuity, and bad faith. I cannot see any authentic relationship between the poignance the *Diary* necessarily had acquired and the burdens of American Jewish culture. Therefore I will confine my own observations on the *Diary* to my Editor's Note, where I consider the reactions of others, from Bruno Bettelheim, an equivocal healer, to Cynthia Ozick, a distinguished writer of fictions. In the remainder of this Introduction, I will return to Nathan Zuckerman's vision of Anne Frank, largely because as a literary critic I judge Philip Roth to be one of the handful of novelists now at work in the United States who will matter most to posterity. The author of *Zuckerman Bound, Operation Shylock, Sabbath's Theater,* and *American Pastoral* is of the eminence shared by Thomas Pynchon, Don DeLillo, and Cormac McCarthy. Roth's sense of Anne Frank, or rather of her image, should help the rest of us to clarify our own relation to that image.

In *Reading Myself and Others* (1985), Roth, interviewed by Hermione Lee, remarks that: "It wasn't easy to see that Amy Bellette as Anne Frank was Zuckerman's own creation." He later expanded upon this difficulty:

> I had trouble getting that right. When I began, in the third person, I was somehow *revering* the material. I was taking a high elegiac tone in telling the story of Anne Frank surviving and coming to America. I didn't know where I was going so I began by doing what you're supposed to do when writing the life of a saint. It was the tone appropriate to hagiography. Instead of Anne Frank gaining new meaning within the context of my story, I was trying to draw from the ready store of stock emotions that everybody is supposed to have about her. It's what even good actors sometimes will do during the first weeks of rehearsing a play—gravitate to the conventional form of presentation, cling to the cliche while anxiously waiting for something authentic to take hold. In retrospect, my difficulties look somewhat bizarre, because just what Zuckerman was fighting against, I was in fact succumbing to—the officially authorized and most consoling legend. I tell you, no one who later complained that in *The Ghost Writer* I had abused the memory of Anne Frank would have batted an eye had I let those banalities out into the world. That would have been just fine; I might even have got a citation. But I couldn't have given myself any prizes for it. The difficulties of telling a Jewish story—How should it be told? In what tone? To whom should it be told? To what end? Should it be told at all?—were finally to become *The Ghost Writer*'s theme. But before it became a theme, it apparently had to be an ordeal. It often happens, at least with me, that the struggles that generate a book's moral life are naively

enacted upon the body of the book during the early, uncertain stages of writing. That is the ordeal, and it ended when I took that whole section and recast it in the first person—Anne Frank's story told by Amy Bellette. The victim wasn't herself going to talk about her plight in the voice of "The March of Time." She hadn't in the *Diary,* so why should she in life? I didn't want this section to *appear* as first-person narration, but I knew that by passing it through the first-person sieve, I stood a good chance of getting rid of this terrible tone, which wasn't hers, but mine. I did get rid of it. The impassioned cadences, the straining emotions, the somber, overdramatized, archaic diction—I cleared it all out, thanks to Amy Bellette. Rather straightforwardly, I then cast the section *back* into the third person, and then I was able to get to work on it—to write rather than to rhapsodize or eulogize.

Amy Bellette's story, precisely because it is *not* Anne Frank's, but a fictive revision, is refreshingly free of the cadences of a saint's life. And of course, Amy's story is a passionate lie, "her consuming delusion," akin to Nathan Zuckerman's mad ambition somehow to marry Anne Frank by distracting Amy away from her obsession with Lonoff. What Philip Roth accomplishes, here as with his broodings on Kafka, is not a reimagining of Anne Frank, but a heightening of our awareness of how difficult it has become to tell *any* Jewish story, this late in so long and so complex a cultural history.

DAVID BARNOUW

The Authenticity of the Diary

The earliest attacks on the authenticity of Anne Frank's diary we could discover in print come in two articles published in November 1957 in the Swedish paper *Fria Ord*[1] under the heading of *"Judisk Psyke—En studie kring Anne Frank och Meyer Levin* [Jewish Psyche—A Study Around Anne Frank and Meyer Levin]." Their author was Harald Nielsen, a Danish literary critic. Basing himself on a brief factual report in *De Telegraaf* of April 11, 1957, Nielsen alleged that the diary owed its final form to Meyer Levin. In support of this opinion, he produced such spurious arguments as the claim that Anne and Peter were not Jewish names. He went on to delve into the Jewish background of Meyer Levin's writing. He concluded his articles with the comment that Levin's reminiscences, published in 1951 in a book entitled *In Search*,[2] had the advantage of undisputed authenticity.

In March 1958 the Norwegian paper *Folg og Land,* the organ of the former SS Viking Division, referred to Meyer Levin's lawsuit and went on to allege that Anne Frank's diary was very probably a forgery.[3] One month later, part of this article was published in translation in the *Europa Korrespondenz*[4] in Vienna, and another month later it appeared in *Reichsruf, Wochenzeitung für das nationale Deutschland*,[5] the weekly journal of the extreme right-wing *Deutsche Reichspartei*,[6] founded in 1950.

The Diary of Anne Frank: The Critical Edition, eds. David Barnouw and Gerrold van der Stroom, trans. by Arnold J. Pomerans and B. M. Mooyaart (London: Viking, 1989), pp. 84–101. Copyright © 1989 David Barnouw.

It is not clear whether Otto Frank himself or any of his publishers ever saw these or other attacks on the diary; in any case no legal action was taken by any of them.

This was not the case with Lothar Stielau, a high school teacher of English at the Lübeck *Oberschule zum Dom*. Stielau, who was born in 1908, had joined the NSDAP (Nazi Party) and the SA (storm troopers) in 1932 and had been a Hitler Youth leader. Ten years after the war he joined the *Deutsche Reichspartei* and in 1957 he became district chairman of the party in Lübeck.[7] On October 10, 1958, he wrote a review of the play *Tom Sawyers grosses Abenteuer (The Adventures of Tom Sawyer)* for the *Zeitschrift der Vereinigung ehemaliger Schüler und der Freunde der Oberschule zum Dom e.V. Lübeck* (Journal of the Association of Former Students and Friends of the Lübeck *Oberschule zum Dom*), which contained the following passage:

> The forged diaries of Eva Braun, of the Queen of England and the hardly more authentic one of Anne Frank may have earned several millions for the profiteers from Germany's defeat, but they have also raised our own hackles quite a bit.[8]

One month later Fischer Verlag had its attention drawn to Stielau's article by the *Zentralrat der Juden in Deutschland* (Central Council of German Jews) and a week later Otto Frank, who had come to the publishing house for a meeting, heard about it as well.[9]

The Ministry of Culture in the federal state of Schleswig-Holstein then decided to determine whether Stielau, who had clearly "caused offense," had also breached his professional obligation of political neutrality. On December 5, Stielau was given the opportunity to explain the passage objected to in front of a senior official. At this interview he conceded that there was no doubt that Anne Frank had kept a diary, but went on to allege that none of the published versions of any of the diaries was anything like the original. He referred to the earlier article in the *Reichsruf* and said that he should have used the word *verfälscht* instead of *fälschen* (while *fälschen* signifies that something is entirely fake, *verfälschen* refers to an original to which greater or smaller alterations have been made). For the rest he insisted that he had been punctilious in the performance of his pedagogic duties.[10]

That was also the view of Heinrich Buddeberg, chairman of the *Deutsche Reichspartei* in Schleswig-Holstein, who wrote a letter to the *Lübecker Nachrichten,* published on January 6, 1959, in which he described Stielau as a political victim of the Social Democrats who, with others, had been pressing for Stielau's suspension. And he, too, came up with the distorted account of the Meyer Levin story, quoting this time from the *Deutsch-Amerikanische Bürger-Zeitung* of October 2, 1958.[11]

Buddeberg, born in 1893, was a farmer at Woltersdorf über Büchen in Schleswig-Holstein. Unlike Stielau, he refused during the preliminary examination to say anything about his political past other than that from 1933 to 1945 he had been *Kreisbauernführer* (District Farmers' Leader), which had earned him two years' internment.[12]

On the day Buddeberg's letter was published, the first official steps were taken to have Stielau disciplined. He was alleged to have neglected his duties and to be unworthy of the respect and confidence to which the teaching profession is entitled. As a teacher, he had propagated political attitudes in conflict with his educational duties. The Ministry of Culture ordered his temporary suspension.[13]

In January 1959, Dr. A. Flesch, a Frankfurt advocate acting for Otto Frank, and a few days later for the two publishing houses as well, laid criminal charges against Stielau and Buddeberg before the public prosecutor of the Lübeck *Landgericht*. The charges included libel, slander, insult, defamation of the memory of a dead person and anti-Semitic utterances. Dr. Flesch stated in his indictment that the manuscripts written by Anne Frank were in Amsterdam and that their authenticity could be checked. He next explained the difference between the actual diary and the Hacketts' dramatization, and emphasized that what Stielau had done was to impugn the authenticity of the diary itself and not that of the play.[14]

The public prosecutor's office reacted very quickly: within two days of the complaint being lodged it confirmed receipt and inquired when Otto Frank had first become aware of Stielau's article.[15]

That same month, too, the Federal Minister of Justice in Bonn asked the Schleswig-Holstein Minister of Justice to keep him informed because of the special interest of the case.[16] The preliminary examination could begin.

In April the public prosecutor set out at the end of a long preamble the reason why it was necessary to determine the authenticity of the diary by court action, namely:

> "Given the delicate nature of the attitude of foreign countries towards Germany and her people due to their National Socialist past, a judicial inquiry is the only way of arriving at a satisfactory conclusion."[17]

If there were a conviction the court would have to take into account the accused's inner attitude *("innere Einstellung")* toward Jews, toward the persecution of the Jews and toward Anne Frank. Moreover, Stielau's attitude as a teacher would also be a factor.

The public prosecutor further noted that an inquiry into the authenticity of the diary would prove extraordinarily difficult, and referred to a recent article in *Der Spiegel*.[18] The magazine, which had focused attention on Cauvern, quoted the latter as saying: "At the beginning I made a good many changes." It also claimed that the well-known clergyman J. J. Buskes had served as a spiritual guide to Otto Frank, who had granted him "censorship rights." The impression that the translation was inadequate was confirmed by a number of obvious inconsistencies in it. The article ended with the following statement by Baschwitz: "I believe that the solution of this case lies in the speedy publication of a word-for-word edition of the diary."

Stielau's first appearance before the examining magistrate, on June 18, was entirely devoted to establishing his background, past and political views. He declared that, because he had considered communism a grave threat, he had joined the NSDAP before the war, but "I was never particularly interested in questions of race, the Jewish question included." After the war he had looked for a party that suited him, one that was "unreservedly pro-German," and had ended up in the *Deutsche Reichspartei*.

Seven days later, when the examination was resumed, Stielau made the astonishing allegation that in his article he had not been referring to the published version of the diary, *Das Tagebuch der Anne Frank*, but to the play. The examining magistrate pointed out that this was something he had failed to mention to the Ministry of Culture.

Stielau wisely refused to be drawn, although he had to admit that at the time he himself had neither read the play nor seen a performance of it. He referred, however, to a number of articles in the press that had given him cause to doubt the authenticity of the diary.[19]

It was not until April 25 of the next year that Stielau was examined again. He now refused to discuss the statements of other witnesses or the expert opinion that had meanwhile been prepared, and stuck by his earlier declaration that in 1958 he had been referring to the play.[20] Otto Frank had been interviewed two weeks after the examination, on July 2, 1959, of one of Stielau's colleagues about the *Journal of the Association of Former Students*.[21] Frank stated on what date he had first been told about Stielau's article and then explained what his daughter had written originally, that those writings had been handed to him by Miep after the war, and what he had done with them after that. According to him, Cauvern had merely corrected Germanisms and grammatical errors, and that was all there was to the claim by *Der Spiegel* that Cauvern had "made a good many changes." Otto Frank had himself given information to *Der Spiegel* but was not very happy with the way his words had been reported.

The next day, during his continued examination, Otto Frank denied that any pressure had been put on him "by the clergy." He did not know the Reverend J. J. Buskes personally. He was in favor of an official investigation into the authenticity of Anne's writings; an expert was free to study all the relevant documents in Basle. The dispute with Meyer Levin was also brought up. Finally, Otto Frank agreed to appear as a witness in Lübeck if that proved necessary; all he wanted was to help remove any doubts about the authenticity of his daughter's diary.[22]

On September 29, Bep Voskuijl and Miep and Jan Gies were heard. Each of them gave a separate account of events in the Annexe at 263, Prinsengracht, declared they had known about Anne keeping a diary, and mentioned the discovery of the diaries and the loose sheets and their return to Otto Frank.[23]

For an expert opinion on the authenticity of the diary, the examining magistrate turned to the *Institut für Zeitgeschichte* in Munich. The Institute, however, advised that the case called for philological and graphological rather than historical expertise. Moreover, since no member of the Institute was proficient in the Dutch language they could do no more than recommend two professors of Dutch studies, one in Münster and the other in Berlin.[24]

It was decided to look closer to home, and at the end of September 1959, Dr. Annemarie Hübner of Hamburg University declared herself willing to prepare an expert assessment of *Das Tagebuch der Anne Frank*. She would investigate whether there had been crucial changes between the so-called Typescript II and the German edition, and what the omissions and additions amounted to. In addition she would try to determine whether the German could be considered a "true" and "faithful" translation of the original.

The Hamburg handwriting expert Minna Becker, for her part, was asked to determine whether the diaries in the possession of Otto Frank and the loose sheets had been written by the same person who had written a letter on December 13, 1940, and two postcards on July 25, 1941, and July 5, 1942, all of which had been signed "Anne."

After formal instruction on October 13, 1959, Dr. Hübner, Mrs. Becker and Dorothea Ockelmann—who had been added by the examining magistrate to the panel of experts at a later stage—traveled to Basel to make their investigations on the spot. Mrs. Becker and Mrs. Ockelmann concluded in their report, dated March 7, 1960, and running to 131 pages, that all the written entries in Diaries 1, 2 and 3, including the pages that had been pasted in, the loose sheets and all improvements and additions were "identical" with the specimen handwriting of Anne Frank. They did not mention that a pasted-in letter from Otto Frank, a card from "Jacque" and a birthday card from Ruth Cauvern had been included in Diary 1.

The examining magistrate also asked them to determine which had been written first—Diaries 1, 2 and 3 or the loose sheets? Mrs. Becker and Mrs. Ockelmann both concluded that the loose sheets had not been written before Diaries 1, 2 and 3.[25]

A month later Dr. Hübner handed in her report to the examining mag-istrate.[26] Although it had not been part of her brief, she had perforce looked first of all into the relationship between the manuscripts and Typescript II. Her conclusion:

> The text of the printed manuscript [=Typescript II] must be considered authentic by virtue of its substance, the ideas expressed in it and its form.[27]
>
> The translation must be considered to correspond [to the original] and on the whole to be factually correct. There are mistakes in translation and these are to be deprecated, but most of them can be considered minor faults which are immaterial to an understanding of the total context.[28]

Dr. Hübner concluded that "the text published in German translation as *Das Tagebuch der Anne Frank* may be considered true to its sources in sub-stance and ideas."[29]

Stielau was defended by Professor Dr. Noack and by Dr. Noack, both from Kiel. In May 1960, they submitted their objections to Dr. Hübner's opinion to the examining magistrate in writing. They questioned Dr. Hübner's quali-fications, arguing that her academic status (*"Dozent ohne Lehrauftrag,"* liter-ally "lecturer without a teaching assignment") was not such as to entitle her to give an expert opinion in the field of "comparative philology." Her opinion was therefore dismissed by them as "worthless."[30] This argument appeared to impress the public prosecutor, who communicated it to the Schleswig-Holstein Minister of Justice and added that it seemed advisable, even dur-ing the preliminary investigation, to appoint an *Obergutachter* ("senior assessor").[31]

One month later the public prosecutor commented on Dr. Hübner's actual findings. There were two central questions, namely, whether *Das Tage-buch der Anne Frank* was authentic in "documentary" respects (which seemed unlikely in view of the changes) and whether it was authentic in literary re-spects. The second question could not be answered by Dr. Hübner because she lacked the qualifications to do so.[32]

In July 1960, Professor Dr. Friedrich Sieburg, a well-known publicist and a contributor to the *Frankfurter Allgemeine Zeitung,* was formally asked to be the senior assessor and to prepare an expert opinion, though the precise terms of his brief were not made clear.[33]

Stielau's lawyers had other strings to their bow. In a letter to the ex-amining magistrate they complained that the preliminary investigation had started from the wrong premise, since the article to which the plaintiff ob-jected had referred to the play, not to the book. Moreover, Stielau had been shocked by the fact that adaptations not faithful to the text had been used to make money, and also by the fact that the U.S. edition had contained a photograph, not of Anne, but of one of the actresses who had played her. Further, Noack and Noack submitted that Albert Hackett, and to a lesser extent his wife, had been Communist fellow travelers since 1937; their source for this information was a series of reports by the California Un-American Activities Committee. In the circumstances, it was not at all surprising that Stielau had not wanted to see the play.[34]

Although Noack and Noack had argued earlier that Dr. Hübner's opinion was "worthless" they felt free to make use of it. After all, she had discovered differences between the original "document" and the translation, and Noack and Noack concluded that the translation was no longer "a document": "A document must be authentic word for word, or else it is not a document."[35]

On October 30, 1960, Sieburg concluded his expert opinion, and Noack and Noack turned their attention to it in December that year. They argued, with justification, that it was difficult to come to grips with the expert opinion since it had not been addressed to any specific question: "It is impossible to tell from the opinion which question the expert is actually trying to answer, nor is it known which question he should have answered."[36]

Sieburg had confined himself in his report to the content and the importance of *Das Tagebuch der Anne Frank;* he did not consider it his task to review the manuscripts or the quality of the translation, not least because he had no Dutch. He did nevertheless refer to Diaries 1, 2 and 3, the loose sheets and the "Tales," though his comments were clearly based on Dr. Hübner's opinion, a fact he failed to mention. Sieburg seemed to think that, in view of the large number of loose sheets (which he had never seen), it must have been necessary to make a selection from them. However this selection in no way affected the picture that Anne Frank had drawn of her life.

An important part of Sieburg's evidence concerned the absurdity of forging the diary of a completely unknown person. Moreover the diary contains references to events, for instance the persecution of the Jewish people, which had been confirmed from thousands of historical sources.

Noack and Noack dismissed this expert opinion, too, as completely "worthless," and returned to the changes discovered by Dr. Hübner, the better to prove that the diary "lacked youthfulness and had been schematized and systematized."[37]

* * *

In fact, Mrs. Becker's and Mrs. Ockelmann's conclusion that everything in the diary was by Anne's hand was not correct, in view of the pasted-in letter, the postcard and the birthday card, none of which had been written by her. The reader is referred to the report of the State Forensic Science Laboratory.

There are also several objections to Dr. Hübner's conclusion that the German translation must be judged by its substance and the ideas expressed. There is no doubt that the translator made Anne "more adult" than she was and omitted items from the translation that the German public might have found "embarrassing."

The purpose of Sieburg's expert opinion remains unclear. His contribution is no more than an essay on the importance of *Das Tagebuch der Anne Frank*.

A few weeks after Noack and Noack's last letter, the public prosecutor was ready to present his case against Stielau and Buddeberg. The indictment was characterized by its thoroughness. It contained a summary of what the accused had done, what the witnesses had stated, and of the evidence three of the expert witnesses had submitted. Next it went into why Stielau's belated assertion that he had been referring to the play and not to the diary was unacceptable. Stielau's wording, the comparison with the two other diaries, the framework within which the remark had been made, Stielau's statement to the official in the Ministry of Culture, the newspaper articles he had quoted, none of which dealt with the play, together with the fact that Stielau was not even familiar with the dramatization of the diary—all served to rebut the submissions of the defense.

Stielau and Buddeberg had furthermore been guilty of *"üble Nachrede"* (libel: Article 186 of the German Penal Code) by denying the authenticity of the diary, and of *"Beleidigung"* (defamation: Article 185) by using the term "profiteers from Germany's defeat." These offenses were punishable with a fine or a maximum prison sentence of two years. The public prosecutor asked for the case to be heard before the *Landgericht* (regional court) in Lübeck.[38]

* * *

In their objection Stielau's lawyers repeated that their client had been referring to the play and not to the book. For an opinion of the play they asked the court to call Hans Gomperts, drama critic of *Het Parool*, who, according to *Der Spiegel* of October 10, 1956, had described the dramatic adaptation as "Kitsch sailing under false colors."[39] Now, Gomperts had admittedly used these words in his review of the U.S. premiere of the play, but he reversed that opinion in his review of the Dutch premiere.[40]

In June the Third Criminal Division of the Lübeck *Landgericht* concluded that Stielau and Buddeberg had a case to answer.[41]

In the end, on October 17, 1961, three years after Stielau had published his article, the whole case simply petered out. Before it had a chance to come to court, Stielau's and Buddeberg's lawyers on the one hand, and Otto Frank's and the publishers' lawyers on the other, had arrived at a settlement. All that the court had left to do was to assess costs. The settlement was put in writing.

Stielau and Buddeberg declared that the preliminary investigation had convinced them that Stielau had had no grounds for claiming that the diary was a forgery—the expert opinions and the evidence of witnesses had persuaded them of the contrary. They expressed regret for their statements, which they had made with no attempt at verification. Stielau also withdrew the phrase "profiteers from Germany's defeat" with expressions of regret.

Stielau and Buddeberg declared further that they had meant no offense to either Otto Frank or the publishers, or to sully the memory of Anne Frank. Otto Frank and the publishers, for their part, acknowledged that preliminary examination had revealed no anti-Semitic tendencies on the part of the defendants.

The defendants agreed to the publication of the terms of this settlement, and Otto Frank and the publishers declared that they would drop criminal proceedings. Stielau agreed to contribute DM 1,000 to the legal costs.[42]

From newspaper reports about the case[43] and statements made later by Otto Frank it appeared that the presiding judge had pressed them to reach a settlement. He had argued that if the injured party declared itself satisfied with a public apology by the offender this was to be preferred to a judicial sentence. Moreover, according to the judge, the continuation of the case would have raised domestic and foreign issues which, although not directly, or at most marginally, connected with it, could have invited unwelcome repercussions.

This was a nebulous argument but one that was given more concrete form perhaps by a letter from Otto Frank to Heinz Roth in which we read that his lawyer had told Otto Frank on October 17 that, had the case been continued, the defendant would have received a very light sentence. The judge was afraid that he would then have been accused by a large section of the press of being too lenient in his treatment of Nazis. Because he, Otto Frank, was not concerned with revenge but only with the authenticity of the diary, he had agreed to the settlement.[44]

The question of the high costs of the preliminary examination was also settled in a somewhat unsatisfactory manner. Stielau offered to contribute DM 1,000, but Buddeberg refused to pay anything, and the bench agreed that he need not. The remaining sum, DM 10,000, would be paid by the state.[45]

On the day after the hearing, *Vrij Nederland* quoted approvingly a headline from the West German *Bildzeitung:* "High school teacher libels Anne Frank [...] but judge lets him off."[46]

Otto Frank may have been satisfied at the time, but later he regretted the settlement. "Had I but known that there would be people who would consider a settlement in this case as insufficient proof [of the authenticity of the diary], I should certainly not have dropped the case."[47]

* * *

The fact that the bench had established the authenticity of Anne Frank's diary did not put an end to the allegations.

In January 1959, even before the Stielau case, the Vienna *Europa Korrespondenz* had published an article with the title *"Der Anne Frank-Skandal. Ein Beitrag zur Wahrheit* [The Anne Frank Scandal. A Contribution to the Truth]," in which Dr. Louis de Jong, until 1979 director of the Netherlands State Institute for War Documentation, was alleged to have been the real author of the diary.

> The father came back to Amsterdam after the war, learned about the alleged diary, did not want to publish it, but was practically forced to do so by his friends. The Dutch journalist Louis de Jong, now director of the Netherlands State Institute for War Documentation, was crucially involved in the diary, and from the publications it is clear that De Jong is the author of the book.[48]

In October 1957, De Jong had admittedly written an article on Anne Frank which had appeared in the *Reader's Digest,* and later in foreign editions of that magazine, but there is nothing to indicate that De Jong ever had anything to do with the publication of *Het Achterhuis.*

In the course of the next few decades the authenticity of the diary was to be challenged in various journals and writings.

Thus, in the summer of 1967, Teressa Hendry took aim at the diary's authenticity in the *American Mercury.* She claimed that its real author had been Meyer Levin and went on to quote in English what was allegedly a summary of the *Fria Ord* articles published in the *Economic Council Letter* on April 15, 1959:

> History has many examples of myths that live a longer and richer life than the truth, and may become more effective than truth.
>
> The Western World has for some years been aware of a Jewish girl through the medium of what purports to be her personally written story, "Anne Frank's Diary." Any informed literary inspection of this book would have shown it to have been impossible as the work of a teenager.
>
> A noteworthy decision of the New York Supreme Court confirms this point of view, in that the well known American Jewish writer, Meyer Levin, has been awarded $50,000 to be paid him by the father of Anne Frank as an honorarium for Levin's work on the "Anne Frank Diary."

> Mr. Frank, in Switzerland, has promised to pay to his race-
> kin, Meyer Levin, not less than $50,000 because he had used the
> dialogue of Author Levin just as it was and "implanted" it in the
> diary as being his daughter's intellectual work.[49]

However, neither the judgment of the court nor the sum mentioned appeared in the two *Fria Ord* articles.

The *American Mercury* article is typical of the way in which right-wing extremists have challenged and continue to challenge the authenticity of the diary: they like to refer to earlier publications and to quote from them in such a way as to suggest that what has merely been alleged is "really true." Several years later the article in the *Economic Council Letter* was used again, in a pamphlet called *Did Six Million Really Die? The Truth at Last.*[50] Its author was Richard Harwood, a pseudonym of Richard Verrall of the extreme-right-wing British National Front.[51] German and Dutch translations of the pamphlet were published in 1975 and 1976 respectively.

Teressa Hendry had used a question mark at the end of the title of her article: "Was Anne Frank's Diary a Hoax?"; Harwood, however, wrote unequivocally: "Best-seller a hoax." His article ended with: "Here, then, is just one more fraud in a whole series of frauds in support of the 'Holocaust' legend and the saga of the Six Million."[52]

In 1975, David Irving, the extreme-right-wing British historian, had this to say in the Introduction to his book *Hitler und seine Feldherren* (Hitler and His Generals):

> Many forgeries are on record, as for instance that of the "Diary of
> Anne Frank" (in this case a civil lawsuit brought by a New York
> scriptwriter has proved that he wrote it in collaboration with the
> girl's father).[53]

Otto Frank protested successfully to the publishers, and the passage was omitted when the book was reprinted. However, because a large number of copies of the first impression had been sold, Otto Frank also asked for damages to be paid to the Anne Frank Foundation in Amsterdam; this too was done.[54]

That same year Richard Harwood's publishers brought out a book by an American, A. R. Butz, called *The Hoax of the Twentieth Century*, a mainly demographic study in which the author denied the "Final Solution." He went at length into the existing literature, the better to suggest that he was a serious scholar. Here again Anne Frank's diary played a part, albeit a subsidiary one:

The question of the authenticity of the diary is not considered important enough to examine here; I will only remark that I have looked it over and don't believe it. For example, already on page 2 one is reading an essay on why a 13 year old girl would start a diary, and then page 3 gives a short history of the Frank family and then quickly reviews the specific anti-Jewish measures that followed the German occupation in 1940. The rest of the book is in the same historical spirit.[55]

The first book of any size to be devoted exclusively to the so-called unmasking of the diary appeared in 1978. *Anne Frank Diary—A Hoax?* was written by Ditlieb Felderer[56] from Sweden, whose own publishing house, Bible Researcher, had also published such books as *Zionism The Hidden Tyranny*.

Felderer conceded that there was no truth in the story that Meyer Levin had written the diary but used a different line of attack, as witness some of his chapter headings: "Drug Addict at Tender Age" ("proven" by the fact that Anne wrote on September 16, 1943, that she swallowed valerian pills every day); "Anne's Character—Not Even a Nice Girl"; "Teenage Sex"; "Sexual Extravaganza" (Anne's entries about her growing love for Peter are styled by Felderer "the first child porno"). Felderer went on to "unmask" the diary as "a forgery, a monstrous travesty."[57]

In the United States people were not yet ready to drop the Meyer Levin myth; on May 1, 1978, Teressa Hendry's article was reprinted in the Washington weekly *The Spotlight*.[58]

That year also saw the foundation of the Institute for Historical Review in Torrance, California, by Willis Carto, director of the Noontide Press, a man closely involved in the *American Mercury* and the Liberty Lobby, publishers of *The Spotlight*.[59] The Institute championed the so-called revisionist approach to history, and to the history of the Second World War in particular. Now, there had been a trend among a small group of American historians ever since the First World War to take a special interest both in the question of war guilt and in why the United States had become involved.[60] This trend resurfaced after the Second World War. It included serious historians, who, for example, reexamined the causes of, and responsibility for, the outbreak of the war, as well as a number of persons who wrote of Nazi Germany in nothing but positive terms, minimizing Nazi war crimes. This second group took on itself the title of "revisionists." The group's "revisions" were so many denials of the persecution of the Jews and the existence of the gas chambers.

The Institute for Historical Review tried to act as an umbrella organization for all these separately operating "revisionists" by distributing "revisionist" and blatantly Nazi literature and, from 1979 onward, by organizing an annual Revisionist Conference at which European "revisionists" were also welcome.

The first issue of the quarterly *Journal of Historical Review*, devoted in the main to the lectures delivered at the annual conferences, appeared in 1980.

The obvious purpose of all these activities was to provide anti-Semitism and neo-Nazism with an ostensibly scientific foundation.[61]

* * *

In Germany, too, there were fresh stirrings. In 1976, Anne Frank's diary was again the subject of a court case, heard this time by the *Landgericht* in Frankfurt following the activities of Heinz Roth, an architect from Odenhausen, north of the city.

In 1975, Roth, whose own publishing house issued neo-Nazi brochures, began to distribute pamphlets with such titles as *Anne Franks Tagebuch— eine Fälschung (Anne Frank's Diary—A Forgery)* and *Anne Franks Tagebuch— der grosse Schwindel (Anne Frank's Diary—The Big Fraud)*. Quoting Irving and Harwood, he referred again to the old story that Otto Frank had written the diary with the help of a New York playwright. In December 1975 a quotation from one of his pamphlets appeared in the *"Leserbriefe"* (readers' letters column) of the Austrian periodical *Neue Ordnung*. When Otto Frank heard about this, he made a request to the editor of *Neue Ordnung* that a letter by himself be published in the same column setting out the successful outcome of his protests against David Irving's Introduction, and stating that the Lübeck *Landgericht* had established the authenticity of the diary.[62] We do not know whether or not this letter was in fact published.

Otto Frank sent a copy of his letter to Heinz Roth, who continued to maintain in the ensuing correspondence that he was concerned with the *"reine historische Wahrheit* [pure historical truth]," and continued to refuse to enter into Otto Frank's detailed arguments.[63]

Roth's activities had not escaped the notice of the German Department of Justice, and after a preliminary legal investigation had been ordered against a distributor of one of Roth's pamphlets, the Bochum public prosecutor inquired of Otto Frank in February 1976 if he had already laid criminal charges. The public prosecutor wanted to know when Frank had first heard about the pamphlet in question; this because of the statute of limitations.[64] Otto Frank replied a few weeks later; he had first heard about the pamphlet in September 1975 and although he had been indignant he had taken no steps because of his age and his health. He enclosed photocopies of his correspondence with Wappen Verlag, the publishers of *Neue Ordnung* (who had not replied), and with Roth, and added that the latter was "stubborn and intractable." This was written by Otto Frank following a performance of the Anne Frank play on February 3, 1976, in Hamburg at which Roth's pamphlet had been distributed, and he asked if it would be possible to proceed not only against the distributor of Roth's pamphlet but also against Roth himself.[65] On July 16, 1976, following the publication of one of Roth's later pamphlets, *Das Tagebuch der Anne Frank—Wahrheit oder Fälschung? (The Diary of Anne Frank—Truth or Forgery?),* Otto Frank applied for an injunction to restrain Roth from using certain expressions in the future.

From the information available, we gather that the Frankfurt *Landgericht* decided on July 22, 1978, that Heinz Roth would incur a maximum fine of DM 500,000 or a maximum prison sentence of six months if he repeated any of the following statements in public:

a) "Anne Frank's diary—a forgery."
b) "This world-famous best-seller is a forgery."
c) "Millions of schoolchildren have been forced and are still being forced to read this fake . . . —and now it turns out that it is the product of a New York scriptwriter in collaboration with the girl's father!"
d) "This fraud was exposed for the first time not just recently but over a decade ago!"[66]

From its deliberations it appears that the bench considered the expert opinions given at the preliminary examination in Lübeck and the statements of the various witnesses carried sufficient weight to refute Roth's allegations. Roth's lawyers had also submitted an expert opinion, which was to play an important part over the years in attacks on the authenticity of the diary. It took the form of a study by Robert Faurisson, to which we shall now turn our attention.

* * *

Faurisson, of the Department of Literature at the University of Lyons, produced his expert opinion, written in German, in 1978. It was published two years later in France under the title of *Le Journal d'Anne Frank est-il authentique? (The Diary of Anne Frank—Is It Authentic?).*[67] In 1985 a Dutch translation was published in Belgium under the title of *Het Dagboek van Anne Frank—een vervalsing (The Diary of Anne Frank—a Forgery),* this time without the question mark.[68] For the purposes of his investigation, Faurisson had examined the published diary in the French translation, compared the Dutch edition with the German, spoken to Otto Frank in Basle and gone into the circumstances of those who had been in hiding and of their arrest in August 1944.

It goes without saying that a life in hiding carried countless risks; the possibility of discovery was ever present, and many thousands of those who hid from the Germans did indeed fall into enemy hands as a result of betrayal, accident or their own carelessness.

From the diary it appears that the inhabitants of the Annexe, too, had to brave many dangers, not least the chance that they might make too much noise and be overheard. Faurisson, however, did not examine the overall picture of life in hiding in any depth, or concern himself greatly in this context with the fact that the Frank family and their fellow fugitives were in the end arrested. On the contrary, he used his findings only in order to demonstrate that it must have been impossible to hide in the Annexe and that therefore the diary could not have been written by Anne Frank.

A typical example of his approach is the way in which he examined the problem of noise as presented in *Het Achterhuis:*

> Let us take the case of noise. The people in hiding, we are told, are not allowed to make the slightest noise, to the extent that if they cough they are made quickly to take some codeine. The "enemies" might hear them. The walls are so "thin" (March 25, 1943). The "enemies" are very numerous: Lewin, who "knows the whole building well" (October 1, 1942), the men in the warehouse, the clients, the tradesmen, the postman, the *charwoman*, Slagter the *nightwatchman*, the sanitary department, the bookkeeper, the police flushing people out of their homes, neighbors near and far, the owner of the building, etc. It is therefore improbable, even inconceivable, that Mrs. van Daan should have been in the habit of using the *vacuum cleaner* daily at 12:30 (August 5, 1943). Vacuum cleaners at that time were exceptionally noisy. I must ask: "Is this credible?" My question is not just a formality. It is not rhetorical. Its purpose is not to astonish. My question is simply a question. An answer will have to be found. That question could be followed by forty others concerning noise. The use of an *alarm clock*, for instance, needs explanation (August 4, 1943). The noisy *carpentry* must be explained: dismantling wooden stairs, turning a door into a movable cupboard (August 21, 1942), making a wooden candlestick (December –, 1942). Peter chops wood in the loft in front of the open window (February 23, 1944). There is mention of making "a few little cupboards for the walls and other odds and ends" with wood from the attic (July 11, 1942). There is even talk of building a little compartment in the attic as a place to work in (July 13, 1943). There is the almost constant noise of the *radio*, the *slamming of doors*, the *incessant shouting* (December 6, 1943), the *rows*, the *crying*, the *clamor*, the "*noise . . . enough to waken the dead*" (November 9, 1942), "*a great din and disturbance followed* [. . .] I was doubled up with *laughter*" (May 10, 1944). The episode described on September 2, 1942, cannot be reconciled

with the need for keeping quiet and for discretion. We see the people in hiding sitting at table. They *chatter* gaily. Suddenly there is *a piercing whistle* and they hear Peter's voice *calling* down the chimney saying that he isn't coming down anyway. Mr. van Daan springs to his feet, his napkin falls to the floor and scarlet in the face he *shouts:* "I've had enough of this." He goes up to the attic and then we hear *a good deal of resistance and stamping.* The episode recorded on December 10, 1942, was of the same type. We see Mrs. van Daan being attended to by the dentist, Dussel. With his scraper he touches a bad tooth. Mrs. van Daan utters "incoherent cries." She tries to pull the thing out of her mouth. The dentist stands with hands against his sides calmly watching the little comedy. The rest of the audience *"roared with laughter."* Anne is not in the least anxious about the screams and the roars of laughter. Instead she says: "It was rotten of us, because I for one am quite sure that I should have screamed even louder."[69]

Given the above extract, we have no need to subject all the examples mentioned by Faurisson to review. We shall make use of just three examples in order to highlight Faurisson's method.

A comparison with the diary will show that to prove his point Faurisson relates his chosen examples in part only. Thus the fact that Mrs. van Daan should have used the vacuum cleaner daily at twelve-thirty (August 5, 1943) is indeed mentioned by Anne on that date, but the sentence before reveals: "The warehousemen have gone home now."

On December 6, 1943, Anne refers to "resounding ... laughter" (the "incessant shouting" is our translation of Faurisson's *"cris interminables"* whereas the French translation of *Het Achterhuis* has *"éclats de rire interminables"*). Again Faurisson fails to mention that Anne sets this scene on a Sunday evening (December 5).

On November 9, 1942, Anne recorded that a sack of brown beans had burst open and that "the noise was enough to wake the dead." Faurisson omits to quote the next sentence: "(Thank God there were no strangers in the house.)"

In the spring of 1977, Faurisson called on Otto Frank, and in the presence of Frank's wife asked a number of questions concerning his time in hiding and the way *Het Achterhuis* had come to be written. Faurisson's account of this conversation gives the impression that Otto Frank was entangled in all sorts of contradictions: "The interview turned out to be grueling for Anne Frank's father."[70] Eighteen months later Otto Frank, in a written commentary on Faurisson's study and in particular on Faurisson's report of their conversation, challenged most of what Faurisson had put into his mouth.[71]

A few items examined by Faurisson have already been discussed. They concern the background of *Het Achterhuis,* the disparities between *Het Achterhuis* and the translations, particularly the German, and the course of events surrounding the arrest of the Frank family.

One point will suffice to clarify Faurisson's work method. In his story of the arrest he mentions a witness "who, I believe, is well informed and of good faith and at the same time has a good memory. [...] I have promised to keep his name secret. [...] The name and address of this witness [...] have been noted in a sealed envelope."[72] A photograph of this sealed envelope is printed as an appendix to Faurisson's "investigation," albeit only in the French version of 1980; the publisher of the Dutch version had the sense to leave out this piece of evidence.

In the same year that the French edition of Faurisson's study appeared, his new book, *Mémoire en défense,* was published in Paris.[73] In it he denied, not for the first time, the existence of the gas chambers and defended himself against those who accused him of falsifying history. The introduction by Noam Chomsky, the distinguished U.S. linguistic philosopher and well-known opponent of United States policy in Vietnam, caused a sensation. Chomsky declared that he would defend freedom of speech everywhere and at all times, even if Faurisson were an anti-Semite or a fanatical Nazi apologist.

In 1981, Faurisson was called before a French judge in order to substantiate his statement on the radio and in various publications that the gas chambers had never existed. He received a three-month suspended prison sentence and was ordered to pay fines and damages for defamation, incitement to discrimination, race hatred and racial violence.[74] The sentence was confirmed on appeal.[75]

* * *

And it was Faurisson's study that was presented as expert evidence during Roth's appeal to the Frankfurt *Oberlandesgericht* (Higher Regional Court) against his sentence. Roth continued to insist that his doubts concerning the authenticity of the diary were justified. He based that claim on the *Der Spiegel* article of April 1959 and also on statements by Harwood, Butz and Faurisson. The court, however, did not seem very impressed and found that Roth had been unable to substantiate his allegations. His appeal was rejected on July 5, 1979; after having taken all the submissions into consideration, the court concluded:

"From the foregoing we must concur with the *Landgericht* that the accused has not succeeded in establishing the truth of his allegations, and that he has failed to submit any evidence that would result in a different conclusion. As a consequence the plaintiff is entitled to demand that he cease from making these claims and from propagating them in the future."[76]

Although Roth had died in November 1978,[77] the *Bundesgerichtshof* (the Federal High Court) referred the case back to the Frankfurt *Oberlandesgericht* on December 6, 1980. In the view of the *Bundesgerichtshof* the case concerned not only the good name of Otto Frank but also the not unimportant role of "proprietary interests," by which the court was probably referring to royalties, although no specific mention of them was made. Otto Frank died on August 19, 1980, so that the question now involved his heirs. The *Bundesgerichtshof* took the view that the court had confined itself to the question of whether Meyer Levin and Otto Frank had jointly written the diary, a claim that had proved to be false. Roth had not, however, been given enough opportunity to prove his allegations that the diary was a "*Fälschung* [forgery]"; he was to be given that opportunity during the review of the case.[78] The fact that the accused had been dead for two years was plainly irrelevant.

* * *

While the case against Roth came to a rather unsatisfactory conclusion, two other cases actually ended in aquittals. In July 1978, E. Schönborn, chairman of the extreme-right-wing *Kampfbund Deutscher Soldaten* (Combat League of German Soldiers), distributed pamphlets outside the Anne Frank Schools in Frankfurt and Nuremberg claiming, *inter alia,* that the diary of Anne Frank was "a forgery and the product of a Jewish anti-German atrocity propaganda campaign intended to support the lie about the six million gassed Jews and to finance the state of Israel." So read the report in *De Volkskrant.*[79]

According to the same daily newspaper, the prosecution asked for a ten-month suspended sentence, but the judge held that Schönborn, too, had the right of free speech. Schönborn, the judge went on to say, had acted within the law inasmuch as he had not denied human rights to any Jews. He was therefore acquitted. The judge, according to *De Volkskrant,* did not exonerate Schönborn, he had simply held that a sentence for defamation must be consequent upon charges being laid by those personally affected.[80]

The second case was heard in Stuttgart. Here a former Hitler Youth leader called Werner Kuhnt, who after the war became editor-in-chief of the extreme-right-wing monthly *Deutsche Stimme,* was charged with *Volksverhetzung* (incitement of the people) and defaming the memory of a dead person. Kuhnt had stated in the issue of October 1979 that Anne Frank's diary was "a forgery" and "a fraud," that it had not been written by Anne and that it was the result of "collaboration between a New York scriptwriter and the girl's father." In June 1980, Kuhnt was acquitted by the Stuttgart *Amtsgericht* (district court). The public prosecutor entered an appeal.[81]

On October 27, 1980, the appeal was heard before the Stuttgart *Landgericht* (regional court), which found that the charge of inciting the people could not be substantiated, that there had been no evidence of anti-Semitism and that Kuhnt had in no way insulted human dignity. As far as the misleading statement in Kuhnt's article was concerned, the bench found that Otto Frank should have lodged a complaint, which he had failed to do. The appeal was therefore dismissed and Kuhnt acquitted.[82]

At the end of February and the beginning of March 1976 it came to the notice of the police in Hamburg that pamphlets had been handed out after performances of the play there. The pamphlets were headed "Best-Seller— a Fraud" and repeated the old Meyer Levin allegation. The pamphlet was, in fact, a reprint of two pages from the German translation of Harwood's *Did Six Million Really Die? The Truth at Last*, and had been distributed, it appeared, by Ernst Römer, born in 1904. On January 13, 1977, almost a year later, Römer was fined DM 1,500 for defamation by the Hamburg *Amtsgericht*. He appealed, and his case was heard on August 21, 1978, before the Hamburg *Landgericht*. During the hearing the journalist Edgar Geiss, born in 1929, distributed pamphlets in the courtroom alleging in effect that the diary was "a fraud."

Geiss was also taken to court, and in April of the following year the *Amtsgericht* sentenced him to one year in prison for defamation. His sentence was more severe than Römer's because he had several previous convictions.

Geiss, too, appealed, and three months later the *Landgericht* decided to hear the cases of Römer and Geiss jointly.

The *Bundeskriminalamt* (the BKA, or Federal Criminal Investigation Bureau) in Wiesbaden was charged with preparing an expert opinion on whether it was possible "by an examination of paper and writing material to establish that the writings attributed to Anne Frank were produced during the years 1941 to 1944."

The investigation—in the spring of 1980—was therefore restricted by this limited brief. The BKA came to the conclusion that the types of paper used, including the covers of Diaries 1, 2 and 3, as well as the types of ink found in the three diaries and on the loose sheets, were all manufactured before 1950–1951 (and could thus have been used during the stated period). On the other hand:

> Some of the corrections made subsequently on the loose pages were [. . .] written in black, green and blue ballpen ink. Ballpen ink of this type has only been on the market since 1951.[83]

The BKA report ran to a mere four pages. The precise location of the corrections on the loose sheets and their nature and extent are not mentioned, nor is the number of such corrections.

In itself this was a less than sensational report and did not touch upon the authenticity of the diary as such. That was not, however, the view of *Der Spiegel*, which on October 6, 1980, published a long article with the following introductory paragraph printed in bold type:

> Proved by a *Bundeskriminalamt* report: "The Diary of Anne Frank" was edited at a later date. Further doubt is therefore cast on the authenticity of that document.[84]

It was a suggestive article in other respects too. Without asking when the writing in ballpoint had been made on the loose sheets, what the nature of these corrections was or whether they had been incorporated in the published texts, the author of the article, instead of referring to *Korrecturen* (corrections) as the BKA had done, wrote of "additions to the original that up till now had always been considered to be in the same hand as the rest of the text."

In support of the phrase "up till now had always been considered," the reader was referred to Minna Becker's mistaken 1960 opinion. *Der Spiegel* added: "Now if the handwriting of the original entries matched that of the additions, then there must have been an impostor at work," which, the magazine generously conceded, "cannot be seriously maintained even now in view of the controversial nature of graphological evidence."

It is only towards the end of the article that *Der Spiegel* quotes briefly from the BKA report and uses the term *"Korrekturen"*; before that, however, the reader had been told that the published diary had been subjected to countless *"Manipulationen* [manipulations]."

True, *Der Spiegel* also pointed out that those who had cast doubt on the authenticity of the diary had done so for the purpose of establishing "the truth about the persecution of the Jews," in the manner, as the magazine remarked critically, of "one of the pamphlet distributors at the Römer trial who wanted to put a stop to the 'gas chamber fraud.'"

David Irving, too, was portrayed critically, as was the "oft-repeated legend" that Otto Frank had incorporated quotations from a film script (what was meant, of course, was from the text of a play) into the diary.

The article aroused great interest both in Germany and abroad. *Der Spiegel*'s message seemed clear: there was something wrong. Members of the Anne Frank Foundation let it be known in the Dutch press that, at the request of Otto Frank, Kleiman had made minor corrections to the manuscript after the war but that these had simply been clarifications.[85]

We have just called the *Spiegel* article suggestive. The magazine had, however, been indirectly encouraged to take this line by the failure of the *Bundeskriminalamt* to publish the concrete data on which it had based its findings, thus rendering any kind of verification impossible.

We asked the *Bundeskriminalamt* to put these data at our disposal. The reply was that no such data were in their possession.

On December 20, 1985, at our request, the BKA then used the State Forensic Science Laboratory of the Netherlands Ministry of Justice in Rijswijk in an attempt to give concrete expression to the findings of their report.

They were in part successful. The reader is referred to Chapter VI of the State Forensic Science Laboratory's report, which also discusses the relevance of the ballpoint writing to the authenticity of the diary.

The BKA was unable to indicate where just one alleged correction in green ballpoint ink was to be found.

Notes

1. *Fria Ord*, November 9 and 11, 1957. Lübeck *Landgericht*, Stielau/Buddeberg dossier.

2. Meyer Levin, *In Search* (London-Paris: Constellation Books, 1951).

3. *Folg og Land*, March 1, 1958. Lübeck *Landgericht*, Stielau/Buddeberg dossier.

4. *Europa Korrespondenz*, April 1958. Lübeck *Landgericht*, Stielau/Buddeberg dossier.

5. *Reichsruf. Wochenzeitung für das nationale Deutschland* [Weekly of National Germany] May 17, 1958. Lübeck *Landgericht*, Stielau/Buddeberg dossier.

6. P. R. A. van Iddekinge and A. H. Paape, *Ze zijn er nog* (Amsterdam: De Bezige Bij, 1970), p. 148.

7. Examination of Stielau, June 18, 1958. Lübeck *Landgericht*, Stielau/Buddeberg dossier.

8. *Zeitschrift der Vereinigung ehemaliger Schüler und der Freunde der Oberschule zum Dom, e. V.*, Lübeck, October 10, 1958. Lübeck *Landgericht*, Stielau/Buddeberg dossier.

9. Examination of Otto Frank, July 16, 1959. Lübeck *Landgericht*, Stielau/Buddeberg dossier.

10. Record of interview, December 5, 1985. Lübeck *Landgericht*, Stielau/Buddeberg dossier.

11. *Lübecker Nachrichten*, January 6, 1959. Lübeck *Landgericht*, Stielau/Buddeberg dossier.

12. Examination of Buddeberg, July 7, 1959. Lübeck *Landgericht*, Stielau/Buddeberg dossier.

13. Dr. A. Flesch, Otto Frank's lawyer, to public prosecutor at the Lübeck *Landgericht*, January 14, 1959. Stielau/Buddeberg dossier.

14. Ibid.

15. Letter from public prosecutor, Lübeck *Landgericht*, to Flesch, January 16, 1959. Lübeck *Landgericht*, Stielau/Buddeberg dossier.

16. Letter from Federal Minister of Justice to Schleswig-Holstein Minister of Justice, January 29, 1959. Lübeck *Landgericht,* Stielau/Buddeberg dossier.

17. Memorandum by Lübeck public prosecutor, April 1959, p. 11. Lübeck *Landgericht,* Stielau/Buddeberg dossier.

18. *Der Spiegel,* April 1, 1959, pp. 51–55.

19. Examination of Stielau, June 18 and 25, 1959. Lübeck *Landgericht,* Stielau/Buddeberg dossier.

20. Ibid., April 25, 1960.

21. Examination of Erich Heim, July 2, 1959. Lübeck *Landgericht,* Stielau/ Buddeberg dossier.

22. Examination of Otto Frank, July 16 and 17, 1959. Lübeck *Landgericht,* Stielau/Buddeberg dossier.

23. Examination of Bep Voskuijl, September 29, 1959; examination of Miep Gies, September 29, 1959 and examination of Jan Gies, September 29, 1959. Lübeck *Landgericht,* Stielau/Buddeberg dossier.

24. *Institut für Zeitgeschichte* to examining magistrate, July 1, 1959. Lübeck *Landgericht,* Stielau/Buddeberg dossier.

25. Expert handwriting opinion in proceedings for defamation against: 1. *Studienrat* Stielau from Lübeck; and 2. farmer Buddeberg from Woltersdorf. Lübeck *Landgericht,* Stielau/Buddeberg dossier.

26. Memorandum by examining magistrate, April 14, 1960. Lübeck *Landgericht,* Stielau/Buddeberg dossier.

27. Expert opinion in the preliminary examination of 1. *Studienrat* Lothar Stielau; and 2. farmer Heinrich Buddeberg, p. 29. Lübeck *Landgericht,* Stielau/ Buddeberg dossier.

28. Ibid., p. 34.

29. Ibid.

30. Noack and Noack to examining magistrate, December 12, 1960. Lübeck *Landgericht,* Stielau/Buddeberg dossier.

31. Lübeck public prosecutor to Schleswig-Holstein Minister of justice, June 14, 1960. Lübeck *Landgericht,* Stielau/Buddeberg dossier.

32. Ibid., July 3, 1960.

33. Expert opinion in criminal proceedings against *Studienrat* Stielau, p. 1. Lübeck *Landgericht,* Stielau/Buddeberg dossier.

34. Noack and Noack to examining magistrate, July 29, 1960. Lübeck *Landgericht,* Stielau/Buddeberg dossier.

35. Ibid.

36. Ibid. December 12, 1960.

37. Ibid., p. 6.

38. Indictment, Lübeck public prosecutor, Lübeck *Landgericht,* Stielau/ Buddeberg dossier.

39. Noack and Noack to examining magistrate, February 20, 1961. Lübeck *Landgericht,* Stielau/Buddeberg dossier.

40. *Het Parool,* November 28, 1956.

41. Decision of Third Criminal Division of Lübeck *Landgericht,* June 1, 1961. Lübeck *Landgericht,* Stielau/Buddeberg dossier.

42. Report of open session of Third Criminal Division of Lübeck *Landgericht,* October 17, 1961. Lübeck *Landgericht,* Stielau/Buddeberg dossier.

43. *Het Vaderland,* October 8, 1961, and *Vrij Nederland,* October 28, 1961.

44. Otto Frank to Heinz Roth, January 21, 1976. Frankfurt *Landgericht*, Roth dossier.

45. Lübeck public prosecutor to Schleswig-Holstein Minister of Justice, October 17, 1961. Lübeck *Landgericht*, Stielau/Buddeberg dossier.

46. *Vrij Nederland*, October 28, 1961.

47. Otto Frank to Heinz Roth, January 21, 1976. Frankfurt *Landgericht*, Roth dossier.

48. *Europa Korrespondenz*, January 1959. Lübeck *Landgericht*, Stielau/Buddeberg dossier.

49. From the Summer 1967 issue of the *American Mercury*, in Ditlieb Felderer, *Anne Frank Diary—A Hoax?* (Taby [Sweden]: Bible Researcher, 1978).

50. Richard Harwood, *Did Six Million Really Die? The Truth at Last* (Richmond [Surrey]: Historical Review Press, 1974), p. 19.

51. Jan Barnes, "Revisionism and the Right," in *Contemporary Affairs Briefing*, Vol. 1, No. 1 (January 1982), p. 7.

52. Harwood, op. cit., p. 19.

53. David Irving, *Hitler und seine Feldherren* (Frankfurt-am-Main, Berlin, Vienna: Ullstein Verlag, 1975), p. 111.

54. Otto Frank to David Irving, October 23, 1979.

55. A. R. Butz, *The Hoax of the Twentieth Century* (Richmond [Surrey]: Historical Review Press, 1975), p. 37.

56. Under the slightly altered title of *Anne Frank's Diary—A Hoax*, Felderer's book was reprinted by the Institute for Historical Review, Torrance, California.

57. Felderer, op. cit., p. 29.

58. *The Spotlight*, May 1, 1978.

59. Colin Holmes, "Historical Revisionism in Britain: the Politics of History," in *Trends in Historical Revisionism* (London: Centre for Contemporary Studies, 1985).

60. M. C. Brands, *"Revisionistische bewegingen in de Amerikaanse historiografie,"* in *Theoretische Geschiedenis*, 2 (1977), pp. 77–92.

61. Vera Ebels-Dolanová, ed., *The Extreme Right in Europe and the United States* (Amsterdam: Anne Frank Foundation, 1975).

62. Otto Frank to Wappen Verlag, December 17, 1975. Hamburg *Landgericht*, Römer-Geiss dossier.

63. Correspondence between Otto Frank and Heinz Roth, January 18 and 25, 1975, and January 8, 15, 21 and 26, 1976. Frankfurt *Landgericht*, Roth dossier.

64. Bochum public prosecutor to Otto Frank, February 20, 1976. Frankfurt *Landgericht*, Roth dossier.

65. Otto Frank to Bochum public prosecutor, March 3, 1976. Frankfurt *Landgericht*, Roth dossier.

66. Verdict of Frankfurt *Landgericht*, March 22, 1978. Frankfurt *Landgericht*, Roth dossier.

67. In Serge Thion, *Vérité historique ou vérité politique?* (Paris: La Vieille Taupe, 1980). For a more moderate version, see Hervé le Goff, *Les grands truquages de l'histoire* (Paris: Jacques Grancher, 1983), pp. 53–40.

68. Robert Faurisson, *Het Dagboek van Anne Frank—een vervalsing* (Antwerp: Vrij Historisch Onderzoek, 1985).

69. Ibid., pp. 9–10.

70. Ibid., p. 18.

71. Reply to the document submitted by Professor Faurisson on July 4, 1978, and Comments on the motion to receive evidence by the Counsel for the defense, dated November 1978. Frankfurt *Landgericht*, Roth dossier.

72. Faurisson, op. cit., p. 58.

73. Robert Faurisson, *Mémoire en défense. Contre ceux qui m'accusent de falsifier l'Histoire. La question des chambres à gaz* (Paris: La Vieille Taupe, 1980).

74. *Le Monde*, July 18, 1981.

75. *Le Monde*, April 28, 1983.

76. Verdict of Frankfurt *Oberlandesgericht*, July 5, 1979, p. 14. Frankfurt *Oberlandesgericht*, Roth dossier.

77. Christiaan Raabe (notary) to Netherlands State Institute for War Documentation, April 24, 1985.

78. Press communiqué of the *Bundesgericht*, December 16, 1980. *Bundesgesgerichtshof*, Roth dossier.

79. *De Volkskrant*, March 23, 1979.

80. Ibid.

81. Verdict of Stuttgart *Landgericht*, October 27, 1980. Stuttgart *Landgericht*, Roth dossier.

82. Ibid.

83. Opinion of Federal Criminal Investigation Bureau, May 28, 1980. Hamburg *Landgericht*, Römer/Geiss dossier.

84. *Der Spiegel*, October 6, 1980.

85. *Het Algemeen Dagblad, De Telegraaf, Trouw*, October 7, 1980.

DEBORAH E. LIPSTADT

Twisting the Truth: The Diary of Anne Frank

Anne Frank's diary has become one of the deniers' most popular targets. For more than thirty years they have tried to prove that it was written after the war. It would seem to be a dubious allocation of the deniers' energies that they try to prove that a small book by a young girl full of musings about her life, relationship with her parents, emerging sexuality, and movie stars was not really written by her. But they have chosen their target purposefully.

Since its publication shortly after the war, the diary has sold more than twenty million copies in more than forty countries. For many readers it is their introduction to the Holocaust. Countless grade school and high school classes use it as a required text. The diary's popularity and impact, particularly on the young, make discrediting it as important a goal for the deniers as their attack on the gas chambers. By instilling doubts in the minds of young people about this powerful book, they hope also to instill doubts about the Holocaust itself.

On what do these deniers and neo-Nazis build their case? A brief history of the publication of the diary, and of some of the subsequent events surrounding its production as a play and film, demonstrates how the deniers twist the truth to fit their ideological agenda.

Anne Frank began her diary on June 12, 1942. In the subsequent twenty-six months she filled a series of albums, loose sheets of paper, and exercise and

Denying the Holocaust (New York: Free Press, 1993), pp. 229–235, 270–271. Copyright © 1993 Deborah E. Lipstadt.

29

account books. In addition she wrote a set of stories called *Tales From the Secret Annex*.* Anne, who frequently referred to her desire to be a writer, took her diary very seriously. Approximately five months before the family's arrest, listening to a clandestine radio she heard the Dutch minister of education request in a broadcast from London that people save "ordinary documents—a diary, letters from a Dutch forced laborer in Germany, a collection of sermons given by a parson or a priest." This would help future generations understand what the nation had endured during those terrible years. The next day Anne noted, "Of course they all made a rush at my diary immediately."[30] Anxious to publish her recollections in book form after the war, she rewrote the first volumes of the diary on loose copy paper. In it she changed some of the names of the principal characters, including her own (Anne Frank became Anne Robin.[31])

When Otto Frank was liberated from Auschwitz and returned from the war, he learned that his daughters were dead. He prepared a typed edition of the diary for relatives and friends, making certain grammatical corrections, incorporating items from the different versions, and omitting details that might offend living people or that concerned private family matters, such as Anne's stormy relationship with her mother. He gave his typed manuscript to a friend and asked him to edit it.[32] (Other people apparently also made editorial alterations to it.) The friend's wife prepared a typed version of the edited manuscript. Frank approached a number of publishers with this version, which was repeatedly rejected.** When it was accepted the publishers suggested that references to sex, menstruation, and two girls touching each other's breasts be deleted because they lacked the proper degree of "propriety" for a Dutch audience. When the diary was published in England, Germany, France, and the United States, additional changes were made. The deniers cite these different versions and different copies of the typescript to buttress their claim that it is all a fabrication and that there was no original diary. They also point to the fact that two different types of handwriting—printing and cursive writing—were used in the diary. They claim that the paper and the ink used were not produced until the 1950s and would have been unavailable to a girl hiding in an attic in Amsterdam in 1942.

But it is the Meyer Levin affair on which the deniers have most often relied to make their spurious charges. Levin, who had first read the diary while he was living in France, wrote a laudatory review of it when Doubleday published it. Levin's review, which appeared in the *New York Times Book Review*, was followed by other articles by him on the diary in which he urged that it be made into a play and film.[33] In 1952 Otto Frank appointed Levin his literary agent in the United States to explore the possibility of producing a play. Levin wrote a script that was turned down by a series of producers. Frustrated by Levin's failures and convinced that this script would not be accepted, Frank awarded the production rights to Kermit Bloomgarden, who turned, at the suggestion of American author Lillian Hellman, to two accomplished MGM screenwriters. Their version of the play was a success and won the 1955 Pulitzer Prize.

Levin, deeply embittered, sued, charging that the playwrights had plagiarized his material and ideas. In January 1958 a jury ruled that Levin should be awarded fifty thousand dollars in damages. However, the New York State Supreme Court set aside the jury's verdict, explaining that since Levin and the MGM playwrights had both relied on the same original source—Anne's diary—there were bound to be similarities between the two.[34]

Since it appeared that another lawsuit would be filed, the court refused to lift the freeze that Levin had placed on the royalties. After two years of an impasse, Frank and Levin reached an out-of-court settlement. Frank agreed to pay fifteen thousand dollars to Levin, who dropped all his claims to royalties and rights to the dramatization of the play. Levin remained obsessed by his desire to dramatize the diary.*** In 1966 he attempted to stage a production in Israel, though he did not have the right to do so, and Frank's lawyers insisted that it be terminated.[35]

* * *

It is against this background that the deniers built their assault on the diary. The first documented attack appeared in Sweden in 1957. A Danish literary critic claimed that the diary had actually been produced by Levin, citing as one of his "proofs" that names such as Peter and Anne were not Jewish names.[36] His charges were repeated in Norway, Austria, and West Germany. In 1958 a German high school teacher who had been a member of the SA and a Hitler Youth leader charged that Anne Frank's diary was a forgery that had earned "millions for the profiteers from Germany's defeat."[37] His allegations were reiterated by the chairman of a right-wing German political party. Otto Frank and the diary's publishers sued them for libel, slander, defamation of the memory of a dead person, and antisemitic utterances. The case was settled out of court when the defendants declared that they were convinced the diary was not a forgery and apologized for unverified statements they had made.[38]

In 1967 *American Mercury* published an article by Teressa Hendry, entitled "Was Anne Frank's Diary a Hoax?" in which she suggested that the diary might be the work of Meyer Levin and that if it was, a massive fraud had been perpetrated.[39] In a fashion that will by now have become familiar to readers of this book, Hendry's allegations were repeated by other deniers as established fact. This is their typical pattern of cross-fertilization as they create a merry-go-round of allegations. In *Did Six Million Really Die? The Truth at Last,* Harwood repeated these charges, unequivocally declaring the diary to be a hoax.[40] In one short paragraph in his book, Arthur Butz likewise stated that he had "looked it over" and determined that the diary was a hoax.[41]

In his 1975 attack on the diary, David Irving relied on the familiar charge that an American court had "proved" that a New York scriptwriter had written it "in collaboration with the girl's father." In 1978 Ditlieb Felderer, publisher of the sexually explicit cartoons of Holocaust survivors, produced a book devoted to certifying the diary as a hoax. He repeated the Levin charge but then went on to label Anne a sex fiend and the book "the first child porno." (Some of his chapter titles are indicative of his approach: "Sexual Extravaganza" and "Anne's Character—Not Even a Nice Girl." Felderer's charges are designed to build on what is often part of the inventory of antisemitic stereotypes: Jews, unnaturally concerned about sex, are also producers of pornography designed to corrupt young children.)

In 1975 Heinz Roth, a West German publisher of neo-Nazi brochures, began to circulate pamphlets calling the diary a forgery actually written by a New York playwright. He cited Irving's and Harwood's findings as "proof" of his charges. When asked to desist by Otto Frank, he refused, claiming, in the familiar defense used by deniers, that he was only interested in "pure historical truth." At this point Frank took him to court in West Germany. Roth defended himself by citing statements by Harwood and Butz declaring the diary to be fraudulent. In addition, Roth's lawyers produced an "expert opinion" by Robert Faurisson, among whose charges to prove the diary fictitious was that the annex's inhabitants had made too much noise. Anne wrote of vacuum cleaners being used, "resounding" laughter, and noise that was "enough to wake the dead."[43] How, Faurisson asked, could people in hiding, knowing that the slightest noise would be their undoing, have behaved in this fashion and not been discovered?[44] But Faurisson quoted the diary selectively, distorting its contents to build his case. When Anne wrote of the use of the vacuum cleaner, she preceded it by noting that the "warehouse men have gone home now."[45] The scene in which she described resounding laughter among the inhabitants of the annex took place the preceding evening—a Sunday night—when the warehouse would have been empty.[46] When she wrote that a sack of beans broke open and the noise was enough to "wake the dead," Faurisson neglected to quote the next sentence in the diary: "Thank God there were no strangers in the house."[47]

In his description of his visit to Otto Frank, Faurisson engaged in the same tactics he used in relation to his encounter with the official from the Auschwitz museum. He tried to make it appear as if he had caught Frank in a monstrous lie: "The interview turned out to be grueling for Anne Frank's father."[48] Not surprisingly Frank's description of the interchange differs markedly, and he challenged the veracity of much of what Faurisson claimed he said. Faurisson also claimed to have found a witness who was "well informed and of good faith" but who refused to allow his name to be made public. Faurisson assured readers that the name and address of this secret witness had been placed in a "sealed envelope." As proof of this evidence he included a photograph of the sealed envelope as an appendix to his "investigation."[49] In 1980 the court, unconvinced by Faurisson's claims, found that Roth had not proved the diary false.

In 1977 charges were again brought against two men in the West German courts for distributing pamphlets charging that the diary was a hoax. The Bundeskriminalamt (The BKA, or Federal Criminal Investigation Bureau) was asked to prepare a report as to whether the paper and writing material used in the diary were available between 1941 and 1944. The BKA report, which ran just four pages in length, did not deal with the authenticity of the diary itself. It found that the materials had all been manufactured prior to 1950–1951 and consequently could have been used by Anne. It also observed, almost parenthetically, that *emendations* had been made in ballpoint pen on loose pages found with the diary. The ink used to make them had only been on the market since 1951.[50] (The BKA did not address itself to the substance of the emendations, nor did it publish any data explaining how it had reached this conclusion. When the editors of the critical edition of the diary asked for the data they were told by the BKA that they had none.[51])

Given the history of the editing of the diary it is not surprising that these kinds of corrections were made. This did not prevent *Der Spiegel* from publishing a sensationalist article on the diary which began with the following boldface paragraph: "'The Diary of Anne Frank' was edited at a later date. Further doubt is therefore cast on the authenticity of that document." The author of the article did not question whether these corrections had been substantive or grammatical, whether they had been incorporated into the printed text, or when they had been made. Nor did he refer to them as corrections as the BKA had. He referred to the possibility of an imposter at work and charged that the diary had been subjected to countless "manipulations."

These sensationalist observations notwithstanding, *Der Spiegel* dismissed the charge made by David Irving and other deniers that Levin wrote the diary as an "oft-repeated legend." It also stressed that those who wished to shed doubt on the diary were the same types who wished to end "gas chamber fraud."[52]

On Otto Frank's death in 1980, the diary was given to the Netherlands State Institute for War Documentation. By that time the attacks on it had become so frequent and vehement—though the charges that were made were all essentially the same—that the institute felt obliged to subject the diary, as well as the paper on which it was written, glue that bound it together, and ink to a myriad of scientific tests in order to determine whether they were authentic. They also tested postage stamps, postmarks, and censorship stamps on postcards, letters, and greeting cards sent by Anne and her family during this period (in addition to the diary the institute examined twenty-two different documents containing writings by Anne and her family). Forensic science experts analyzed Anne's handwriting, paying particular attention to the two different scripts, and produced a 250-page highly technical report of their findings.

The reports found that the paper, glue, fibers in the binding, and ink were all in use in. the 1940s. The ink contained iron, which was standard for inks used prior to 1950. (After that date ink with no, or a much lower, iron content was used.) The conclusions of the forensic experts were unequivocal: The diaries were written by one person during the period in question. The emendations were of a limited nature and varied from a single letter to three words. They did not in any way alter the meaning of the text when compared to the earlier version.[51] The institute determined that the different handwriting styles were indicative of normal development in a child and left no doubt that it was convinced that it had all been written in the same hand that wrote the letters and cards Anne had sent to classmates in previous years.

The final result of the institute's investigation was a 712 page critical edition of the diary containing the original version, Anne's edited copy, and the published version as well as the experts' findings. While some may argue that the Netherlands State Institute for War Documentation used an elephant to swat a fly, once again it becomes clear that the deniers' claims have no relationship to the most basic rules of truth and evidence.

Notes

* The Secret Annex was the name Anne gave to the family's hiding place.

** Even after the diary was published to wide acclaim in Europe, American publishers were wary. Ten rejected it before Doubleday published it in 1951. It was an immediate success.

*** In fact, in 1973 he wrote a book, *The Obsession*, about the entire episode.

Notes

30. March 29, 1944, *Diary of Anne Frank: The Critical Edition* (New York: 1989), p. 578 (hereafter cited as *Diary of Anne Frank*).

31. Gerrold van der Stroom, "The Diaries, *Het Achterhuis* and the Translations," *Diary of Anne Frank*, pp. 59–61.

32. Ibid., p. 63.

33. *New York Times Book Review*, June 15, 1952; *Congress Weekly*, Nov. 13, 1950; *National Jewish Post*, June 30, 1952; David Barnouw, "The Play," *Diary of Anne Frank*, p. 78.

34. *New York Law Journal*, Feb. 27, 1959 cited in Barnouw, "The Play," p. 80.

35. *New York Times*, Nov. 27, 1966: Meyer Levin, *The Obsession* (New York, 1973), p. 262.

36. David Barnouw, "Attacks on the Authenticity of the Diary," *Diary of Anne Frank*, p. 84.

37. Ibid., p. 84.

38. Ibid., p. 84–89.

39. Teressa Hendry, "Was Anne Frank's Diary a Hoax?" *American Mercury* (Summer 1967), reprinted in *Myth of the Six Million*, pp. 109–111.

40. Harwood, *Did Six Million Really Die?* p. 19.

41. Hoax, p. 37.

42. Ditlieb Felderer, *Anne Frank's Diary—A Hoax?* (Taby, Sweden, 1978). When the book was reprinted by the IHR the question mark was omitted from the title.

43. Dec. 6, 1943, *Diary*, pp. 424, 425.

44. Robert Faurisson, *Le Journal d'Anne Frank est-il authentique?* in Serge Thion, *Vérité historique or vérité politique?* (Paris, 1980), Barnouw, "Attacks on the Authenticity," pp. 94–95.

45. Aug. 5, 1943, *Diary of Anne Frank*, p. 385.

46. Dec. 6, 1943, Ibid., p. 424.

47. Nov. 9, 1943, Ibid., p. 301.

48. Robert Faurisson, *Het Dagboek van Anne Frank—een vervalsing* (The diary of Anne Frank—a forgery) (Antwerp, 1985), p. 18, cited in Barnouw, p. 95.

49. Barnouw, "Attacks on the Authenticity," p. 96.

50. Opinion of Federal Criminal Investigation Bureau, May 28, 1980; Hamburg, Landgericht, Romer/Geiss dossier, cited in Barnouw, "Attacks on the Authenticity," pp. 97–98.

51. Barnouw, "Attacks on the Authenticity," p. 99.

52. *Der Spiegel*, Oct. 6, 1980, cited in ibid., p. 98.

53. H. J. J. Hardy, "Document Examination and Handwriting Identification of the Text Known as the Diary of Anne Frank: Summary of Findings," *Diary of Anne Frank*, p. 164.

SHELBY MYERS-VERHAGE

Postmarked from Amsterdam—
Anne Frank and Her Iowa Pen Pal

As World War II loomed over Europe, an innovative Iowa educator was bringing the situation home to her students. One spring day in 1940, the seventh- and eighth-grade teacher at the Danville Community School in Des Moines County offered her students the chance to correspond with pen pals overseas. One of her students, Juanita Wagner, drew the name of a ten-year-old girl in the Netherlands—Anne Frank.

The name "Anne Frank" resonates for us today because of the diary of the young Jewish girl kept while in hiding from the Nazis during World War II. First published nearly fifty years ago, the diary is the story of an ordinary teenage girl facing extraordinary circumstances. She details in her diary the usual adolescent fears about growing up, falling in love, and being misunderstood by her parents. Yet she also writes as a Jew hiding from the Nazis as the war raged outside. Readers of the diary all over the world have come to see her as a heroine of the war because, in spite of all she suffered, she still felt that people were inherently "good at heart." Her words have touched generations of people who continue to struggle to understand the complexities of a world war in human terms. Few realize, however, that long before *The Diary of a Young Girl* became legendary, a few pages of Anne Frank's thoughts came to Danville, Iowa, in the spring of 1940.

The Palimpsest, Volume 76, Number 4 (Winter 1995): pp. 152–159. Copyright © 1995 University of Colorado.

This brief connection between Amsterdam and Danville was because of the work of Birdie Mathews to bring those worlds together. By 1940, Mathews was a veteran teacher. She had been teaching since age eighteen, having begun her career at the nearby Plank Road rural school, where she taught grades kindergarten through eighth until she was past forty. About 1921, she moved to the Danville Community School, where she taught seventh and eighth grades. Over two decades at a country school, where she had taught a wide range of curriculum and varying ages and levels of students, no doubt made her a seasoned teacher. But Mathews had accumulated other experiences as well, overcoming the professional isolation that particularly plagued rural and small-town teachers.

These teachers had few opportunities to interact with colleagues outside of their buildings. Even help from the Iowa State Department of Education seemed distant; only local administrators could make requests for its limited materials. In an effort to bring new teaching practices and ideas to rural teachers, the State University of Iowa and other colleges brought traveling workshops, called Tri-County Institutes, to regional locations each fall. Similar to today's in-service days, the institutes met for a half- or whole-day session of speakers and workshops. The institutes minimized the isolation of rural teachers and furthered their professional growth.

Birdie Mathews most likely participated in some of these sessions, since they were often required of all staff. Yet she also spent summers studying at Iowa State Teachers College in Cedar Falls and Colorado State University, as well as Columbia University in New York, where, according to her 1935 diary, she took three courses—"Education and Nationalism," "Modern Trends in Classroom Practices" and "Character and Personality Testing." Few teachers had the time, resources, or incentive for this level of professional education.

"Miss Birdie," as her students called her, acquired more teaching resources through travel. She was even a bit of a local celebrity when she sent home lengthy letters to the *Danville Enterprise* detailing her 1914 trip to Europe. Her letters became front-page news, and her travel experiences became classroom lesson plans. Her students remember fondly the afternoons when they would gather around Mathews to hear her adventures. Opening their eyes to the world beyond, she frequently sent postcards to her students from her travels overseas and across the country, and it is believed that on one of these trips she acquired the names of potential pen pals for her students.

* * *

Because pen-pal writing as a classroom practice was still fairly rare at this time, only creative teachers such as Birdie Mathews would have set up situations in which their students could learn firsthand about the world. Some

Danville students wrote to other children in the United States, but many, including Juanita Wagner, chose to write to overseas pen pals.

In her introductory letter in the spring of 1940, Juanita, age ten, wrote about Iowa, her mother (a teacher), sister Betty Ann, and life on their farm and in nearby Danville. She sealed the letter and sent it to Anne Frank's home address in Amsterdam.

In a few weeks Juanita received not one, but two overseas letters. Anne had written back to Juanita, and Anne's sister Margot, age fourteen, had written a letter to Betty Ann, Juanita's fourteen-year-old sister. "It was such a special joy as a child to have the experience of receiving a letter from overseas from a foreign country and a new pen pal," Betty Ann Wagner later recalled. "In those days we had no TV, little radio, and maybe a newspaper once or twice a week. Living on a farm with so little communication could be very dull except for all the good books from the library."

The Frank sisters' letters from Amsterdam were dated April 27th and the 29th and were written in ink on light blue stationery. Anne and Margot had enclosed their school pictures. The letters were in English, but experts believe that the Frank sisters probably first composed their letters in Dutch and then copied them over in English after their father, Otto Frank, translated them.

In her letter Anne told of her family, her Montessori school, and Amsterdam. She must have pulled out a map of the United States because she wrote, "On the map I looked again and found the name Burlington." Enclosing a postcard of Amsterdam, she mentioned her hobby of "picture-card" collecting: "I have already about 800."

Anne made no mention of the political situation in Europe. Her sister, Margot, however, wrote Betty Ann that "we often listen to the radio as times are very exciting, having a frontier with Germany and being a small country we never feel safe." Referring to their two cousins in Switzerland, Margot remarked, "We have to travel through Germany which we cannot do or through Belgium and France and in that we cannot do either. It is war and no visas are given."

"Needless to say we were both thrilled to have established communications with a foreign friend, and we both wrote again immediately," Betty Ann recalled years later. The Wagner sisters anxiously awaited a second reply postmarked "Amsterdam." But no reply came. Although they did not know that the Frank family was Jewish and therefore in grave danger as the Third Reich advanced, Betty Ann did consider that mail might be restricted or censored. Wondering what had happened to their new Dutch pen pals, the Wagner sisters waited.

Anne's April 29th letter to Juanita had been written just three weeks after Germany had invaded Denmark and Norway—that spring had proved to be a successful one for the Nazi campaign in northern Europe. On May 10, eleven days after Anne wrote her letter, the Dutch surrendered to the Nazis.

At first, little seemed changed in the Netherlands except for the presences of soldiers on the streets. Yet Jews slowly began to feel the effects of the Third Reich. By October 1940, Otto Frank as a Jew would be required to register his business. By June 1941, when Anne Frank would be turning twelve, Jews would be forced to carry identity cards stamped with the letter "J." In the fall of 1941, Anne and Margot, like other Jewish children in Holland, would have to attend a separate school.

* * *

Europe's volatile situation seemed far removed from the world of Juanita and Betty Ann Wagner, where students thought of the war in Europe as they thought of ancient history, that is, as hardly relevant. Yet gradually, the war became more of a reality for the Wagner sisters, their teacher Birdie Mathews, and other southeastern Iowans. Scattered articles about the war in Europe began to appear in the *Burlington Hawkeye Gazette* and *Des Moines County News*. In 1940, a war munitions plant was built between Danville and nearby Middletown. The munitions plant was somewhat controversial: on the one hand it brought new jobs to the local economy; on the other, it took almost a dozen family farms in the area. Temporary housing was constructed for people moving to the area for the jobs. Draft notices began arriving. On Fridays, "Current Events Day," students in Birdie Mathews's class and other classrooms discussed articles and radio broadcasts about the war in Europe.

Suddenly, in December 1941, the bombing of Pearl Harbor catapulted the United States—and Danville, Iowa—into the war. Worried that something had happened to Anne and Margot, Betty Ann and Juanita Wagner still waited for a reply as winter dragged on. No letters came.

By the spring of 1942, in Anne and Margot Frank's world across the Atlantic, Jews were now forced to wear the yellow star of David on all of their clothing and were forbidden to use public transport. Soon many other restrictions came. Anne would write in her diary: "Jews must hand in their bicycles . . . must be indoors from eight o'clock in the evening until six o'clock in the morning; Jews are forbidden to visit Theaters, cinemas and other places of entertainment." Anne was just entering adolescence, and such restrictions surely affected her budding social life. Later she would record in her diary her friend's comment that "you're scared to do anything because it may be forbidden."

When the Frank family received an arrest notice for Margot, they were scared enough to go into hiding on July 6, 1942. Otto Frank planted clues around their apartment to suggest the family had fled to Switzerland. Their hiding place was the rear part of the building where Otto Frank had his business in the heart of Amsterdam. The door to the "Secret Annex," as Anne called it, was hidden behind a bookcase in one of the offices.

A business acquaintance, Herman van Pels, and his wife and son, Peter, also joined them. A few months later a Jewish dentist, Fritz Pfeffer, also moved into the annex (making a total of eight people hiding in four small rooms and a watercloset). Four of Otto Frank's coworkers knew about the annex above their offices; they supplied the families with food and news of the outside world. Although her letter writing to Danville had long since ended, Anne wrote faithfully in her diary.

On August 4, 1944, while Danville residents were reading about the Polish underground and the Nazis' flight from Florence in the *Burlington Hawkeye Gazette*, German police entered the secret annex and arrested the Frank and van Pels families and Fritz Pfeffer. Within a month, they were transported by train with many other Dutch Jews to Auschwitz, the death camp in Poland. The men and women were separated, but Anne and Margot were allowed to stay with their mother until October 1944, when the sisters were transferred to Bergen-Belsen. Their mother died in January 1945.

At Bergen-Belsen, conditions were atrocious, food was scarce, and thousands were dying from disease. Anne discovered an old school friend in another section of the camp; the two girls talked through the barbed wire separating them. As winter ended, typhus swept through the camp. Margot became ill first and died in March 1945. A few days later, just weeks before the British liberated the camp, sixteen-year-old Anne died.

Ten-year-old Anne Frank writes to Juanita Wagner in Iowa:
Amsterdam 29 April Monday
Dear Juanita,

I did receive your letter and want to answer you as quick as possible. Margot and myself are the only children in our house. Our grandma is living with us. My father has an office and mother is busy at home. I have not far from school and I am sitting in the fifth class. We have no hour-classes we may do what we prefer, of course we must get to a certain goal. Your mother will certainly know this system, it is called Montessori. We have little work at home.

On the map I looked again and found the name Burlington. I did ask a girl friend of mine if she would like to communicate with one of your friends. She wants to do it with a girl about my age not with a boy.

I shall write her address underneath. Did you yourself write the letter I received from you, or did your mother do it? I include a post-card from Amsterdam and shall continue to do that collecting picture-cards I have already about 800. A child I used to be at school with went to New-York and she did writh [sic] a letter to our class some time ago. In case you and Betty get a photo do send a copy as I am curious to know how you look. My birthday is the 12th of June. Kindly let me know yours. Perhaps one of your friends wil [sic] write first to my girl friend, for she also cannot write English but her father or mother will translate the letter.

Hoping to hear from you I remain your Dutch friend Annelies Marie Frank.

P.S. Please write me the address of a girl. [Anne ends with the name and Amsterdam address of her own friend, Susanne Ledermann.]

* * *

After the war was over, Betty Ann Wagner was teaching in a country school in eastern Illinois. Still curious about the Dutch pen pals, she wrote again to Anne's address in Amsterdam. A few months later, she received a long, handwritten letter from Otto Frank. He told about the family hiding, of Anne's experiences in the "secret annex," and how Anne had died in a concentration camp. This was the first time Wagner learned that Anne had been Jewish. "When I received the letter I shed tears," Wagner recalled, "and the next day took it with me to school and read Otto Frank's letter to my students. I wanted them to realize how fortunate they were to be in America during World War II."

By 1956, Wagner had settled in California and was driving home from work one day when she heard a review on the radio of a new Broadway play called *The Diary of Anne Frank*. Thinking it might be the same Anne Frank, she rushed to order a copy of the play. As soon as it arrived she realized it was indeed her sister's pen pal; a photo similar to the one from Anne appeared on the cover.

Although Otto Frank's letter had been misplaced during one of the Wagner family's frequent moves, Betty Ann had carefully kept Anne and Margot's letters safe. In the late 1980s the letter became part of the collections of the Simon Wiesenthal Center in Los Angeles, where they are now on display.

* * *

And what of Birdie Mathews, the small-town teacher who by a combination of innovative teaching and pure chance briefly connected the Wagner sisters and the Frank sisters? "Miss Birdie" had retired the year the war ended, having built a local reputation as a devoted teacher who never hesitated to create special opportunities for her students. Years earlier, she had started what she considered the county's first drivers' education program: during recesses, she taught farm boys how to drive her car. The trade-off was that now that they knew how to drive and could borrow Mathews's car, they had to keep coming to school despite seasonal demands of farm work. When the Great Depression hit in the 1930s, Mathews had refused her salary so that fuel could be brought to keep the school heated and open. She often organized class picnics and wiener roasts at a park or her home. One former student recalled when "Miss Birdie" took her to a state spelling contest and an overnight stay at the University of Iowa—a truly exciting trip for a youngster from Danville, population 309 in 1940.

Because Danville was a small community and Mathews came from a large family, she taught many of her nieces and nephews; they often remarked that she was tougher on them than on the other pupils in an effort to avoid favoritism. Although revered by her students, she was known as a strong disciplinarian. One former student recalled her response to a particularly obnoxious boy: "Miss Birdie took him in the hallway and shook him until his shirt buttons popped off."

After her retirement in 1945, Mathews's sense of exacting detail and organization translated easily into her long-time love of needlework and gardening. A meticulous gardener, she believed that "flowers do something for a person—brightens up a home." Every year she shared her abundant vegetable crops with friends and relatives, and she continued to volunteer at the Danville Congregational Church, where she and her family had deep roots. She remained involved in the lives of her many nieces and nephews. With more time to travel, she took several trips to sunny locations during long Iowa winters. She had always kept travel diaries. Now retired, she took more care to keep her day-to-day dairies current. As the years progressed, Mathews traveled less, yet she continued an active correspondence with friends and former students. She died in 1974, at age ninety-four.

Today, Betty Ann and Juanita Wagner continue to tell their story about their brief connection to Margot and Anne Frank, aware that even the most ordinary person can be a part of extraordinary situations. Against a backdrop of an approaching world war, three human impulses briefly connected: "Miss Birdie" Mathews's vision to broaden her students' world view; Juanita Wagner's desire for an overseas pen pal; and Anne Frank's eagerness to respond as "your Dutch friend," as she signed her letter. As a result, a few letters were exchanged and a few friendships sprouted one spring a half-century ago, when Amsterdam came postmarked to Iowa.

In early July 1942, when Anne's family decided to go into hiding, Anne wrote in her diary about packing hurriedly: "The first thing I put in was this diary, then hair curlers, handkerchiefs, schoolbooks, a comb, old letters; I put in the craziest things with the idea that we were going into hiding, but I'm not sorry, memories mean more to me than dresses." Could some of the "old letters" she packed have been postmarked "Danville, Iowa"?

Thirteen-year-old Margot Frank writes to Betty Ann Wagner:
Amsterdam 27th April 1940.
Dear Betty Ann,

I have only received your letters about a week ago and had no time to answer right away. It is Sunday to day, so I can take time to write. During the week I am very busy as I have to work for school at home every day.

Our school begins at 9 a.m. till noon then I go home by my bicycle (if the weather is bad I go by bus and stay at school) and return for the class beginning at half past one; we then have class until three o'clock. Wednesday and Saturday afternoon we are free and use our time to play tennis and to row. In the winter we play hockey or go skating if it is could *[sic]* enough. This year it was unusually cold and all the canals were frozen; to day is the first really spring day, the sun shining bright and warm. Generally we have lot of rain.

In summer we have a two months holiday, then a fortnight at Christmas and so on Easter; Whitsuntide only four days.

We often listen to the radio as times are very exciting, having a frontier with Germany and being a small country we never feel safe.

In our class most of the children comunicate *[sic]* with one or the other so I do not know children who would want to take up correspondence. I only have two cousins, boys living at Basel, Switserland *[sic]*. For American ideas this is not far but for us it is. We have to travel through Germany which we cannot do or through Belgium and France and in that we cannot either. It is war and no visas are given.

We live in a five room flat attached to the only sky scraper of the city being twelve storeys high. Amsterdam has about 200000 inhabitants. We are near the sea-shore but we miss hills and woods. Every thing being flat and a great part of the country lying below sea-level; therefore the name Netherland.

Father is going to business in the morning and returns about 8 p.m.; Mother is busy at home. My grandmother is living with us and we rented one room to a lady.

Now I think I have told you quite a lot and I am expecting your answer.

With kindest regards your friend.
Margot Betti Frank.
P.S. Many thanks for Juanita's letter as Anne is writing to her I need not write myself. Margot.

RACHEL FELDHAY BRENNER

Writing Herself Against History: Anne Frank's Self-Portrait as a Young Artist

Perhaps we are at the end of an era where narrating no longer has a place
. . . because human beings no longer have any experience to share. . . .
And yet . . . Perhaps, in spite of everything, it is necessary . . . to believe
that new narrative forms, which we do not yet know how to name, are
already being born. . . . For we have no idea of what a culture would be
where no one any longer knew what it meant to narrate things.

—Paul Ricoeur[1]

Introduction: Problems of Reception

Strictly speaking, the *Diary of Anne Frank* is not a testimony of the
Holocaust atrocity. In contrast with ghetto diaries and concentration camp
memoirs, Frank's text depicts the anticipation of the Holocaust persecution.
It is a story of the victim coping with the inexorable awareness of the Final
Solution. The eventual encounter with the persecutors and the physical
destruction itself are not part of Frank's narrative.

As Alvin Rosenfeld sees it, the absence of the tragic end in the text
seems to have reduced Anne Frank to a symbol of moral and intellectual convenience.[2] The particular position of the text which ends in medias res, at the
threshold, so to speak, of the deportation camp, allows to attenuate and even
to abstract the horror that awaited the author. The concentration camp in the
testimonies of Elie Wiesel, Pelagia Lewinska, Primo Levi, and other victims

Modern Judaism, Volume 16, Number 2 (May 1996): pp. 105–134. Copyright © 1996 Rachel
Feldhay Brenner.

of the Final Solution exposed an unimaginable horror. The Annexe, however, retained a semblance of normalcy which helped to insist on continuing faith in humanism.

The reading of the *Diary* as a lesson in liberal-humanist Weltanschauung was established very early. *The Critical Edition of the Diary* quotes the 1946 response by the writer Jan Romein. "How [Frank] died, I do not wish to ask," Romein says, "The way she died is in any case not important." What is important, according to Romein, is that Frank's fate makes us reject fascism and reminds us that the future solution lies in "the building of a society in which talent is no longer destroyed, repressed and oppressed, but discovered, nurtured, and assisted, wherever it may appear."[3]

The reception of the *Diary* as an edifying, universal message to humanity contributed to its classification as adolescent literature.[4] The tenor of optimism is noticeable in the *Diary*'s adaptation into a play and into a successful film. Anne Frank herself became a standard presence in the writings and the events produced in commemoration of the Holocaust. She is considered the symbol of universal victimization and, at the same time, an emblem of prevailing humanism.

The critical responses focused on the politics of the *Diary*'s theatrical and cinematic adaptations. Meyer Levin raised the question of the universalization of Jewish suffering. Levin was instrumental in the first publication of Frank's *Diary* in the United States in the 1950s. In the famous court case, he claimed that the dramatized version was a distortion of the *Diary*'s Jewish character.[5] Levin's extraordinary, thirty-five-year-long struggle against the de-judaisation of Anne Frank has been recently documented in Lawrence Graver's study of his obsession.[6]

Judith Doneson argues that the stage and film productions of the *Diary* reflects America's ideological crisis in the 1950s. The ambivalence regarding the Jewish aspect of the *Diary* should be considered in the context of the McCarthy era. Doneson claims that the play's emphasis on Frank's faith that "people are good at heart" promoted the ideal of democratic liberalism by turning the Holocaust victim into a symbol of humanistic fortitude.[7] Sidra Ezrahi argues that the universalization of Jewish suffering signals the reluctance of the assimilated American Jews to single out the Holocaust as Jewish experience. Like Doneson, Ezrahi maintains that the play's emphasis on human goodness reaffirms trust in the endangered tenet of democratic freedom and equality.[8]

Another trend of critical response draws attention to Frank's own universalism. Critics point to her assimilationist background and her lack of Jewish education. Sandor Gilman dismisses Levin's arguments about the *Diary*'s "Jewishness" and maintains that "Anne Frank was typical of assimilated Jews . . . [her language] is no specific marker for her identity . . . she does not speak with a Jewish accent, does not mix bits of Hebrew in her discourse."[9] According to Gilman, the de-emphasis of the Jewish component in the theatrical production is congruent with Frank's upbringing and orientation.

The notion of the language as a marker of Jewish identity emerges in James Young's discussion of Holocaust diaries. Young highlights the Jewish authenticity of those diarists who wrote in Hebrew and in Yiddish in contrast with "Anne [who] was assimilated, non-Zionist, and wrote in Dutch."[10] Young reads the *Diary* as "alternately jaded and optimistic."[11] He argues that "in the context of her assimilated world view" Frank emerges as "[a] member of the human community and not as one who identified herself as part of a collective Jewish tragedy."[12]

It is important to note that the controversy concerning the "Jewishness" of the *Diary* provided ammunition to the deniers of the Holocaust. As Gilman notes, Levin's court case fuelled the revisionist claim that the *Diary* was a fabrication and thus a proof that the Holocaust never happened.[13] In response to these claims, the authenticity of Anne Frank's work was definitively reconfirmed in the *Critical Edition of the Diary* prepared by the Netherlands State Institute for War Documentation published in 1989.

At the psychological level, the controversy of the *Diary* signaled the difficulty to accept the reality of the Holocaust. In this sense, Bruno Bettelheim's essay, "The Ignored Lesson of Anne Frank," exemplifies a denial of the irrevocability of the Final Solution. It is true that Bettelheim first sees the play's concluding affirmation of human goodness as an implication that "there never really was an Auschwitz."[14] Then, however, Bettelheim claims that Anne Frank need not have died had Otto Frank resorted to different tactics of escape and hiding, which he inexcusably failed to consider. Bettelheim's argument met with an outraged critical response. As Rosenfeld notes, "Bettelheim's charge that the Jews, in effect, had prepared the way for their own victimization was received in a hostile manner."[15]

The reluctance to confront the horror emerges also in postwar American Jewish literary treatment of Anne Frank. Nathan Zuckerman, the protagonist-writer in Philip Roth's *The Ghost Writer*, denies Frank's death. His fantasy of Frank, alive and well, demonstrates the fearfulness of the North American Jew to confront the true meaning of the European catastrophe. The portrayal of Frank as a survivor signals the wish to deny the event of the Holocaust. Like her theatrical image constructed to symbolize humanistic faith, the novelistic figuration of Frank as a living character communicates the need to abstract the horror of the Holocaust.

The fictional representations of Frank imply unwillingness, or perhaps inability, to face the author of the *Diary*. Even the opponents of the transformation of the *Diary* into a humanistic manifesto of a child-victim invariably focus on the cinematic and theatrical adaptations. Systematic critical examinations of the original text are rare.

Among the few who have tried to grapple with the *Diary* itself,[16] John Berryman seems to offer the most thoughtful and relevant analysis of the text. In contrast with the Jewish critics, Berryman, who was not Jewish, does not concern himself with Frank's ethnic or religious authenticity. Nor does he question Frank's Jewishness. What attracts him is the *Diary* itself which he considers an extraordinary piece of writing produced by an extraordinary writer under extraordinary circumstances. And he is amazed that the artistic and ethical qualities of the text have been virtually ignored. "I am obliged to wonder," Berryman admits, "whether Anne Frank has *had* any serious readers, for I find no indication in anything written about her that anyone has taken her with real seriousness. . . ." He is certain that she deserves genuine critical attention:

> At first it is necessary to discover what she is writing about. Perhaps . . . she is not truly writing about anything—you know, 'thoughts of a young girl,' 'Jews in hiding from the Nazis,' 'a poignant love affair'; but such is not my opinion.[17]

Berryman dismisses the notion of the *Diary* as a work of a young girl. He also rejects the play's sentimental emphasis on child victimization in the Holocaust. In contrast, Berryman considers the *Diary* a unique literary event produced by a person who becomes "more mature than perhaps most persons ever become."[18] It is a credit to Berryman's critical astuteness that his appreciation of the *Diary* was made on the basis of the early, partial publication of Frank's papers. He had no opportunity to consider the complete work as it appears in the *Critical Edition of the Diary*.

Nonetheless, Berryman shows a deep understanding of the uniqueness of the text. He sees Frank's *Diary* as a narrative of developmental conversion. His point of comparative reference is St. Augustine's *Confessions*, a text of religious conversion. Berryman compares "the originality and ambition and indispensability of the two books *in the heart of their substances*." He suggests that the subject of Frank's *Diary* is "the conversion of the child into a person" and maintains that, in that sense, Frank's account is "more mysterious and fundamental than that of St. Augustine's."[19]

Berryman then proceeds to analyze the psychological aspects of Frank's development.[20] His discussion is based on a close textual reading. He not only calls attention to the process of Frank's emotional maturation, but highlights her growth as a talented writer. Most significantly, however, Berryman is aware of the ironic futility of his efforts to place the *Diary* in a referential context.

The Augustinian and Freudian models of conversion and development are inadequate in the case of Frank's narrative. According to Berryman, because of the "very special circumstances" under which this particular personality was developing "we have been tracing a psychological and moral development to which, if I am right, *no close parallel can be found.*"[21]

Berryman's assertion of the uniqueness of the *Diary* is enlightening. His view highlights the interpretive problematic regarding a text which has "no close parallel." The unprecedented historical circumstances under which the text was composed posit the *Diary* as a category of its own. It is a life narrative which resists and, at the same time, is shaped by the projected narrative of awaiting deportation and death.

The poignancy of Frank's writing, therefore, emerges from her awareness of the terrifying historical reality against which, as a Jew, she writes her life story. As we shall see, she becomes increasingly conscious of the impossibility to communicate the tensions, the dangers, and the terrifying prospects that she and those with her are facing. This consciousness forges Frank's artistic skills and shapes her ethics. As a story of "psychological and moral development," in Berryman's definition, the *Diary* is also, to recall Ricoeur, a quest for a "new narrative form" which would make it possible to "share an experience" to which a parallel cannot be found.

This discussion of the *Diary* will proceed along the lines suggested in Berryman's reading. I suggest that the *Diary* is a work of art, which defiantly contravenes the fearful hiatus which brought it into being. It is not our "reduction of Anne Frank to a symbol of moral and intellectual convenience," to recall Rosenfeld, that allows us to read optimism into Frank's life narrative. It is, rather, her valiant artistic accomplishment and her courageous ethical vision that enables us to read triumph into her losing battle against fear and despair.

I should mention here that in my appreciation of Frank's writing I was fortunate to be able to use the two versions of Frank's *Diary* and the text of the first publication of her papers as they appear in the *Definitive Edition.*[22]

The Language(s) of an Unparalleled Situation

Comparative reasoning enables us to approach unfamiliar phenomena. The ability to draw comparisons communicates a fundamental belief that no phenomenon is inherently new; phenomena may be new only in terms of our personal experience. Reference to previous experiences evokes a network of corresponding patterns, assimilating the new experience in a familiar context.

Kafka's story "Metamorphosis" illustrates human inability to break away from patterns of thinking grounded in analogues, even in an unprecedented situation. As Tzvetan Todorov tells us, despite the incomprehensible nature of Gregor's transformation, both the protagonist and his family continue to behave as if their misfortune were of perfectly ordinary nature. Through its representation in ordinary language, "a shocking, impossible event . . . ends by becoming possible."[23] The ordinary language allows us to approach the event in the sphere of the "normal."

In the case of the *Diary,* the desire to situate the experience within the boundaries of the "normal" is evident in the dramatized adaptation of the text. The ending on a hopeful note in the stage production attenuates the Holocaust circumstances. A similar intention is communicated in the wording of the title and in the synopsis which appears on the cover of the pocket-book edition.[24]

The title of the paperback reads: *Anne Frank: The Diary of a Young Girl.* The attempt to fictionalize the diary is signaled in the qualifier "Young Girl" and in the absence of any reference to the Holocaust. The wording of the title places the content in the realm of the "normal." The omission to mention the Holocaust circumstances of the life narrated in the *Diary* is conspicuous in the phrase "young girl" which associates with longevity and hope.

The synopsis on the back cover re-emphasizes the evasion of the Holocaust. The content summary does not mention Frank's death as a Holocaust victim; in fact, it does not mention her death at all. The focus is on Frank's romantic involvement with Peter. Indeed, the back cover tells us that the *Diary* "is not a lament but a song of love." Such an interpretation, clearly designed to lure the prospective buyer of the book, misrepresents both the content of the *Diary* and the circumstances of its composition.

It is very interesting to note that Frank anticipated the postwar attempts to place the *Diary* in the context of conventional literary categorization.

In response to the official announcement that private papers relating to the war experience would be collected and published once the war was over, Frank considered submission of her diary. The title of her publication, she decides, will be *Het Achterhuis* [The Secret Annexe]. She then remarks jokingly that "the title alone would be enough to make people think it was a detective story." The significant comment that follows, however, demonstrates Frank's awareness that her tale of hiding and suspense could not comply with the detective story convention:

> But, seriously, it would seem quite *funny* ten years after the war
> if we Jews were to tell how we lived and what we ate and talked
> about here. (*D* 578, my emphasis).[25]

Nonetheless, on May 20, 1944, Frank decides to tell her tale. She writes that "at long last after a great deal of reflection I have started my "Achterhuis" (*D* 653). In fact, she started rewriting her diary on loose sheets. This version became the second version of the *Diary* in the *Critical Edition* (*D* 61). Clearly, she saw publishing the story of her war experience as a step toward becoming a writer.

The story of the Secret Annexe tells of suspense which does not classify it as a conventional detective story. Frank's story depicts the perilous situation of the Annexe inhabitants as both Dutch citizens under Nazi occupation and as Jews under the threat of the Final Solution. At one level, the suspense reflects the helplessness of the endangered and starved Dutch population at large. At another level, it reflects the particular plight of the hunted, condemned-to-death Jewish population.

Anne describes the fear when "350 British planes dropped half a million kilos of bombs on Ijmuiden and the houses trembled like a wisp of grass in the wind"; she talks about the epidemics, the "indescribable" shortage of food, the doctors who are under "incredible" pressure, the burglaries and thefts which are "beyond belief," the "wanton destruction by youth," etc. (*D* 578–579).

A future writer struggling to find the language to portray an "indescribable" reality, Frank is aware of the "unreality" of this situation to anybody distanced from the world at war. She finds herself in the predicament of a writer afraid of failing her reader.

In a direct comment to Kitty, the imaginary 26 addressee of her testimony, Frank addresses her misgivings, "You don't know anything about all these things, and I would need to keep on writing the whole day if I were to tell you everything in detail" (*D* 578–579). This hyperbole as well as the recourse to such modifiers as "indescribable," "incredible," and "beyond belief,"[27] signal Frank's sensitivity to the limitations of her vocabulary. She seeks terminology to narrate a reality which escapes the accepted linguistic connotations.

In this reality, the intended haven of the Annexe speaks the language of a frightful entrapment. "Everyday our living space grows smaller," Frank observes. "Will it be over soon enough, before we suffocate and die of hunger?" (*D* 581). The hardship of the war which affects everybody intensifies incomparably for the Jewish victims. Frank is aware that for the Jews the alternative to deprivation and air raids is deportation and gas chambers.

The consciousness of premeditated Jewish annihilation emerges as early as October 1942. In this entry Frank reports about Jewish friends who have been rounded up and sent to Westerbork, and about transports to Eastern Europe where Jews are being gassed (*D* 272).

The story of the "Secret Annexe" diverges therefore from the detective's search for "who's done it." Rather, it poses a poignant query: "how much longer?" In Frank's "detective story," the suspense is not evoked by the expected discovery and elimination of a wily criminal. Rather, it generates from the threat of discovery and elimination of the innocent victim.

For the Jewish population, therefore, the entrapment is absolute. The sense of inescapable doom emerges poignantly at the time of an especially powerful air raid. As Frank describes it, "the house rumbled and shook, and down came the bombs." At that moment of fear, she realizes that

> there's nowhere we can go. If ever we come to the extremity of fleeing from here, the street would be just as dangerous as an air raid. (*D* 375)

Literally a "death trap," the Annexe illustrates the Jewish fate under Nazi occupation. Far from acting and writing as an inauthentic, assimilated Jew, Frank demonstrates full understanding of the terrible situation of the Jews. Furthermore, she demonstrates solidarity with the Jewish plight. As she bitterly points out, her situation reminds her time and again that "we are Jews in chains, chained to one spot, without any rights" (*D* 600).

Frank's decision to record the story of the "Secret Annexe" for a postwar readership confronts her with the complexity that such a testimony entails. While the text strives at a mimetic representation of the situation, it also demonstrates its author's search for an appropriate narrative form and an adequate linguistic expression. Fully conscious of her fate as a Jew, Frank seeks a rhetoric which would both name and defy the unparalleled reality of horror.

The "Indescribable" Reality of the Imminent Apocalypse

In a letter to Kitty written a year after going into hiding, Frank observes that "everything" in the "Secret Annexe" is "so different from ordinary times and from ordinary people's lives" that "it is quite indescribable." Nevertheless, in an attempt to communicate the "out of the ordinary" experience of hiding, Frank decides to "give . . . a slightly closer look into our lives," and to present Kitty with "a description of an ordinary day" (*D* 381). The next two entries offer detailed accounts of the meal times, sleeping arrangements, and daily tasks of the Annexe inhabitants.

In a way, Frank's description of an ordinary day seems to reveal nothing out of the ordinary. If anything, it demonstrates the remarkable determination of the individuals in hiding to lead normal lives. They go about their activities, trying to work, read, and study, while striving to adjust to the cramped setup of the Annexe.

What, then, causes Frank to sense the "indescribable" quality of her existence? I suggest that her decision to describe the "ordinary" indicates a conscious wish to defuse the notion of the anomalous situation of hiding. The meticulous listing of regular schedules, activities, and arrangements communicates the desire to hold on to the semblance of normalcy.

It is as if the account of the routine could fend off the invading sense of the futility of hiding. The account of the "ordinary" registers the need for a sense of control and purposefulness to contravene the debilitating sense of helplessness.

It is significant that Frank's decision on Aug. 4, 1943 to describe the daily routine in the Annexe follows the entry of Aug. 3. There Frank describes Mrs. Van Daan, "shaking like a leaf" after the third air raid that day, and quotes her saying, "A terrible end is better than no end at all" (*D* 380). We should note that the same sentiment is reiterated by Frank herself at a later date, in May 1944, when she wonders "how long have we still to put up with this almost unbearable, ever increasing pressure?" (*D* 660) and admits her growing despair:

> Again and again I ask myself, would it not have been better for us all if we had not gone into hiding, and if we were dead now and not going through all this misery . . . I hope something will happen soon now, shooting if need be—nothing can crush us *more* than this restlessness . . . (*D* 662, italics in the text)

The hiding place incurs such mental hardship that it evokes the death wish. The anticipation of the end has become too terrible to endure.

As the ordeal of hiding goes on, it becomes increasingly evident that the main source of anguish, strain, and hopelessness is rooted in a self-inflicted erasure from history and even from one's own life story. The decision to disappear from the social scene signifies severance of all social patterns which define one's sense of belonging.

Ironically, the opposition to the Nazi plan of Jewish elimination signified, in fact, deliberate self-elimination from normal life. In order to remain alive, the Jews in the Annexe had to cease to exist as members of society. They had to detach themselves from their personal past and identity. They were coerced into the role of condemned, ghostlike figures, allowed to come to life only at night.

With past annulled, the growing sense of doom precluded the future. The horrific news of the systematic destruction of the Jews incurred fear which was exacerbated with each of the increasingly frequent air raids. The diminishing chances of survival engendered despair, rendering plans, dreams, and prospects for after the war meaningless to the point of the absurd.

In her moving memoir, Miep Gies, the woman who helped to hide the Frank family, remembers Mrs. Frank admitting to her in private that "she was suffering under a great weight of despair." Miep recalls that "although the others were . . . making games of what they would do when the war was all over, Mrs. Frank confessed that she was deeply ashamed of the fact that she felt the end would never come."[28]

An entry in the *Diary* makes clear that Mrs. Frank's sense of despair was shared by her daughter. Indeed, as Frank writes on Nov. 8, 1943, planning for the future has turned into a meaningless exercise; the memories of the past have also become meaningless:

> I simply can't imagine that the world will ever be normal for us again. I do talk about "after the war," but then it is only a castle in the air, something that will never really happen. If I think back to our old house, my girl friends, the fun at school, it is just as if another person lived it all, not me. (*D* 416)

The merciless implementation of the Final Solution not only stripped the hiding Jews of their past, but robbed them of the hope for the future. In a sense, it "froze" the victims' time by imprisoning them in the present of constant dread.

In this situation, the "ordinary" day seems out of the ordinary because it lacks a future direction. In the atmosphere of the end constantly about to come, the people in the Annexe are helplessly suspended in the situation of "no exit." They are doomed to lead an "indescribable" life of exclusion from the continuum of time.

A brief discussion of life narrative as a metonymic construct of human-kind's progression in history will help to elucidate the "new form," to recall Ricoeur's term, of Frank's timeless life narrative. Speaking about temporal constituents of emplotment, Ricoeur distinguishes between the "episodic dimension of the narrative" and its "configurational dimension." The former is made of events; the latter transforms the events into a story. "The configurational arrangement," claims Ricoeur, "transforms the succession of events into one meaningful whole."[29]

According to Ricoeur, such a "whole" renders the story meaningful because it determines its beginning, middle, and end. The notion of start and conclusion moves the narrative along. In this sense the narrative concurs with the notion of history as teleological, that is, meaningful, linear progression from beginning to end, as decreed by the divine Providence.

By his own admission, Ricoeur follows in the footsteps of Frank Kermode. In his *Sense of Ending*, Kermode postulates that eschatological closure is inherent in any story, as it reflects the prototypical narrative of the Bible. According to Kermode, the configuration of the biblical story reflects the paradigm of human history which begins with Creation and ends with the vision of apocalyptic destruction.[30] But the apocalypse, that is, the ending of history, is constantly deferred. As Kermode says, "[the apocalypse] is disconfirmed without being discredited."[31] History has continued to evolve despite the anticipated ending of time, and so modern theological thought perceives the apocalypse "as immanent rather than imminent."[32]

The sense of the immanent apocalypse affects the individual life story. The consciousness of ending shapes our life as "fiction," the evolution of which reminds us of the temporarily deferred reality of our death. As long as it remains in the sphere of the abstract, the myth of the apocalypse infuses sense in life by teaching us a useful lesson about our mortality. An attempt to actualize the myth, however, brings forth destruction. Kermode observes that such an attempt produces a "consciously false apocalypse," such as the Third Reich, "which projected death upon others."[33]

In the context of Kermode's discussion, therefore, the "projection of death" upon Jews in the Holocaust was meant to actualize the prophecy of the apocalypse. Through fascism, says Kermode, "the world is changed to conform with a fiction, as by the murder of Jews." The destruction of Jews identified by the "medieval apocalyptic movements" as "the demonic host of the prophecies"[34] marks the Holocaust as an attempt to end the history of the Jewish people.

The end of history amounts to the arrest of the time flow. The timelessness which marks the end of human history signifies the lifelessness of a world devoid of its future. For the inhabitants of the Annexe—the targets of the apocalyptic scheme of the Third Reich—time had stopped, as they were approaching the end designated as the Final Solution.

In the normal course of events, humanity's position on the historical paradigm is, as Kermode sees it, in "the middest," that is, between the "imaginatively recorded past [the Creation] and imaginatively recorded future, [the Apocalypse]."[35] The anomaly of the "false apocalypse" of the Nazi terror transferred the position of the Jews onto the pole of the hitherto only "recorded future" of the apocalypse. The imagined apocalyptic ending has become the concrete reality of the present. Thus, in terms of the Creation-Apocalypse paradigm, the hiding Jews in the Annexe are no longer "in the middest"; rather, they move inexorably towards the sphere of the destruction.

The apocalyptic situation of the Jews in the Annexe turns the configurational dimension of the "ordinary," everyday life in the Annexe into a purposeless, "episodic" existence. Divested of everything that connects them to the past, deprived of the future, the inhabitants of the Annexe follow their daily schedules which, increasingly, turn into perfunctory, repetitious, and meaningless motions.

The temporal stasis compounded by the spatial confinement marks an existence empty of meaning. The purposelessness of such an existence is apocalyptic in itself, because it evokes the self-destructive wish for an ending. Indeed, the tragic fulfillment of this wish reconfirmed the ordeal of hiding as a preamble of the apocalyptic termination. The eventual betrayal, deportation, and annihilation of the Annexe inhabitants enhance the ironic futility of an attempt to defy the reality of the Final Solution.

The Jewish Holocaust undermines the sense of teleological meaningfulness. The unwillingness to acknowledge the irrevocable concreteness of the destruction emerges, as demonstrated earlier, in the evasive reader-response to the tragic fate of the *Diary*'s author. I suggest that Frank's death constitutes a crucially important addendum to her story. The consciousness of her death in Bergen Belsen confronts us with the reality of the decreed catastrophe and thus highlights the heroic quality of her artistic struggle with the "indescribable" life narrative.

The Apocalyptic "Stillness" and the Voice of Art

As a rule, autobiographers write their lives in order to understand their motivations and attain an extent of self-understanding. They draw upon their past experiences to illuminate their present situation and to gain a measure of foresight. Frank, whose young age could hardly offer a sustaining perspective of the past, drew support and strength from her aspiration to become an artist. Despite the imminence of death, writing seemed to afford her a sense of future.

Frank treated her desire to become a writer with utmost seriousness. As mentioned before, in preparation for the possible publication of *Het Achterhuis* after the war, she started to recopy and to edit her diary. The seriousness about her future vocation is also evident in the frequency of the entries, the range of topics, and the insistence on an accurate portrayal of life in the Secret Annexe. Methodically and meticulously, Frank created a record of a world in the throes of terror, a world which, as she knew very well, was on the brink of collapse.

To persist at creating such a record meant a constant struggle against despair. The fear that dominated the Annexe was so overwhelming that it often put the diarist in a state of utter desperation. In a moving entry of Oct. 29, 1943, Frank portrays herself as "a songbird whose wings have been clipped and who is hurling himself in utter darkness against the bars of his cage." Depressed, she lies down to sleep, "to make the time pass more quickly, and the *stillness* and the terrible fear, because there is no way of killing time" (*D* 411, my emphasis).

The sense of the end is so palpable that soon after it transforms into a truly apocalyptic vision of destruction. On Nov. 8, 1943, Frank wrote:

> I see the eight of us with our "Secret Annexe" as if we were a little piece of blue heaven, surrounded by heavy black rain clouds. The round, clearly defined spot where we stand is still safe, but the

clouds gather more closely about us and the circle which separates us from the approaching danger closes more and more tightly. Now we are so surrounded by danger and darkness that we bump against each other, as we search desperately for a means of escape. We look down below, where people are fighting each other, we look above, where it is quiet and beautiful, and meanwhile we are cut off by the great dark mass, which will not let us go upwards, but which stands before us as an impenetrable wall; it tries to crush us, but cannot do so yet. I can only cry and implore: "Oh, if only the black circle could recede and open the way for us!" (*D* 416)

This poetic visualization presents a surprisingly lucid picture of reality. The apocalyptic tenor of the vision calls attention to Frank's lack of self-delusion. The act of writing, therefore, was by no means a panacea. Despite her youth, Frank was capable of articulating a poignant and unsparing assessment of the circumstances.

Frank's imagination and intelligence enabled her to assume a detached "bird's eye view" which she articulated in a striking, poetic language. A remarkable confluence of sensitivity, integrity, and artistic inspiration precluded escape into self-deception and false optimism. Insistence on a faithful and systematic representation of the experience compelled the diarist to re-live her fear in the act of writing.

Frank's determination to confront reality in writing raises the question of the rationale for this re-immersion in the terrifying situation. Why would the young victim feel the need to tell about her world coming to its end? What would make her write about a reality in which both recounting and foretelling became meaningless?

To understand the telos of Frank's writing we need to remember that the time span that she sets out to describe is the present of immediate, direct menace and dread. It is therefore important, first of all, to comprehend the artistic significance of such a foreshortened perspective.

The mimetic representation of the world at the edge of the apocalypse subverts the Aristotelian notion of the mimetic plot as a carefully selected sequence of events. Mimesis, "the medium of imitation," as Aristotle defines it,[36] foregrounds the "unity of plot" and is, therefore, predicated upon the selection of the "probable or the necessary" events which center around "one action."[37] The unity of action results from the process of artistic selection out of the "infinitely various . . . incidents in one man's life."[38] The narrative is directed at the audience and, if effective, the cathartic impact of its mimetic construct, especially in the case of a tragic tale, "will thrill with horror and melt to pity" all those who hear the story.[39]

When applied to the life in the Annexe, the Aristotelian precepts of mimesis highlight the fact that the range of events subject to selection was extremely limited. Needless to say, the expectation to elicit a cathartic sense of horror and pity under the circumstances presented a totally incongruous proposition.

We should mention in passing that the *Diary*'s theatrical production did follow the Aristotelian precepts of the tragic plot. The staging of the text as a tragedy ended with a cathartic relief. The dramatic adaptation complied with Aristotle's injunction that "the tragic plot must not be composed of irrational parts," since "the poet should prefer probable impossibilities to improbable possibilities."[40] The dramatized version of the *Diary* defused the "irrationality" of the Holocaust horror. It suggested the probability of a cathartic response to the Holocaust.

In contrast to its dramatic production, the narrative of the *Diary* focuses on the irrational. The story deals with the unprecedented problematic of the "improbable possibility" of the Holocaust.

The possibility of the Holocaust signifies that history improbably turned life itself into an artifact. Life became an arbitrarily controlled and extremely limited existence in the shadow of the apocalypse. In the Aristotelian *ars poetica*, the function of art is to reshape and refigure life through conscious selection and compression of infinite number of events. In contrast, the terrible confines of the *univers concentrationnaire* of the Holocaust ineluctably reduced life in the Annexe to the lifelessness of an absolute lack of choice. The arrest of the time flow in the apocalyptic tremendum effected a stagnant existence suffused with the fear of imminent destruction. Consequently, the inversion of the Aristotelian paradigm points to the "improbable possibility" of art-as-life in the death-in-life existence in the Annexe.

The courage that we detect in Frank's poetic rendition of the fear of death highlights the energizing power of art in the presence of death. The humanistic message in the *Diary* should not be sought in its subject matter but, rather, in its artistic form. In other words, the act of literary representation of the Annexe presents literary creativity as a life sustaining system.

Indeed, time and again, Frank affirms her writing as a life line which saves her from despair. On March 16, 1944, she confides in Kitty that writing enables her to endure the unbearable situation:

> Yes, Kitty, Anne is a crazy child, but I do live in crazy times and under still crazier circumstances. But, still, the brightest spot of all is that at least I can write down my thoughts and feelings, otherwise I would be absolutely stifled! (*D* 540–541)

Frank shows a full awareness of the role that the *Diary* plays in her life. In the entry of April 4, she reports she has overcome a spell of incapacitating misery and depression. She reasserts herself as a writer who defeats fear through writing:

> I can shake off everything if I write; my sorrows disappear, my courage is reborn . . . for I can recapture everything when I write, my thoughts, my ideals and my fantasies. (*D* 587–588)

Paul Tillich offers the observation that "the most fundamental expression of [every encounter with reality] is the language which gives man the power to abstract from the concretely given and . . . to return to it, to interpret and transform it. The most vital being is the being which has the word and is by the word liberated from bondage to the given."[41]

Frank's *Diary* seems to actualize this observation in a moving and poignant way. The entry which describes the terror of a close call that the people in hiding experienced illustrates Frank's perception of art as the sustaining source of the "life wish."

There was a burglary in the offices below and the investigating police came up the stairs to the camouflaged door leading to the Secret Annexe. The terrified people inside discussed what needed to be destroyed in case they should be discovered. Somebody suggested burning the diary. Frank responded to this suggestion with an emotional outburst:

> This [the suggestion] and when the police rattled the cupboard door, were my worst moments. "Not my diary; if my diary goes, I go with it!" (*D* 595)

The connection that she makes between the destruction of the *Diary* and physical destruction reiterates dramatically Frank's view of writing as a life-giving activity. Her behavior illustrates Tillich's belief that the ability to abstract, to interpret, and to transform through language signals the vitality of being. In Frank's view, the ability to voice helplessness redeems her vitality because it liberates her from the "stillness and the terrible fear" that this very helplessness incurs.

It is therefore important to examine the voice of art in Frank's writing. How does the artist's creative act redeem vitality in the apocalyptic void of paralyzing fear and deepening depression?

To an extent, the answer seems to lie in the understanding of the time factor implied in diaristic writing. As "a book of time,"[42] the diary presents two kinds of time: the period that it records and the actual duration of the recording. I would argue that in the Annexe situation the time of the diaristic recording counteracts the timelessness of the apocalyptic ending.

Let us recall Henri Bergson's notion of the correlation between the inspirational stage of artistic creativity and the stage of the actualization of the work of art. Bergson claims that "to the artist that creates a picture by drawing it from the depths of his soul . . . the duration of his work is part and parcel of his work. . . . The time taken up by the invention is one with the invention itself. . . . It is a vital process, something like the ripening of an idea."[43]

According to Bergson, the effort of artistic creativity comprises the time in which the artist's vision comes into being and the time during which this vision shapes its mode of artistic expression. In this sense, the diaristic mode effects compression of the two aspects of time in a creative continuum.

As Lawrence Rosenwald tells us, the diary is an art of microscopic literary writing,[44] in that every entry is a distinct creative act of its own. Consequently, Frank's constant preoccupation with her diary infuses the duration of hiding with an ongoing artistic invention. Looking at reality as material for diaristic recording elicits a sense of meaningful continuity. The purpose of recording contravenes the episodic disconnectedness of the reality of destruction.

In her diaristic recording, Frank creates an illusion of a "normal" existence. Further, the mode of her writing becomes the signifier of a normally continuing life. By virtue of its calendric recording, the *Diary* reflects a "microscopic" historical continuity which extends into the future and therefore offsets the a-historicity of the apocalyptic ending.

As an evolving record, Frank's *Diary* becomes the Annexe's chronicle. It enables the diarist to read "backward" and write "forward," to draw analogies to formerly described events, and to incorporate the past into the present. In the entry of Jan. 2, 1944, for instance, Frank comments disapprovingly on past events which she recalled when "[she] turned over some of the pages of [her] diary." By re-reading past entries, Frank can re-evaluate her past experiences. The sense of the past enters and affects her present, as she observes:

> This diary is of great value to me, because it has become a book
> of memoirs in many places, but on a good many pages I could
> certainly put "past and done with." (*D* 438)

The accumulation of memories and events enhances the importance of the *Diary* as a life story. The possibility of maintaining a historical record even in the limited time span allows Frank to infuse the stagnant existence in the Annexe with a meaningful theme worthy of an artistic representation. The re-reading and also, let us recall, the re-writing of the *Diary* in preparation for future publication, defer, even if for a short while, the diarist's listless anticipation of the end.

Thus, the *Diary's* artistic construct countervails the deathlike tenor of its subject matter. In this sense, the *Diary* is an inversion of the Aristotelian concept of art modeled on life. The creativity of diaristic writing infuses the notion of vitality into an otherwise atrophied, lifeless existence.

The entry of May 3, 1944 is a case in point. After having reported about meals consisting of rotten lettuce and rotten potatoes, Anne ponders "despairingly" the human "urge to destroy, an urge to kill, to murder and rage." She suggests that "until all mankind, without exception, undergoes a great change, wars will be waged, everything that has been built, cultivated, and grown will be destroyed and disfigured" (D 627–628).

At this very point, when "the sense of an ending" threatens to invade and when despair is about to take over, the consciousness of life as narrative intervenes, allowing the author to feel, even if only temporarily, in charge of her art and life:

> I have often been downcast but never in despair. I regard our hiding as a dangerous adventure, romantic and interesting at the same time. In my diary I treat all the privations as amusing. . . . My start has been so very full of interest, and that is the sole reason why I have to laugh at the humorous side of the most dangerous moments. . . . I am young and strong and am living a great adventure; I am still in the midst of it and can't grumble the whole day long. . . . I have been given a lot, a happy nature, a great deal of cheerfulness and strength. Why, then, should I be in despair? (D 628–629)

The process of gaining control over life through art points to the reflective function of the *Diary*. Frank's autobiographical story is also the story of her growth as an artist. As the entries follow each other, Frank crystallizes and defines the autobiographical purpose of her writing. In the above quote, she sees her writing as an act of self-assertion. Life writing reverts an existence of incapacitating helplessness and despair into a humorous adventure.

Like the foremost Yiddish storyteller, Sholom Aleichem, who proscribed tears and prescribed laughter to heal suffering and pain,[45] Frank exercises her authorial prerogative to re-view the world that surrounds her. She neutralizes her fear by establishing an alternate point of view. In her ongoing struggle with despair, she enlists humor to cope with the desperate situation.

The choice of the humorous perspective is concomitant with the qualities of "cheerfulness and strength" that she constantly strives to develop. The hopeful passages do not support therefore, the popular notion of Frank's naive faith in the goodness of man. Rather, they disclose the subtext of an immense effort to affirm meaning in the meaningless, hopeless ordeal.

Frank refers to her struggle when she says: "Everyone must try to be the master of his own moods. . . . My work, my hope, my love, my courage, all these things *keep my head above water* and keep me from complaining"

(*D* 603, my emphasis). Significantly, the list of things that sustains her starts with "work," that is, her writing.[46] However tenuous and temporary, the victory over despair signals the vitality of creative imagination.

Writing infuses potency. The transformation of "hiding from the Gestapo" into a literary theme of "life in the Secret Annexe" allows Frank, to distil, in Ricoeur's terms, the "configurational dimension" out of the "episodic dimension." The ability to ascribe the meaning of a "romantic adventure" to Jewish existence at the time of the Holocaust engenders a sense of control. And the capability of experiencing her "adventure" through the act of writing reinforces the hope to develop the inner discipline to become "the master of her moods."

The perception of life as a humorous adventure attests to Frank's imaginative attempt to transform the miserable existence in the Annexe. The epistolary form of the *Diary* illustrates an even more significant aspect of the freedom of imagination. The *Diary* takes the form of letters to an imaginary addressee, Kitty. Frank structures Kitty as a character outside the reality of occupied Europe. The literary construct of a close friend, yet a distant addressee, functions on multiple narrative levels.

The addressee is a naive listener, occasionally presented as an interlocutor. She has the knowledge of neither the horror of the raging war nor of the systematic destruction of European Jews. At the same time, her presence is reaffirmed in each entry by the heading "Dear Kitty" and the signature "Yours, Anne." Moreover, the direct statements, comments, and questions, such as, "I must tell you," "I think you should know," "You asked me . . . so I must reply," etc., reinforce the sense of closeness between the writer and the addressee.

These direct phrases imply a dialogic situation, whereby the writer enlightens the naive reader-outsider. The construct of "Kitty" attests to Anne's need to share her "adventure."

The *Diary* as a testimonial directed to a distant reader defines Frank as a witness-victim. In this respect, therefore, "Kitty," the reader-outsider, represents all of us, the postwar readers of Frank's *Diary*. In this respect, the diarist's intention to inform and teach does not differ from the intention of other witnesses-victims of the Holocaust who wished to bequeath their testimony to posterity.

However, the placement of the addressee in the text calls attention to the uniqueness of the *Diary* as a Holocaust testimony. As the marker of the epistolary form of the *Diary*, "Kitty" communicates Frank's need for an audience. Writing to a particular, singled-out reader highlights the therapeutic function of the imagined addressee.

In this respect, it is, perhaps, not so much the need to inform posterity, as the urgency to alleviate the specter of despair that motivates Frank's constant dialogue with her imaginary friend. The special friend, a confessant ready to hear, but not to condemn, indicates Frank's ingenuous search for support in art.

The addressee as a naive listener highlights further the complexity of this artistic effort. In Kitty, the author creates a mind unaffected by the horror. This intentional creation of a tabula rasa receiving consciousness ineluctably affects the manner and the voice in which the narrative unfolds.

The construct of an ignorant addressee incurs the need to devise adequate narrative strategies. The complete unawareness of the addressee regarding the reality of the Holocaust de-intensifies the teller's emotional involvement with her tale. The naivete of the addressee compels the writer to innovate, diversify, infuse comic relief—in brief, to seek literary devices to ensure the accessibility of the story.

Let us recall once more Sholom Aleichem who, as a rule, defuses the tragic tenor of his narrator's tale of woe by invariably incorporating into his story the character of an unimplicated narratee. In a similar way, Frank achieves respite from feelings of despondency and hopelessness by focusing on communication with her remote addressee. To communicate, she must distance herself from misery and despair. She must gain control over her subject matter and see it, even if only for a moment, as "a romantic adventure." The role of the teller that she constructed for herself by devising a naive "Kitty" allows Frank the freedom to exercise her creativity and imagination as a writer.

The Ethical Self at the Time of De-Humanization

As a continuing, daily activity, Frank's diaristic writing becomes a source of vitality. In this sense, Frank's testimonial defies the Final Solution. Her creative energy, persistence, and artistic ability to record this world carve an enclave of normalcy in the midst of uncontrollable madness of destruction. As a coherent narrative as well as a dialogue, the *Diary* records and, at the same time, contravenes the terror. The rhetorical strategies in the work indicate an effort to maintain meaningfulness even in the situation of the apocalypse. Thus, against all odds, Frank attempts to create the time span characteristic of an autobiographical self-representation.

Georges Gusdorf claims that in autobiographical writing "I exercise a sort of right to recover possession of my existence now and later . . . for the past drawn up into the present is also a pledge and a prophecy of the future."[47] In light of Gusdorf's definition, the *Diary* is not merely an autobiographical story of a Jewish girl in hiding. It is also, against all hope, "a pledge and a prophecy," of this girl as a woman. Considered as a pledge for the future, the *Diary* offers more than a chronologically unfolding testimonial. It is also a remarkably insightful self-representation of the growing artist.

Beside the factual observations and reports, Frank expresses her expectations, thoughts, and desires. As she sets her goals, she deplores her weaknesses and laments over her disappointments. Above all, she articulates the desire for a spiritual change. Let us keep in mind that Frank's preoccupation with moral self-improvement takes place in the context of increasing certainty of deportation and death.

Diaristic writing demonstrates the need to retell a recent past. This act discloses the writer's teleological sense of self because the act of shaping life into a tale communicates the premise that life has meaning and purpose. The sense of the future is most concrete in a diary where, by definition, each entry sets up the anticipation of a shortly forthcoming sequel. The boundaries between immediate past events and expected developments are often blurred, since the projection of the near future affects the present.

Margaret Farley maintains that "My future, too, changes my present and my past—not when it comes, but while it is the future which I anticipate."[48] As an art of "microscopic writing," the *Diary* highlights the unity of the writing self's recollected past, its unfolding present, and its anticipated future.

Consideration of the self in terms of its past and especially in terms of its future could hardly make sense in the reality of the Final Solution. The Holocaust eradicated the past of the Jewish people. It also intended to eliminate the Jews' "pledge and prophecy for the future." Facing immediate annihilation, the victim lost the sense of her teleological self.

In the limited time that she has, Frank tries to actualize her artistic and moral potential despite the reality of imminent ending. Tragically, she is aware that under the circumstances neither her ethical nor her artistic actualization can be deferred. Conscious of impending death, she knows that it is in the present that she must actualize herself both as a human being and as an artist:

> I want to go on living even after my death! And therefore I am grateful to God for giving me this *gift*, this possibility of *developing myself* and of *writing*, of expressing all that is in me. (*D* 587, my emphasis)

Indeed, the *Diary* presents Frank as a growing and developing person. I am using the term "developing person" advisedly. Let us recall that, as discussed above, most critics read the *Diary* as a text of a precocious young girl. I, however, as mentioned before, concur with John Berryman's notion that Frank's inner struggle to establish a moral Weltanschauung transcends the typically adolescent development.[49]

It is true that Anne experiences physical changes and emotional vicissitudes related to her growth into adolescence (menstruation, the discovery of sexuality, defiance of the adult world, mood fluctuations, etc.). Yet, it seems impossible to explain the seriousness and the integrity of her ethical self-examination as characteristic of a thirteen- or fourteen-year-old. And, as I shall demonstrate, it seems equally difficult to describe her ethical Weltanschauung as precocious.

Despite her young age, both Frank's self-perception and her perception of others reveal remarkable maturity. As Berryman asserts, "most people do not grow up, in any degree that will correspond to Anne Frank's growing up."[50]

Ironically, the intention to dehumanize Jews by stripping them of their identity, reducing them to non-persons, and in Frank's particular case, forcing her into hiding, had a countereffect on Frank's process of individuation. As a written and re-written text, the *Diary* defiantly affirms Frank's dignified self-perception as an individual whose story deserves to be recorded. Even further, her understanding of self-writing as a vehicle of ethical self-development demonstrates Frank's self-assertion against the tyranny of depersonalization.

Steven Kagle claims that "the life of a diary is often born of a tension ... [which] is a sustaining force of a diary."[51] The life of Frank's *Diary* seems to derive from the tension between the indelible sense of self-worth and the indignity of the life in hiding, between the certainty of the unalienable right-to-be and the knowledge of having been doomed to non-being.

The need to defy the hatred that enforced the self-image of a hunted, terrified Jew "in chains" engages Frank in a rigorously sustained process of shaping her moral values. In view of Frank's complete awareness of her situation, her uncompromising and unsparing quest for self-knowledge and for moral self-improvement assumes heroic dimensions.

The Ethical Self Vis-à-Vis Others

Frank's inward journey becomes a struggle of the conflicting needs for independence and for connectedness. On the one hand, she constantly seeks separation from those who surround her; on the other hand, she yearns for close relationships with others. This twofold search is informed by her adherence to a highly demanding value system.

Frank consistently refuses to compromise and accept norms that do not measure up to her world of ethics. The people close to her fail to provide support to maintain her moral vision. Eventually, she understands the extent of solitude and self-sufficiency that her uncompromising ethical outlook entails. The tenor of dejection in the final entries of the *Diary* testifies to Frank's growing sense of loneliness and defeat.

The view of Frank as a precocious adolescent gains support from her companions in hiding. As it emerges in Frank's own reporting, she was perceived as an outspoken, boisterous girl. However, Frank's argumentation against this perception raises doubts about the astuteness of this critical attitude:

> Although I'm only fourteen, I know quite well what I want, I know who is right and who is wrong, I have my opinions, my own ideas and principles, and although it may sound pretty mad from an adolescent, I feel more of a person than a child, I feel quite independent of anyone. (*D* 534)

Frank asserts her maturity. She claims to be able to form and articulate her ethical norms as well as evaluate the ethical make-up of others. She sees herself as a morally discerning person of solid convictions. Therefore, in order to assess the validity of her claim to be "independent of anyone," it is necessary to investigate Frank's increasing alienation from her father, mother, and Peter.

Frank's eventual estrangement from her father is rooted in what she experiences as his incapability of empathic understanding. The earlier, oedipal stage of her clinging to her "ideal" father[52] develops into a critical assessment of their relationship. Towards the end of the *Diary* Frank reaches the conclusion "that Daddy was never any support to me in my struggle," that "he hasn't realized that for me the fight to get on top was more important than all else," that "he is not able to feel with me like a friend, however hard he tries" (*D* 690–691).

As Frank sees it, her father failed her by not allowing their relationship to develop beyond father-child patterns. Ironically, the teenage daughter is mature enough to discern and articulate her father's inability to establish a mutually respectful relationship with her. She frankly admits to herself that he never accepted her as "Anne-on-her-own-merits," and acknowledges that, "I don't feel I can tread upon more intimate ground with him." She consciously and painfully detaches herself from him, "for my peace of mind . . . I concealed from Daddy everything that perturbed me; I never shared my ideals with him" (*D* 691).

While her father fails her on emotional grounds, her mother does not provide the intellectual model that Frank requires. The daughter becomes disappointed in her mother[53] when she feels ready for her mother's friendship and example. Eventually, she is capable of an unsparing, yet quite objective, assessment of her mother's limitations. Frank feels able to "discuss things and argue better" than her mother. She claims that she is not "so prejudiced," does not "exaggerate so much," and that she is "more precise and adroit" than her mother (*D* 544).

Frank, who plans to be a journalist and a writer, feels no respect for her mother who has not actualized herself professionally. "I can't imagine," she wonders, "that I would have to lead the same sort of life as Mummy and Mrs Van Daan and all the women who do their work and are forgotten." And in a truly feminist fashion she vows, "I must have something besides a husband and children, something that I can devote myself to" (D 587).

While her parents do not provide Frank with the emotional and intellectual support that she needs, in Peter she discerns a lack of integrity that she cannot accept. She condemns his inability to develop self-discipline. She passes judgment on Peter's weak moral values and his derogatory views of religion (D 684–685).

It is remarkable, especially in view of her young age, that, despite her affection for Peter, Frank does not let love blind her. She finds it inexcusable that Peter appears to be "afraid of his own weakness" and so she decides not to indulge his dependency: "Peter's beginning to lean on me a bit and that mustn't happen under any circumstances. A type like Peter finds it difficult to stand on his own feet" (D 683). Eventually, Peter's apparent lack of moral fiber causes Frank to withdraw emotionally from the relationship.

Frank realizes that her closest companions do not give her the support she seeks. Her unwillingness to compromise is all the more significant in view of her intense need to create meaningful contacts with others (D 180–181), to have someone's complete confidence (D 683), to make a real friendship (D 693).

This desire for meaningful, trusting relationships reminds us of Hannah Arendt's observation that "the remedy for unpredictability, for the chaotic uncertainty of the future, is contained in the faculty to make and keep promises."[54] As Arendt sees it, relationships grounded in the premise of loyalty and truthfulness maintain the telos of human existence. The failure to establish honest relationships threatens to eliminate the sense of order and direction.

Frank confirms Arendt's view of friendship as a condition for a meaningful existence. She realizes that the need for trust, confidence, and security motivated her relationship with Peter: I needed a *living person* to whom I could pour out my heart; I wanted a friend who'd help to put me on the right road (D 693, my emphasis).

Frank's desire for friendship with Peter was rooted in the need for a loyal, reliable friend. But even more significantly, her need for Peter's companionship was predicated upon an inner drive for moral self-improvement. The extent of Frank's maturity emerges in her unsparing criticism of her own failings and her desire to become a better person.

A living friend, rather than the imaginary Kitty, might have helped Frank to overcome her weaknesses. An empathic friendship would have shaped her character according to the ethics that inform her world picture. In the absence of such a person, the *Diary* became the substitute for a friendly response and it functioned as both a receptacle of confidence and as an ethical corrective.

Frank's writing as constant self-examination results in a critical, objective self-evaluation. "I can watch myself and my actions, just like an outsider," she claims. "The Anne of every day I can face entirely without prejudice, without making excuses for her, and watch what's good and what's bad about her" (*D* 689).

Her insistence on moral self-improvement takes the form of a solitary, difficult struggle "to put herself on the right road" rather than to join others on the "easy road" of emotional, intellectual, and ethical passivity. The need to create her own self-evaluating measure, rather than submit to the judgment of others, gradually becomes the goal of Frank's lonely struggle. On Nov. 7, 1942, in beginning of the hiding period, Anne makes an important decision:

> I must become good through my own efforts without examples and without good advice. Then later on I shall be all the stronger. . . . I frequently feel weak, and dissatisfied with myself; my shortcomings are too great. I know this, and every day I try to improve myself, again and again. (*D* 296–297)

In the final entry of Aug. 1, 1944, the inner battle still goes on. Addressing Kitty for the last time, Frank tells her imaginary friend of her failure to become her ideal self:

> I've already told you before that I have, as it were, a dual personality . . . This side is usually lying in wait and pushes away the other which is much better, deeper and purer. My lighter superficial side will always be too quick for the deeper side of me and that's why it will always win. You can't imagine how often I've already tried to push this Anne away, to cripple her, to hide her, because after all, she's only half of what is called Anne. (*D* 697–698)

Frank presents here a complex three-tiered construct of self. The discrepancy between the "ideal 'I'" that she struggles to become and the "flawed 'I'" which obstructs her progress is narrated by the "third eye/I" of the narrator. The narration of the dialogic-adversarial relations of the split self highlights Frank's capability of self-critical perspective. The objectivity of her uncompromising insight conflates with her desire to correct her weaknesses and shortcomings. The narrative "eye/I" watches the inner struggle for self-improvement and admits defeat.

The diaristic form of Frank's narrative, however, questions such a categorical admission of failure. It is interesting to consider Frank's self-insight in light of André Gide's view of a diary's function. Writing in his journal, Gide observes:

> rather than recounting his life as well as he has lived it, [the artist] must live his life as he will recount it. In other words, the portrait of him formed by his life must identify itself with the ideal portrait he desires.[55]

If the "ideal portrait" represents the absolute, then Frank's objective to become absolutely good is humanly impossible and therefore doomed to failure. If, however, the process of enabling the "deeper, better and purer" self to emerge is all important, then Frank in her struggle for self-improvement becomes this "ideal portrait." Frank's struggle for the ideal, despite and perhaps because of the situation of the Holocaust, paints an "ideal portrait" of a remarkable self-development.

In this respect, Frank's narrative of her struggle reconfirms her ethical self. Indeed, Margot's and Peter's view of Frank corroborates her fighting spirit. As Frank recounts, both her sister and friend comment "again and again" on her self-discipline which they find quite superior to theirs: "Yes," she quotes them saying, "if I was as strong and plucky as you are, if I always stuck to what I wanted, if I had such persistent energy . . ." (D 682). Margot and Peter refer to the inner force that motivates Frank despite the reality which justifies passivity and stagnation. They correctly detect her inner strength.

Frank persists in her ethical conviction of accountability toward oneself and toward the world. In that respect, she sees the self and the world ineluctably interconnected. Succinctly, she summarizes her aspiration and her credo:

> Let me be myself and then I am satisfied. I know that I'm a woman, a woman with inward strength and plenty of courage. If God lets me live. . . . I shall work in the world and for mankind. (D 601)

Against the reality of imminent annihilation, Frank proclaims her uniqueness and assumes responsibility to become a whole human being. Her desire to fulfill herself reminds us of the famous Hasidic rabbi Zusya who said: "In the world to come they will not ask me, 'Why were you not Moses?' They will ask me, 'Why were you not Zusya?'" Like Zusya, Frank knew that true self-improvement entails an utmost effort to actualize one's authentic self. Self-actualization, however, cannot take place in isolation from the world. In the above statement Frank expresses her conviction that self-fulfillment is possible only through a responsible relationship with the world.

Conclusion: Are People Good at Heart?

The final entries in the *Diary* demonstrate Frank's frustrated desire to reconnect with the world. While the world outside becomes increasingly foreboding, life in the Annexe offers no encouragement, consolation, or real friendship.

Frank's last sentence affirms her disappointment in humanity and comes close to an admission of personal defeat: "I keep on trying to find a way of becoming what I would so like to be, and what I could be, if . . . there weren't any other people living in the world" (*D* 699). Whereas the confidence in her potential is still there, her premonition is that in this world of death and alienation this potential will never materialize.

The final sentence appears to contradict the celebrated affirmation written only two weeks before that "in spite of everything I still believe that people are really good at heart" (*D* 694). This hopeful declaration, which concludes the *Diary*'s theatrical production, inscribed the *Diary* as a manifesto of faith in human humaneness even in view of the Holocaust.

My discussion of the *Diary* concludes therefore with a re-examination of the famous statement. I suggest that considered in its context, the statement reveals a struggle with despair that Frank is about to lose.

The section (*D* 693–694) in which the statement appears starts with a saying that Frank remembers having read somewhere, "For in its innermost depths youth is lonelier than old age." She admits to identifying with this statement. She realizes that her sense of loneliness grows out of the difficulty to hold to faith "when people are showing their worst side, and do not know whether to believe in truth and right and God."

In Frank's pessimistic view of the world, the "solution" that young people offer to mend the world is not strong enough "to resist the facts which reduce it to nothing again." As Frank sees it, "ideals, dreams, and cherished hopes rise within us, only to meet the horrible truth and be shattered."

Frank's picture of the hopeless situation reminds us of Arendt's postulation that the fulfilled promise is the antidote to the unpredictability of the future. Frank indicts the world which broke its promises, robbing young people of their ideals, leaving them with no moral support. Her disappointment with the world signals a growing sense of the futility of an ethical system defeated time and again by the powers of evil that have overtaken the world.

In what follows we observe a shift from Frank's general comments on the moral collapse of the world. Now she focuses on her personal confrontation with the reality of physical and spiritual apocalypse.

I quote the passage in its entirety, as it is important to follow the inner dialogue embedded in the text. The dialogue reveals vacillation between the voice of hopelessness and the voice which clings to hope. The italicized phrases indicate Frank's reluctance and hesitation to admit defeat, betraying, in effect, the awareness of her losing battle against despair:

hopelessness
It's really a wonder that I haven't dropped all my ideals, because they seem so absurd and impossible to hope to carry out.

hope
Yet I keep them, because in spite of everything I still believe that people are really good at heart.

hopelessness
I simply can't build up my hopes on a foundation consisting of confusion, misery, and death. I see the world gradually being turned into a wilderness, I hear the ever approaching thunder, which will destroy us too, I can feel the suffering of millions

hope
and yet, if I look up into heavens, I think that it will all come right, that this cruelty too will end and that peace and tranquillity [sic] will return again.

Interestingly, the rhetoric of this apparently optimistic final statement conveys the ultimate admission of defeat. The apocalypse will destroy the world, including the writer herself, and will be followed by heavenly peace.

In Frank's poetic representation, the unfolding catastrophe is likened to the Armaggedon, which, as the biblical story has it, will be followed by the heavenly peace of the end of time. This eschatological vision of the future, however, lies beyond the futureless world of the Holocaust. Frank knows that the Armaggedon will destroy her. Tragically, the implacable Final Solution which interrupted Frank's *Diary* in medias res reaffirmed her vision.

The accidental survival of only one inhabitant of the Annexe highlights the unrelieved tragedy of those who were mercilessly annihilated. Upon his return from "another planet" of the nameless dead, Otto Frank recovered the *Diary*. It was his daughter's disrupted story of her disrupted life. This story named the despair of young people, who, like Anne Frank, demanded "let me be myself" and, who, unlike rabbi Zusya, were deprived of the right to live and to fulfill themselves.

The *Diary*'s legacy of hope, therefore, should not be sought in hard won moments of optimism. Rather it is found in the desire to fight despair through its painful representation in art. In this sense, the *Diary* allows us to experience a "new form" of a life narrative, to recall Ricoeur. By its very existence, this narrative is new as it redefines the heroism of resistance.

The last chapter of Frank's life story was written by Frank's fellow inmate in the concentration camp. Her recollection does not picture Frank extolling the goodness of people. This witness remembers Frank's despair when she wept over gypsy girls driven to the crematoria and over Hungarian children waiting in front of gas chambers.[56] Frank's ability to see and to respond to suffering reinforces the lesson of victory in defeat that her *Diary* teaches so poignantly.

NOTES

1. Paul Ricoeur, *Time and Narrative*, trans. Kathleen McLaughlin and David Pellauer (Chicago, 1984), Vol. 2, p. 28.

2. Alvin H. Rosenfeld, "Popularization and Memory: The Case of Anne Frank," *Lessons and Legacies: The Meaning of the Holocaust in the Changing World*, edited by Peter Hayes (Evanston, 1991), p. 271.

3. Quoted in *The Diary of Anne Frank: The Critical Edition*, p. 67–68. For full bibliographical annotation, see note 25.

4. See for instance Miri Baruch's article, "Anne Frank's *The Diary of a Young Girl*," which discusses the various aspects of *The Diary* as a text by an adolescent appropriate for adolescent readers. *The Melton Journal: Issues and Themes in Jewish Education*, Vol. 23 (Spring 1990), pp. 17–19.

5. Meyer Levin sued Otto Frank and the producer Kermit Bloomgarden who, on the suggestion of Lillian Hellman, hired Albert and Frances Hackett to write the play. Levin recorded his involvement with *The Diary* in his novel *Obsession* (New York, 1973).

6. Lawrence Graver, *An Obsession with Anne Frank* (Berkeley, 1995).

7. Judith E. Doneson, "*The Diary of Anne Frank* in the Context of Post-War America and the 1950s," in *The Holocaust in American Film* (Philadelphia, 1987), pp. 57–85.

8. Sidra DeKoven Ezrahi, *By Words Alone: The Holocaust in Literature* (Chicago, 1980), pp. 200–204.

9. Sander L. Gilman, *Jewish Self-Hatred: Anti-Semitism and the Hidden Language of the Jews* (Baltimore, 1986), pp. 349–350.

10. James E. Young, *Writing and Rewriting the Holocaust: Narrative and the Consequences of Interpretation* (Bloomington, 1988), p. 27.

11. Ibid., p. 27.

12. Young's postulation (p. 29) that Anne showed no affinity with the fate of the Jewish people seems incorrect. Anne demonstrates strong identification with the suffering of Jewish people. See, for instance, the entry of Dec. 13, 1942: "I saw two Jews through the curtain yesterday. I could hardly believe my eyes; it was a horrible feeling, just as if I'd betrayed them and was now watching them in their misery" (*D* 328); and the entry of April 11, 1944: "Who has inflicted this upon us? Who has made us Jews different from all other people? Who has allowed us to suffer so terribly until now? . . . We can never become just Netherlanders, or just English, or

representatives of any country for that matter, we will always remain Jews, but we want to, too" (*D* 600).

13. Gilman, *Jewish Self-Hatred*, p. 353.

14. Bruno Bettelheim, *Surviving and Other Essays* (New York, 1980), p. 251.

15. Rosenfeld, "Popularization and Memory," p. 275.

16. See, for instance, a general overview of the *Diary* in Henry F. Pommer, "The Legend and Art of Anne Frank," *Judaism*, Vol. 9 (1960), pp. 36–46 and the theme of the Jewish woman in the *Diary* in Yasmine Ergas, "Growing up Banished: A Reading of Anne Frank and Etty Hillesum," in *Behind the Lines: Gender and the Two World Wars*, edited by Margaret Randolph Higonnet, Jane Jenson, Sonya Michael and Margaret Collins Weitz (New Haven, 1987), pp. 84–99.

17. John Berryman, *The Freedom of the Poet* (New York, 1980), p. 92 (italics in the text).

18. Ibid., p. 104.

19. Ibid., p. 93 (italics in the text).

20. Ibid., p. 96.

21. Ibid., p. 104 (my emphasis).

22. The editors of the *Critical Edition* explain: "Anne Frank wrote two versions of her diary, the second being based on the first. It was on the basis of these manuscripts that the first Dutch publication of her diaries, *Het Achterhuis*, was brought out in 1947." In the *Critical Edition*, the first version appears at the top of the page, the second version appears under the first and, finally, the English translation of the Dutch publication entitled *Anne Frank: The Diary of a Young Girl* published in 1952 (p. 168; for full annotation of the *Critical Edition*, see note 25).

23. Tzvetan Todorov, *The Fantastic: A Structural Approach to a Literary Genre*, trans. Richard Howard (Cleveland, 1973), pp. 170–172.

24. I am referring to the popular edition of the text, *Anne Frank: The Diary of a Young Girl* (New York, first printing in 1952). This is the translation of the Dutch publication *Het Achterhuis* (1947).

25. All the quotes from Anne Frank's *Diary* are taken from *The Diary of Anne Frank: The Critical Edition*, prepared by the Netherlands State Institute for War Documentation, edited by David Barnouw and Gerrold van der Stroom, English translation by Arnold J. Pomerans and B. M. Mooyart, Doubleday (New York, 1989). The page numbers preceded by the letter *D* appear in the text.

26. Although, as Miri Baruch mentions in her article, that Anne's friend Kitty was found living in South Africa seems correct, we assume that Kitty is Anne's imaginary construct, especially if taking into consideration Anne's own definition: "I want this diary to be my friend, and I shall call my friend Kitty (*D* 181–182).

27. Interestingly, these modifiers were deleted in the second version of the entry; they appear only in the first draft of the entry of March 29, 1944.

28. Miep Gies, *Anne Frank Remembered: The Story of a Woman Who Helped to Hide the Frank Family* (New York, 1987), p. 165.

29. Ricoeur, Vol. 1, pp. 66–67.

30. Frank Kermode, *The Sense of Ending* (New York, 1967), p. 6.

31. Ibid., p. 8.

32. Ibid., p. 30.

33. Ibid., pp. 38–39.

34. Ibid., p. 109.

35. Ibid., p. 8.

36. Aristotle, "Poetics," *Criticism: Major Texts*, edited by Walter Jackson Bate (New York, 1952), p. 20.

37. Ibid., pp. 24–25.

38. Ibid., p. 24.

39. Ibid., p. 27.

40. Ibid., p. 36.

41. Paul Tillich, *The Courage to Be* (London, 1961), p. 77.

42. Lawrence Rosenwald, *Emerson and the Art of the Diary* (New York, 1988), p. 6.

43. Henri Bergson, *Creative Evolution* (London, 1911), pp. 359–360.

44. Rosenwald, p. 22.

45. See, for instance, the conclusion of Sholom Aleichem's story "The Haunted Tailor," which ends with the following address to the reader: "It was not a good ending. The tale began cheerfully enough, and it ended as most such happy stories do—badly. . . . Then let the maker of the tale take his leave of you smiling, and let him wish you, Jews—and all mankind—more laughter than tears. Laughter is good for you. Doctors prescribe laughter." *The Best of Sholom Aleichem*, edited by Irving Howe and Ruth Wisse (New York, 1979), p. 36.

46. Anne sees her writing as work. On April 4, 1944, she writes: "I must work, so as not to be a fool, to get on, to become a journalist, because that's what I want . . . I am the best and the sharpest critic of my own work. I know myself what is and what is not well written" (*D* 586–587). In the April 6, 1944 entry she begins the list of her hobbies: "First of all: writing, but that hardly counts as a hobby" (*D* 589).

47. Georges Gusdorf, "Conditions and Limits of Autobiography," in *Autobiography: Essays Theoretical and Critical*, edited by James Olney (Princeton, 1980), p. 44.

48. Margaret A. Farley, *Personal Commitments: Beginning, Keeping, Changing* (San Francisco, 1986), p. 43.

49. Berryman, p. 104.

50. Ibid., p. 93.

51. Steven E. Kagle, *American Diary Literature 1620–1799* (Boston, 1979), p. 17.

52. See, for instance, the following, statement in the entry of Nov. 7, 1942: "I'm not jealous of Margot, never have been. . . . It is only that I long for Daddy's real love: not only as his child, but for me—Anne, myself" (*D* 295).

53. See in the same entry as above: ". . . I have in my mind's eye an image of what a perfect mother and wife should be; and in her whom I must call 'Mother' I find no trace of that image" (*D* 297).

54. Hannah Arendt, *The Human Condition* (Chicago, 1958), p. 236.

55. André Gide, *Journals*, trans. Justin O'Brien (Harmondsworth, 1978), pp. 18–19.

56. Ernst Schnabel, *Anne Frank: A Portrait in Courage*, trans. Richard and Clara Winston (New York, 1958), pp. 168–169.

JUDITH GOLDSTEIN

Anne Frank: The Redemptive Myth

For millions of people, Anne Frank's history has come to symbolize one of Europe's deadliest conflagrations—a time when one nation set fire to its democratic government, ravaged countries all over the continent, destroyed Jewish life in Eastern Europe, and irreparably damaged Jewish existence in many Western European countries, as well. The outlines of Anne Frank's history are clear: the escape with her family from Germany and resettlement in 1933 in Amsterdam, where her father Otto Frank had a business; German occupation of the Netherlands in May, 1940; and the family's flight in 1942 into hiding in the attic above Otto Frank's office. Then betrayal and capture in August 1944; imprisonment in Westerbork, a transit camp; deportation to Auschwitz in September 1944; and death in Bergen-Belsen a few weeks before liberation in March 1945. Otto Frank's return as the sole surviving member of the family led to publication, in the early 1950s, of the diary found by Miep Gies after the police arrested the Franks and to posthumous fame for Anne and her family.

The Diary of Anne Frank and derivative theatrical productions have made a unique impact on children and adults throughout the world. The writing bespeaks courage, misery, persecution, and resistance. Anne Frank has come to represent the child, in her mid-teens, struggling to maintain hope and faith in mankind, if not in her own future. The most famous quote from her diary

Partisan Review, Volume 70, Number 1 (Winter 2003): pp. 16–23. Copyright © 2003 Judith Goldstein.

is, "In spite of everything I still believe people are good at heart." Sudden capture stopped the testimony of inner thoughts.

An aura of sweet optimism and faith surrounds the *Diary*. Unfortunately, the sentiments are misapplied. Cynthia Ozick's critique is closer to the truth. She described the *Diary* as a "chronicle of trepidation, turmoil, alarm. . . . Betrayal and arrest always threaten. Anxiety and immobility rule. It is a story of fear." People know that Anne, her sister, and her mother were exterminated, but for many readers Anne's story ends with the hope that "people are really good at heart." These words, I believe, are the key to understanding the conversion of her diary and persona into a redemptive myth.

Ian Buruma wrote that Anne Frank has "become a Jewish Saint Ursula, a Dutch Joan of Arc, a female Christ." He concluded, "Anne is a ready-made icon for those who have turned the Holocaust into a kind of secular religion." I would take the comparisons even further. Despite the evolution of Europe's postwar secular spirit, the myth derives much of its force from a deeply ingrained Christian template. Anne's story converges on elements of Christian belief and symbolism: a hidden child, a virgin, a betrayal, the Holocaust as Hell, a form of resurrection through words. The redemptive tale seems tragically simple, but the real history is complex and convoluted. It is part of a national tragedy in a country of contradictions. The German occupation exacerbated passive political and social habits that affected the individual and collective life of the Dutch. The Anne Frank legend has further blurred the history of Dutch Jews and the Dutch nation during the War. A sorting out is long overdue.

In an essay published in early 1981, the American historian Simon Schama highlighted some of those Dutch paradoxes in regard to the Jews. Schama was writing about Rembrandt's time, when Jews were welcomed in Amsterdam but also subject to restrictions in terms of occupation, membership in guilds, political rights, and religious expression. In his introduction to an exhibition of Rembrandt's images of Jews in the Netherlands, Schama wrote, "The relationship of the host culture to its Jewish immigrants was . . . clouded with ambiguities." He continued, "Compared with other seventeenth century options, it cannot be overstressed, the Dutch Republic was a paradise of toleration and security." He described Amsterdam in the seventeenth century as a "relatively benevolent milieu" for Jews—one in which they could develop an identity in the Dutch context.

> For its sheer regularity, the undisturbed ordinariness, with which
> Amsterdam Jews went about marrying, raising their young, burying
> their dead, cleaning their houses before Pesach, gathering together
> in their splendid temples for the Sabbath and the solemn feasts
> and fasts—that testifies most eloquently to the emergence of an

authentic Dutch Jewish culture. In some ways Amsterdam, with its hectic oscillation between mass piety and mass hedonism, was an odd habitat for this Great Calming Down to occur. . . . Despite the golden crown on the spire of the Westerkerk, it wasn't really Jerusalem. But then it wasn't Babylon, either.

With this remarkable advance in acceptance by a European country, the Jewish population in the Netherlands continued to expand and confidently regarded itself as part of the Dutch nation. In Rembrandt's time, the Jewish population was 10,000. Two centuries later, it was 140,000. By 1940, many Jews had attained high levels of prosperity, recognition, and acceptance in Dutch life, although not to the degree characteristic of German Jews before the rise of Hitler. Forty percent of the Jewish population lived in small villages, towns, or cities such as The Hague. The other 60 percent lived in Amsterdam. A large number of them were poor. Through the 1930s, Dutch Jews focused on internal issues of assimilation, integration, and the well-being of the Jewish community despite the fact that Nazi rule in Germany compelled thousands of Jews, such as Otto Frank, to seek refuge in the Netherlands.

The Dutch haven appeared secure until the spring of 1940, when Germany conquered the Netherlands. The Dutch fought for five days and then capitulated. The Queen and government fled to London, established a resistance government in exile, and urged the Dutch at home to oppose the Germans. The presence of thousands of Germans—as administrators, police, and soldiers—the acquiescent Dutch civil service, and the active support of Dutch Nazis quickly turned the Netherlands into a subject state. The government in Berlin put the Dutch under the control of Seyss-Inquart, an accomplished Nazi fresh from anti-Semitic conquests in Austria. From that point on, Amsterdam was neither Jerusalem nor Babylon. It was hell.

It didn't take long for the Germans to differentiate Jews from other Dutch citizens through anti-Jewish decrees and administrative acts: first, prohibition against Jewish civil servants and teachers; then, in 1941, violent assaults against Jews in the Jewish Quarter in Amsterdam. The Germans insisted that the Jews form a Jewish Council to make their community respond to increasingly punitive German demands. Jews were separated from the rest of Dutch society when their rights to property, education, work, and mobility were taken away. Jews were not allowed to use trams or bicycles, enter parks or swimming pools, go to movie houses, or use beaches. Children's schools were segregated, universities were closed to Jewish professors and students, and Jewish musicians and actors were no longer allowed to perform. Shopping was only allowed in narrow time slots. These were the same kinds of restrictions that the Germans imposed upon their own Jews the 1930s.

Initially, German policies of disenfranchisement and persecution infu-
riated the Dutch. In February 1941, they launched a general strike, which
closed down the docks, the transportation system, and industry. This great
spasm of opposition to the Germans—and outrage against the treatment
of the Jews—lasted three days. The punitive German response pushed the
Dutch back into acquiescence and did nothing to stop the increasing physical isolation of the Jews, their economic ruination, and the eventual roundups
and deportations. Resistance flared again in the spring of 1942, when every
Dutch Jew was ordered to buy and wear a yellow star with "Jew" written on
it. Many Dutch non-Jews wore the yellow star or a yellow flower in solidarity. It made a strong impression on Miep Gies, protector of the Frank family.
"The yellow stars and yellow flowers those first few days were so common,"
she wrote in her book *Anne Frank Remembered*, "that our River Quarter was
known as the Milky Way. . . . A surge of pride and solidarity swelled briefly
until the Germans started cracking heads and making arrests. A threat was
delivered to the population at large: anyone assisting Jews in any way would
be sent to prison and possibly executed."

Life for Jews in the Netherlands ground down to a devastating pattern of anxiety and violent roundups for Jews, their protectors, and those in
the resistance movement. Unlike the Jews in Denmark who could escape
to Sweden, the Dutch Jews had nowhere to go. Some, such as the Franks,
withdrew into hiding. They were totally dependent on their Dutch protectors
who resisted the Germans by housing, feeding, clothing, and caring for Jews.
Of the 140,000 Jews in the Netherlands in 1940, about 20,000 went into
hiding. Approximately 7,000 of them were discovered. They shared the fate
of the majority of Dutch Jews: removal to the Westerbork camp and then
deportation to Sobibor and Auschwitz in the East. By the time the process
was complete, 110,000 Dutch Jews had been killed.

The German occupation sorely challenged traditional Dutch attitudes,
built upon a seemingly strong façade of tolerance and compromise. The political and social acceptance of differences obscured the fateful gulf between
tolerance, on the one hand, and disinterest and disengagement, on the other.
In regard to national cohesion and separate ethnic, religious, and political
identities, the war tested the viability of the so-called Dutch pillar society,
based upon separate realms of allegiance among Protestant, Catholic, Social-
ist, and Liberal groups. With insidious understanding of these affiliations
and, above all else, the Dutch yearning for order, the Germans surgically removed the Jews from Dutch life. And so the Jews disappeared from the realm
of moral concern.

Despite the humiliation and anxiety of occupation, only in the last year
of the war did the non-Jewish Dutch—principally those in the large northern cities—suffer acutely from the depletion of goods and the dangers of

forced labor in Germany. The German defeat finally came to the northern part of the country on May 4, 1945. When the Germans finally surrendered, the Dutch celebrated in the streets for days. The Queen returned. "People who had been in hiding came out onto the streets," Miep Gies wrote. "Jews came out of hiding plates, rubbing eyes that were unused to sunlight, their faces yellow and pinched and distrustful. Church bells rang everywhere; streamers flew. . . . To wake up and go through a whole day without any sense of danger was amazing."

And then came the questions and the counting—a new kind of reckoning amid the decay of civilized life. Miep Gies recounted that she and her husband Henk

> and everyone else began waiting to see just who would be coming home to us. Shocking, unimaginable accounts circulated of the liberation of the German concentration camps. Pictures were printed in the first free newspaper; eyewitness information, too. Through the occupation we'd heard rumors of gassings, murder, brutality, poor living conditions in these camps, but none of us could have imagined such atrocities. The facts had far surpassed even our most pessimistic imaginings. . . . I needed to do everything I could to keep my optimism about our friends. It would have been unbearable to think otherwise.

Their friends included nine Jews who had been hiding above the offices where Gies had worked for Otto Frank's firm. Day after day she asked returning Jews if they had seen any of the Frank family. In June, Otto Frank returned to the Netherlands from Auschwitz with the news that his wife had died there. He was unsure about what had happened to his two children, Margot and Anne. Months later he got word from a nurse in Rotterdam that the daughters had not survived their imprisonment in Auschwitz and Bergen-Belsen. The finality of all the deaths mixed into the tortured lives of those who survived. "I heard it said," Gies wrote in her book, "that where the Jews had looked like everyone else before [the war], after what they had endured, those who returned looked different. But people hardly noticed because everyone had been through so much misery that no one had much interest in the suffering of others." Despite the fact that Dutch Jewry lost nearly 75 percent of its population—the highest number of deaths in any Western European country under occupation—despite the fact that the Dutch Jews had lost everything, the few who came back were expected to make do with what they found, or did not find, of their former lives.

Frieda Menco was fifteen when she returned from Auschwitz with her mother. They were the only survivors of their large family that had lived in the Netherlands for over three hundred years. "When we came back," she recalled, "we tried to tell people of our experiences. But nobody wanted to listen. The authorities considered us as a pain in the neck. A Jew who came back and wanted something." The survivors were told to be quiet—to keep their nightmares and losses to themselves. A once thriving Jewish Dutch world of family, community, institutions, and property was gone. The Dutch constructed effective bureaucratic remedies to bury Jewish claims to emotional and full financial restitution. Many survivors retreated into silence as European countries began to rebuild, to cleanse themselves, and to adjust to the development of the Iron Curtain.

Amidst rebuilding civilized life in the postwar world, Europeans and Americans constructed comforting wartime myths, especially myths about resistance. This is particularly true about the Dutch, who sought to restore a viable nation after the trauma of occupation and the erosion of the pillar society. In a seminal essay, Matthijs Kronemeijer and Darren Teshima described this process:

> [This new] identity was built upon the heroic stories of resistance in the Netherlands to the Nazi regime and the belief that Dutch society had stood by and protected its Jewish citizens. While individual acts of heroism and resistance certainly existed, the formation of a national myth focused on these acts and extending this heroism to describe the entire Dutch nation obfuscated the truth of the war experience.

The world thinks that the Franks were emblematic of what happened to the Jews in the Netherlands. From Anne's story, the international public has gained the impression that whole Jewish families could go into hiding together; that most could remain in one place for a few years; that numerous Christian friends or employees could sustain and succor them in hiding; and that the unfortunate hidden Jews were the ones betrayed by some unknown informer. And there was the final impression: that after the war Dutch Jews would be welcomed back to the country in which they had lived.

In the Netherlands, as in all European countries, there were extremes of valor and decency along with villainy, greed, brutality, and cowardice. In the large middle ground there were bystanders who lived with fear and indifference to the threatened minority. At Yad Vashem in Israel and the U.S. Holocaust Memorial Museum in Washington, thousands upon thousands of Dutch are honored as Righteous Gentiles, including Miep Gies. Risking their lives, they had to resist not only the Germans but their fellow citizens as well. Yet Dutch collaborators or Nazis—as well as rogues just desperate for money—hunted Jews down and turned them over to the authorities. In the official report on the Franks, the record simply states that someone was given the pitifully small amount of sixty guilders—seven guilders for each person he turned over in the Frank hideout.

The history of Otto Frank and his family was unique in many ways. Most of the Dutch were too afraid of German terror and punishment to aid those in hiding and most couldn't be sure that their neighbors could be trusted. Most Jewish Families were broken up, as children were sent away by themselves into hiding and people had to move from place to place to escape detection. Many Amsterdam Jewish families were too poor to pay for places to hide, although a considerable number of Dutch protected Jews without initially asking for payment. And then, after the war, most Dutch Jews came back to a society that was largely indifferent or cruelly hostile to what the Jews had suffered. Otto Frank's welcome was an exception. Miep Gies and her husband, who had protected and aided the Franks in hiding, received him warmly, brought him into their family for seven years, and helped him to rebuild his life.

These exceptions never impinge on the myths. In the service of the redemptive legend of Anne Frank, there is a pattern of pilgrimage to 263 Prinsengracht in Amsterdam. People go to Anne Frank's house to have contact with a consecrated space of suffering. The Dutch are somewhat appalled that the Anne Frank House is such an attraction for tourists—especially for Americans who pay homage to Holocaust remembrance. Nonetheless, this flood of attention is a convenience and a distraction for the Dutch—as well as a lucrative source of income. Tourists don't dig deeper into the history, and the Dutch don't push the matter. Few of the visitors explore what happened to the rest of the Dutch Jewry and to the Dutch themselves. There are 800,000 visitors annually at the Anne Frank House, but only 19,000 visit the Hollandse Schouwburg, the former theatre—now a museum and a monument—where the Germans processed many Dutch Jews for deportation.

There is a clear irony here. The 1950s public, including the Dutch, welcomed Anne Frank's miraculously preserved diary. But had she herself returned, few in the Netherlands would have wanted to learn about her suffering. Testimony was not in style. After enduring the occupation and the impoverishment of both the economy and public morale, the Dutch didn't want to hear about the orderly disappearance of 110,000 Jews between 1942 and 1944.

There is, however, one place in Amsterdam, and maybe others as well, where the myth of Anne Frank does not flourish. This is in the social hall of the Liberal Jewish Synagogue. After attending a service in the sanctuary, one goes into an adjoining room to eat and socialize. On the central wall is a picture of Anne Frank at age twelve—one that we have all seen numerous times. There is no written explanation on the wall—no attempt at identification, just a remembrance. The Franks were members of the original Liberal Jewish Synagogue.

No one in the congregation needs any explanation for what happened to her. In this place, there are no misconceptions concerning the symbolic and the real Anne. The burden of living with that past is hard enough. Living in today's somber shadows of Dutch tolerance, indifference, national victimization, and the Anne Frank myth may be almost as hard.

NIGEL A. CAPLAN

Revisiting the Diary:
Rereading Anne Frank's Rewriting

Paul Celan, a Romanian-born, German-speaking Holocaust survivor, exhorts the reader of his poem, "Die Posaunenstelle" ("The Shofar Place"): "hör dich ein / mit dem Mund" ("hear deep in / with your mouth") (Felstiner, *Selected Poems* 360–361). In these two strident triplets, we can hear Celan's challenge to Theodor Adorno's oft-quoted assertion that "to write poetry after Auschwitz would be barbaric" (qtd. in Felstiner, *Paul Celan* 139). Although Adorno later recanted, George Steiner took up this theme; yet to write "the literature of atrocity" (to borrow Lawrence Langer's term) has always been controversial.[1] For Celan, it is possible to write about the Holocaust when readers are engaged enough to hear with their mouths, to add their voices to the text, to be also (re)writers. It is my contention in this article that the process of rereading and rewriting is modeled in the most famous of all Holocaust texts, and that—following Celan—it is precisely this dialogic attention to language that allows a young girl's diary to "[break] through the horrors and [capture] readers' imaginations generation after generation" (Becker B5).[2]

With more than 15 million copies in print today (van der Stroom 74), Anne Frank's *Diary* might well be called the canonical work of children's literature of the Holocaust. However, it has faced a barrage of criticism ever since its first Dutch publication in 1947, from allegations of inauthenticity,

The Lion and the Unicorn, Volume 28, Number 1 (January 2004): pp. 77–95. Copyright © 2004 The Johns Hopkins University Press.

to a needless controversy over Otto Frank's abridgements, to a recent trend which dismisses it as "more a coming of age story of a precocious young adolescent than an insightful look into the horrors of the Holocaust" (Sullivan 51; see also Langer, *Holocaust*). This discrepancy between public enthusiasm and academic recognition can be seen in the United States Holocaust Memorial Museum's ambivalence towards Anne Frank; in 2003, for the first time in its ten-year history, the museum mounted an exhibition on the *Diary*.[3] The publication of a critical edition by the Netherlands State Institute for War Documentation in 1989 allows a reevaluation of this popular book's importance and answers many of its detractors by understanding exactly what sort of text this remarkable document is.

Little did I think when I first read a slim British edition of *Anne Frank: The Diary of a Young Girl* as a child, that I would ever find a 700-page version of Anne Frank's journal. The weighty *Critical Edition* includes a summary of the Dutch State Forensic Science Laboratory's study, which concluded "with a probability bordering on certainty" that Anne did indeed write the diary, notebooks and loose-leaf sheets which Miep Gies recovered in August 1944 (Hardy 141). However, this is by no means "a defensive and hence sorrowful volume" (Ozick 119). The main body of the book prints Anne's personal diary (the "a-text" found in a diary and two exercise books), her incomplete revision, almost certainly intended for publication after the war (the "b-text," written on typing paper), and the first English language edition of 1952 (the "c-text"). We can now therefore glimpse what Anne intended us to read, and analyze the strategies she employed in her rewriting. By reading the *Critical Edition* both synchronically (across the three versions) and diachronically (through the three versions independently), we can "hear deep in" to Anne's writing, and engage with this text as a significant piece of the literature of atrocity.[4]

Anne began keeping her journal in the plaid-covered diary she was given for her thirteenth birthday; less than a month later, on July 5, 1942, the Franks went into hiding to escape deportation. The first book was filled by the end of November, although Anne periodically returned to add comments and fill in blank pages. The second volume of her original diary, covering the subsequent twelve-month period, has never been found and is presumed lost amidst the chaos of the Franks' capture. On December 22, 1943, Anne continued her diary in an exercise book, which lasted until April 17, 1943, and then began the exercise book in which she would make her very last entry, on August 1, 1944.

On March 29, 1944, after hearing Gerrit Bolkstein, Minister for Education, Art and Science of the Dutch government in exile, announce on Radio Oranje that "after the war a collection would be made of diaries and letters dealing with the war," Anne began to consider writing—according to the most widely read translation—a "romance of the 'Secret Annexe'" (578). However, the original Dutch word *roman* is a "romance" only in the sense of an imaginative prose narrative: that is, a novel.[5] *Het Achterhuis* literally means "the house behind," but translators have generally considered "the Secret Annexe" to be the best approximation (*Critical Edition* 578). Only the Dutch edition used Anne's own title for her book, whereas by calling it a "diary," translators and critics have either shied away from the implication that they are dealing with a crafted work of literature, or (probably unwittingly) have perpetuated Anne's own fiction of a day-to-day journal.[6]

That the published book is to some extent fictitious is evident in Anne's rereading and rewriting, as she turns a private diary into a public document. On May 20, 1944, she writes in the a-text (there is no b-text for this period): "At long last after a great deal of reflection I have started my 'Achterhuis,' in my head it is as good as finished, although it won't go so quickly as that really, if it ever comes off at all" (653). This sentence was not included in the published version, perhaps because it foregrounds the constructed nature of the b-text. This is regrettable because we can hear Anne thinking about *Het Achterhuis* as a story she can plot out ("in my head it is as good as finished"), and also expressing her anxiety about the possible ending—"if it ever comes off at all" might also mean "if we ever get out of here at all."

The b-text that she now begins to write opens with a letter to "Kitty" dated June 20, 1942, and ends on March 27, 1944 (which, incidentally, means that at least the revised version of the missing second volume of the diary has been preserved). The proximity of this date to Bolkstein's broadcast two days later may be a sad coincidence (if we follow Gerrold van der Stroom's assumption in his foreword to the *Critical Edition* that she had only reached this point when she was captured), or it might lead us to speculate whether the entries in the a-text after this point were written with publication in mind, and thus did not require further revision.

This is categorically not to cast doubt on the authenticity of the b-text, nor of the events and emotions expressed therein. Barbara Chiarello's assertion that the a-text "seems more truthful because Anne wrote it for herself" (87) is not founded on critical analysis. A close comparison of the texts reveals that the differences are not factual, only occasionally substantial and, as we shall see, mostly strategic. Nonetheless the diary is "a literary work by Anne Frank rather than an autobiographical document *sensu strictu*" (van der Stroom 71), and I propose to analyze the rewritten text (and the later a-text entries) as such. To the best of my knowledge, this represents the first systematic attempt to distinguish systematically the "I" of the narrator (Anne in May–July, 1944) from her thirteen- and fourteen-year-old (re-)creation (the "I" of the narration). By focusing on the a- and b-texts (rather than on the c-text), I intend to avoid the debate over Otto Frank's abridgements, which—as Mirjam Pressler adequately explains—were made in the interests of concision, modesty, and respect for the dead ("Foreword" vi). I do note the few cases where I feel the changes are substantive or unfortunate for the modern reader.

One such change occurs where Anne writes about her understanding of the role of the writer. In an a-text-only passage dated March 25, 1944 (which has been printed in full only in the *Critical Edition*), Anne writes movingly about how she has changed in hiding, and how Peter van Pels "helps me make the best of a bad job" (568) in dealing with her fellow exiles. She continues:

> I also told Peter much less difficult things that I normally keep to myself; thus I told him that I want to write later on, and even if I don't become a writer, I won't neglect my writing while doing some other job. Oh yes, I don't want to have lived for nothing like most people. I want to be useful or give pleasure to the people around me who don't really know me, I want to go on living after my death! And therefore I am grateful to God for giving me this gift, this possibility of developing myself and of writing, of expressing all that is in me! (569; a-text)

Anne does not include this paragraph anywhere in her b-text, but her father appended the words from "I want to go on living after my death" to the entry of April 5, 1944, in the published version (587).[7] Quoted in full and in context, Anne's famous words articulate not so much a yearning for literary immortality, as a very personal desire to be known and understood for what she believed herself to be. In her final entry four months later, she writes about her two personalities—the "giddy clown" mask that she wears in public, and the "better, deeper and purer" Anne (697) whom no one knows, but who "predominates when we're alone" (698). At one level, therefore, Anne has created a literary persona to "[express] all that is in me" (569) because it is only in writing that she feels she will be taken seriously.

The text that Anne Frank envisaged was to be both a personal statement and a record of the circumstances of her life. It was "to be useful or give pleasure," a (probably unconscious) echo of Horace, who claimed that the aim of poetry, and by extension literature, was "to teach and to delight" (qtd. in Rosenblatt, *Reader* 3). This raises the thorny issue of whether the literature of atrocity can teach children about that which it describes. David Russell has claimed that "art of the Holocaust is necessarily didactic art" (268), to which Adrienne Kertzer responded, in the tradition of "adult" writers such as Primo Levi, Elie Wiesel, and Paul Celan, that there is no "why" in the Holocaust: "children's books about the Holocaust seem to function primarily to explain what adult texts often claim is ultimately inexplicable" (239–240). However, Kertzer argues the memoir disturbs this model because it is written without knowledge of the end, and therefore without "the consolation of shaping narrative order" (241).[8]

The *Critical Edition* thus sets the *Diary* in a no-man's-land between fiction and memoir. Anne Frank does not fit Kertzer's description of "the memoirist [who] often claims that she does not comprehend her own experience. How then can she take on the explanatory function so necessary to the child protagonist who often narrates Holocaust fiction for children?" (240). Anne does understand and explain her own experience, but she writes without knowing for certain the end of her story, and without attempting to interpret what happens beyond the secret annex. Minister Bolkstein explained that his collection of personal documents would balance the official history of the war, so that "our descendents [will] fully understand what we as a nation have had to endure and overcome during these years" (qtd. in van der Stroom 59), and the *Diary* is explanatory and didactic only in this limited way. It crossed Anne's mind that *Het Achterhuis* would sound like the title of a detective story (578); but this would offer the wrong model for reading, one which generically ends with closure in the disclosure of the murderer's identity—an explanation. In a diary, each entry is complete in itself, but a diary entry in a *roman* is part of a structure that has an end, and thus an explanation. Anne's novel is "atrocious" precisely because it has no end, no *telos,* and therefore no power to explain.[9] The lack of closure in a novel is marked because a plot is meaningless if incomplete, and read as such, rather than as a diary; it is harder to ignore the painful realization that the story did not end as Anne wanted it to.

Written in a retrospective present without a clear view of the future, the b-text of the *Diary* resists "the well-intentioned impulse to construct an unambiguously hopeful lesson" (Kertzer 245). As we have seen, Anne had doubts in May 1944 whether the text could ever be finished, but she had a sense of its purpose as a document of personal, everyday experience; she selected and condensed her material "to be useful or give pleasure." Literary texts, as Louise Rosenblatt has argued, cannot dictate their readers' response, but only provide a "blueprint [. . .]. The author has looked at life from a particular angle of vision; he [sic] has selected out what he hopes will fulfill his aim, as Conrad phrased it, to make you see, make you hear, make you feel" (*Reader* 86). Anne Frank had to do all this and more:

> While the text [i.e. the *Diary*] strives at a mimetic representation of the situation, it also demonstrates its author's search for an appropriate narrative form and an adequate linguistic expression. [. . .] Frank seeks a rhetoric, which would both name and defy the unparalleled reality of horror. (Feldhay Brenner 112)

Paul Celan too "invented a poetic form singularly appropriate for the substance of his vision" (Langer, *Holocaust* 12), although Anne has the distinction of forging a narrative that would be accessible to millions of readers. A comparison of the manuscripts suggests that her two principal strategies were to make the *Diary* both more vivid (pleasurable) and more public (useful).

Anne exploits the possibilities of the fictitious autobiography by inserting illusions of reality which give the reader a "lived-through experience" (Rosenblatt, "Viewpoints" 102) as if reading the diary as it was actually written. "It's so peaceful at the moment," she adds to her second revised entry (185); later she interjects, "Phew . . . ! Oh dear, oh dear" (537). She also splits longer entries into more succinct, focused letters by breaking off with: "someone is calling me" (218), and "continued tomorrow" (210). More significantly, she creates a completely new entry for the morning of July 5, the day on which her family went into hiding. After relating the latest gossip from school, she signs off with a hurried interjection of the present tense: "There goes the doorbell, Hello's here [Anne's latest would-be suitor], I'll stop / yours, Anne" (205). The doorbell turns out to be the one that precipitates the crisis; it was an S.S. officer delivering call-up papers for her sister Margot. Anne continues her revised diary under the date of July 8 with the added phrase: "Years seem to have passed between Sunday and now" (206), enticing the reader to relive the traumatic—and exciting—experience with her. In a later entry, the original opening words, "yesterday we had another terrible fright," are transformed into a more immediate sentence which better helps the reader see, hear and feel an attempted burglary: "My hand still shakes although it's two hours since we had the shock" (279). It was of course nearly two years, and not two hours, since the shock.

The result is certainly engaging, and so natural that Anne has always tricked readers into believing that she was a precociously talented thirteen-year-old writer, rather than a fifteen-year-old rewriter. To give just one example, John Berryman's attempt to trace Anne's psychological development ("the conversion of a child into a person" [93]) can now be seen to confuse the author and narrator ("I think we ought to form some opinion of the temperament of Anne Frank" [95]). He quotes Anne's letter of November 7, 1942, as an of example of "the second phase of her development" (100), but the *Critical Edition* (to which Berryman did not have access) reveals that this is a b-text letter, written a year and a half later.

As well as drawing the reader into the text, Anne also turns her personal diary into a public document, as the minister had requested. Critics such as Langer and Sullivan have complained that the Diary does not venture beyond 263 Prinsengracht, and that the horrors of Nazi persecution remain peripheral to the book. However, the Holocaust is ever-present in the *Diary*, just as the railway tracks in Jerzy Kosinski's *The Painted Bird* are clearly, but not explicitly, heading for a concentration camp. As Victoria Stewart has recently argued:

> The familiarity of family rows, exchanging of birthday presents, and Anne Frank's hopes and desires is inevitably set against the most unfamiliar series of events, the Holocaust, and it is the ever-threatened eruption of the Holocaust into daily life which *must* give the reader pause. (101; emphasis added)[10]

It is precisely because Anne's life was "pseudo-ordinary" (Berryman 94) that its representation, the *Diary*, is viable as Holocaust literature. This quotation, though, highlights the limitations of text-based literary criticism, which is uncomfortable with real readers. It is impossible to predict with such certainty (see my italics) how individual readers will respond to any text. In the reader-response tradition, we look for clues in the text which "guide and gauge" the reader's experience (Rosenblatt, *Reader* 86).

We can see this guiding hand in the techniques Anne uses to turn her personal diary into a public text. First, she changes her presentation of the unseen horror, which always threatens to erupt into the secret annex. Originally, she listed all the anti-Jewish laws in one long paragraph (226; a-text); this passage was included in the published version, appended to the entry for June 20, 1942 (180; c-text). However, in the rewritten b-text for that date, Anne provides a much neater summary of "recent" events in Holland (writing with the benefits of hindsight and the BBC), which concludes:

> After May 1940 good times rapidly fled, first the war, then the capitulation, followed by the German invasion which is when the sufferings of us Jews really began. Anti-Jewish decrees followed each other in quick succession and our freedom was seriously limited. Yet things were still bearable, despite the star, separate schools, curfew, etc, etc. (183)

Subsequently, though, Anne reincorporates the anti-Semitic laws she has excised here. The effect is subtler, and does not run the risk of disengaging readers by presenting them with a catalogue of misery, but instead provides several brilliantly orchestrated moments which might give anyone pause.

For example, we learn that Jews' access to certain stores has been limited when Anne and her friends go to "the nearest ice-cream shop, Oasis or Delphi, where Jews are allowed" (185). The interdiction on public transport is incorporated into her inserted b-text letter for June 24, 1942 (trams are "a forbidden luxury for Jews" [198]); on July 5, she adds that Jews have to go to special schools (204) and she adds these poignant words to the revised entry describing how her family walked through the rain from their comfortable home to the cramped hiding place:

> We got very sympathetic looks from people on their way to work.
> You could see by their faces how sorry they were they couldn't offer
> us a lift, the gaudy yellow star spoke for itself. (210)

A second strand of Anne's attempt to widen the scope of the diary and thereby be "useful" is in her treatment of politics and the war effort. Largely absent from her personal diary until Bolkstein's radio broadcast, the outside world makes its presence felt more in the b-text and in the later a-text entries through regular war reports, which become noticeably more frequent after D-Day. Often, though, the focus of these entries is not on the events themselves, but on her own feelings and the reactions of those around her, as they ebb and flow with the Allies' progress. Anne was clearly not trying to write a historical document; her focus is inwards, not outwards. On March 19, 1943, for instance, she records a radio report about Hitler, but continues, with her characteristic flair for juxtaposition:

> I dropped [Pfeffer]'s scented soap on the floor. I trod on it and a
> big bit has been lost. I've asked Daddy for compensation on his
> behalf, especially since Pf. only gets 1 bar of soap per month. /
> Yours, Anne. (436)

Hitler is given no more (and arguably less) attention than a bar of soap.

In an earlier entry Anne appears to explain why she resorts to humor and such apparent trivialities:

> Not one of us really knows how to react [to Pfeffer's descriptions of
> deportations]. The news about the Jews had not really penetrated
> through to us until now, and we thought it best to remain as
> cheerful as possible. [. . .] Yet we shall still have our jokes and
> tease each other when these horrors have faded a bit in our minds;
> it won't do us any good or help those outside to go on being as
> gloomy as we are at the moment and what would be the object of
> making our "Secret Annexe" a "Secret Annexe of Gloom"? (317)

Many of the extra passages in the revised text which are not found in the a-diaries consist of charming vignettes of life in hiding:[11] an *Achterhuis* of gloom (the word here is a likely reference to her proposed title) would not fulfill her joint aims of pleasing and being useful.

So far we have seen how Anne added to her original entries. She also deleted passages which she may have felt were too personal (which in itself would justify many of her father's abridgements). As early as January 1944, she is rereading her diary with embarrassment:

> I cannot believe that I was ever such an innocent young thing. [...]
> I really blush when I read the pages with subjects that I'd much better have left to the imagination. I put it all down so bluntly!"
> (304; a-text)

Indeed, we can trace a third and final strand of the public strategy whereby she removes that which she preferred to keep private, particularly concerning her relationship with Peter van Pels.

Peter is largely ignored in the original entries that describe his family's arrival in the annex, but Anne later describes their growing romance at great length in her a-text. However, by the time she set about rewriting the *Diary*, her infatuation with Peter was over. The b-text is thus very different throughout: it contains a few brief, additional references to Peter in August and September 1942, as if to set up their relationship, which is subsequently narrated in much less detail. Long descriptions—ten entries in all between February 16 and March 6, 1944 (489–512)—of their semi-illicit attic meetings are cut completely in the b-text, although they are reinstated virtually in full in the published c-text, and form the basis of the stage and screen plays. An indication of her changing plan for the *Diary* can be seen in her long entry of March 7, 1944, a deep reflection on her life in hiding: in the revised text, she removes all mention of Peter (515–520). The result of these emendations is a more coherent text which does not descend into a sentimental teenage love-story (a "romance of the Secret Annexe" as in the original mistranslation), but retains its dual focus on Anne's personal development and her life in hiding.

There are other instances where the b-text is less intimate than her original entries. On December 29, 1943 she wrote in the a-text about a vivid dream in which her late grandmother and her friend Hannelies appeared, but she deletes this from the rewriting (435). Shortly afterward, she apparently replaces a vitriolic a-text letter about her mother with a far more reasonable description of her fraught relationship with Edith Frank, in which she concedes that "it's true that she doesn't understand me, but I don't understand her either" (439).[12] The author of the original entry is angry, impetuous, even bitter; the constructed writer of the revised letter is more reminiscent of the "better, deeper and purer" Anne (697). This rewritten passage is framed within the context of a rereading ("this morning when I had nothing to do, I turned over some of the pages of my diary" 438) which is either fictitious or an afterthought, as it does not appear in the a-text. It foregrounds the fiction of the narrative persona.

The b-text strikes a delicate balance between the author's dual aims of being useful and giving pleasure. However, it would be inappropriate to conclude that "Anne pulls the reader into her culture each time she begins an entry for a vicarious experience that ends when she signs off in a manner that establishes her immediate presence" (Chiarello 88). Reading *Het Achterhuis* can in no way be described as living vicariously through the fear, discomfort and ever-present threat of capture and death which characterized the Franks' life in hiding. As Daniel Harding has argued, no written text establishes an immediate presence with its author, not even a diary. However much Anne engages us, we are not participants but "onlookers," to borrow Harding's term, and we do not look upon events but upon "representations of events" (137). The rewriting process further distances us, offering a "quasi-experience and partial understanding" (145), but never the experience itself.

James Britton expands on this notion of the reader as onlooker and argues that we use language for two functions: as participants, in order to "do" something, and as spectators when, freed from the demands of participation, we are at liberty to "make" a verbal object, and the reader/listener can appreciate and evaluate the text. Britton defines literature as "writing in the role of spectator—spectator of other men's [sic] lives, of one's own past and future or might-have-been" ("Viewpoints" 325), and claims that the spectator, better than the participant, role allows us to make sense of what is beyond us (*Language* 118). It is important to realize that the reader in the spectator role is not emotionally detached from the text, but rather is "living through the story as a virtual experience" (Galda 262), where the key word is "virtual": the spectator, unlike the participant, does not completely lose sight of the materiality and fiction of the literary work, and does not treat reading as a vicarious experience.[13]

The two authorial versions of the *Diary* can be seen to represent the two roles in Britton's model. In the a-text, Anne writes as a participant in her own story, but in her revision she adopts the spectator role, which, for Britton, is properly the mode of literature. Reading the a-text, her personal diary, it is easy to be caught up in Anne's whirling emotions, her sexual maturation and her often childish reactions to the people and happenings around her. Even critics who profess awareness of Anne's rewriting—such as Chiarello, Ergas, and Ozick—often adopt the participant role in this way. In less than two years, and thanks in part to her voracious appetite for reading (which has been examined by Sylvia Iskander), she developed a style for her rewritten diary which offers the reader sufficient detachment to reflect on her words. By adopting, and thereby encouraging the reader to adopt the spectator role, Anne Frank's revised, literary text can certainly "give pleasure or be useful"

and even, as Harding claimed, "contribute to defining the reader's or spectator's values" (144).

Anne makes it clear that her reader can only ever be a spectator with
partial knowledge of "that which happened" (in Celan's formulation):[14] "although I tell you a lot, still, even so, you know only very little about our
lives" (587). Moreover, the "you" of the *Diary* is not exactly the reader. The
identity of "Kitty," Anne's mysterious correspondent, has been partly solved
by Mirjam Pressler in *Anne Frank: A Hidden Life,* where she observes that
Kitty is a character in Cissy van Marxveldt's *Joop ter Heul* stories, which Anne
devoured. In the original diary, Anne writes letters to a range of characters
from the series, but by September 1942 she has decided that she prefers writing to Kitty, for reasons which remain obscure (*Critical Edition* 240). In the
b-text, Anne excises the other characters, her playful references to their fictitious lives ("Dear Phien [. . .] Are you showing any signs of fertilization, I
hope so, it's not all that easy" 277), and her habit of writing to the characters
about the books in which they appear, thus sparing us dizzying intertextual
complexities. Although it would be naïve to believe that even a personal diary
is written without any thought of a potential (albeit imaginary) public, Anne's
a-text comes close to that paradigm, because it is impossible for any other
reader to adopt the position of these fictitious addressees.

The Kitty of the revised text, however, is a deliberately constructed imaginary correspondent; she is now accessible to real readers, but she is no longer
van Marxveldt's character: Kitty actually becomes the diary. The first entry of
the b-text (and the only one not written as a letter) explains that "the reason
why I started a diary is that I have no such real friend" (180). This clarifies and
replaces the more frequently quoted sentence which she wrote in the front of
the plaid-covered diary, but did not choose to include in the public version ("I
hope I shall be able to confide in you completely" 177; a-text). Kitty's status is
further elaborated in the b-text:

> In order to enhance in my mind's eye the picture of the friend for
> whom I have waited so long I don't want to set down a series of
> bald facts like most people do, but I want this diary itself to be my
> friend, and I shall call my friend Kitty. (181)

Kitty, though, turns out to be more than a name for the diary-friend. One of
Anne's *Tales* is called "Kitty," and she copied it into the b-text for publication
within the framework of the diary (387), although Otto Frank omitted it
from the c-text, presumably for the sake of space (it is more markedly absent
from the *Definitive Edition*). This short story gives us a sketch of her implied
(ideal?) reader. Kitty is the complete opposite of Anne, her *"alter ego"* (Ergas
37). She has blond hair and blue eyes, a loving mother, a dead father and six

siblings; Kitty is sturdy and fights back against her elder brother, Peter, who is strong, manly, fatherly and generous (and possibly therefore Peter van Pels's alter ego). Kitty is an observant Christian, free to wander where she pleases, and wants to work in a factory, marry and have children. Significantly, "Anne structures Kitty as a character outside the reality of occupied Europe" (Feldhay Brenner 121) making her both an intimate and a distant friend, emphasizing her role (and by extension, the reader's) as a spectator.[15]

This story is important in several ways. First, it seems that Anne has fully appropriated Kitty from Cissy van Marxveldt. Second, it stresses that even Kitty, Anne's confidante and implied audience, cannot approach the text as a vicarious participant; and finally, it may leave the reader of the *Diary* with the uncomfortable feeling of being a literary voyeur, reading misdirected letters. The interactive style therefore distances the reader into the spectator role, by making the referent of the "you" a figure from Anne's own fiction. Each entry thus begins with a salutation, which reminds us that we cannot participate in the relationship between the constructed letter writer and her fictitious correspondent.

The *Critical Edition* allows us to observe several curious slips of the pen which further complicate this relationship: in the b-text manuscript, the letter preceding this story opens "Dear Anne," instead of "Dear Kitty" (she makes the same mistake on March 7, 1944). Without wishing to be too Freudian, one might tentatively suggest that, at some level, Anne saw Kitty as an image of herself and wished to be the recipient, not the sender, of the letters.[16]

This is made even more poignant when we realize that Anne's letters could never be answered: "Who besides me will ever read these letters? From whom but myself shall I get comfort?" (297). In this line, she rationalizes her (originally more playful) decision to write to Kitty and the others; initially she even treated the *Joop ter Heul* books as answers to her letters (248; a-text). We can see this deep yearning for an answer in a more intimate way when she writes to her best friend, Jacqueline, in her personal diary (243). Presumably she was not permitted to send the letter: thus it only exists as a fantasy in her a-text. She also seems to invent a reply between the lines, for she immediately writes a second letter (with the same date as the first) beginning: "Dear Jackie / I was very glad to get your letter" (243). Three days later, with the physical end of this volume looming, Anne goes back to fill in pages she had left blank, and finds a real letter which her friend wrote before Anne went into hiding; she adds these words to her original entry:

> This is the only letter I had from Jacqueline van Maarsen, I asked her often enough for a photograph and she said she would look out for me, but now on 28 Sept. 1942 it is too late, as anyone who reads this will know, for we've been in hiding for quite some time. (192)

It is too late for her "to apologize [for not saying goodbye before going into hiding] and to explain things" (192) so she creates this space in her personal diary to console herself. However, as with her guilt at leaving Hannelies behind while she went into the relative safety of the secret annex (436), this was expiation meant for no other eyes.[17]

This close reading of the *Critical Edition* supports the view of the *Diary* as "an extraordinary piece of writing produced by an extraordinary writer under extraordinary circumstances" (Feldhay Brenner 107–108, paraphrasing Berryman). The extent of Anne Frank's literary development can be appreciated by looking at one of her last entries. Anne begins this long letter dated July 15, 1944 by discussing a book she has read called *What Do You Think of the Modern Young Girl?* (689). This leads her into an astonishing retrospective on her life, almost as if she is putting her affairs in order: "I want to lay myself completely bare to you for once" (689). She defines her "one outstanding trait" as the ability to know herself (689), and she steps back into the spectator role to give us a cool appraisal of herself and those around her. She then sums up her relationship with Peter in a mature, analytical manner:

> I committed one error in my desire to make a real friendship: I switched over and tried to get at him by developing it into a more intimate relation, whereas I should have explored all other possibilities. (693)

Next, she turns to a line she remembers from another book: "For in its innermost depths, childhood is lonelier than old age" (693), and uses this to formulate her own version, as a participant, of the challenges of adolescence:

> It's twice as hard for us young ones to hold our ground, and maintain our opinions, in a time when all ideals are being shattered and destroyed, when people are showing their worst side, and do not know whether to believe in truth and right and in God. (693)

Anne is trying very hard to "do" something with her language—to express her fears and doubts to herself and possibly (for Anne never had a chance to revise—that is, "make"—this entry) for a wider audience.

This rumination on the loneliness of childhood develops into a conclusion which, in its apocalyptic terror and premonitionary force, might well prove an uncomfortable, virtual experience, particularly for the reader who recognizes the approaching (premature) end of the book as presaging the end of Anne's life. It is true that she asserts "people are really good at heart" at this point, but as Langer ("Americanization"), Kertzer, and others have noted, the stage and screen adaptations mutilated the diary by ending here. Anne continues:

> I simply can't build up my hopes on a foundation consisting of confusion, misery and death. I see the world gradually being turned into a wilderness, I hear the ever approaching thunder which will destroy us too, I can feel the suffering of millions and yet, when I look up into the heavens, I think that it will all come right, that this cruelty too will end, that peace and tranquility will return again. In the meantime, I must uphold my ideals, for perhaps the time will come when I shall be able to carry them out! Yours, Anne M. Frank. (694)[18]

Alongside her ideals, Anne is fully aware of the "grim reality" (a phrase she uses earlier in this entry) of "confusion, misery and death." Today we know that the very existence of the diary in its present form is predicated on the murder of its author, and the fact that the "approaching thunder" reached her before it could all "come right" makes these words chillingly prophetic. "Perhaps the time will come" is not an expression of childish innocence, optimism and ignorance; it is an adolescent's highly qualified faith. Once we realize that the future she predicts is our past, we can make connections between the text and the world that can be "useful."

On the inside back cover of the last exercise book appears a short sentence in French (the language which gave Anne so much trouble) that has not been published in any other edition:

> Sois gentil et tiens courage! (699)

"Be kind and be brave!" Is this a motto, a message, or an exercise in the French imperative? Is it a command to Kitty, to the reader, or to herself? We do not know. *Het Achterhuis*, "The Secret Annex," was indeed the most appropriate title for this remarkable text, which its author uses to explore herself and her world. Anne was a secret, "a little bundle of contradictions" (696) as she explains in the last entry she had the chance to write:

> What does contradiction mean? Like so many words, it can be interpreted in two ways: a contradiction imposed from without and one imposed from within. The former means not accepting other people's opinions, always knowing best, having the last word; in short, all those unpleasant traits for which I'm known. The latter, for which I'm not known, is my own secret. (697)

Three days after she wrote those words, Anne and the occupants of the secret annex were captured and deported to Nazi concentration camps, where all but Otto Frank were killed.

The *Critical Edition* reveals some of the strategies that Anne appears to have employed when rewriting her diary for publication. Her revised b-text guides the reader in an attempt to entertain and to educate, to give pleasure and be useful. In this way, I suggest that *Het Achterhuis*—in the version that the author plotted out and intended to submit for publication—deserves to retain its place and importance in the canon of the literature of atrocity. No one's experience of this literature should end with the *Diary*, but there can be few better starting points than trying to "hear deep in" to this literary masterpiece.

NOTES

1. Eleven years later, in 1966, Adorno wrote: "it might have been wrong to say that no poem could be written after Auschwitz" (qtd. in Felstiner, *Celan* 232). Steiner was categorical: "The world of Auschwitz lies outside speech as it lies outside reason" (qtd. in Langer, *Holocaust* 15).

2. I acknowledge a sense of unease with the term "Holocaust." As Zev Garber has convincingly argued, its etymology (from the biblical Greek word for a burnt sacrifice) renders it less appropriate than the Hebrew "Shoah" ("destruction"). I am grateful to Dr. Jane Liddell-King of Cambridge University for bringing this to my attention, and also for introducing me to Celan and the literature of the Shoah.

3. The exhibition opened on June 12, 2003, in Washington, D.C. (Becker B1). I am grateful to this journal's anonymous reader for bringing this newspaper report to my attention.

4. All quotations and page references are from the *Critical Edition*, and are taken verbatim from the b-text where available, and if not, from the a-text, unless otherwise indicated.

5. The *Critical Edition* reproduces Mooyart-Doubleday's use of "romance," compounding the acceptance of this mistranslation; Susan Massotty correctly translates *roman* as "novel" in the *Definitive Edition*.

6. Rachel Feldhay Brenner's article is a notable exception; she begins "the *Diary* is a work of art" (108). However, even her astute reading does not distinguish between the original and rewritten manuscripts.

7. The 1952 translation mistakenly dated this entry April 4; the correct date is given in the *Definitive Edition*.

8. Daniel Mendelsohn, in a recent *New York Times Magazine* article, discovers that the version he knew of his relatives' betrayal to the Nazis was not true, but rather derived from "the desire for a story." He concludes: "a narrative of greed and naïveté and bad judgment was better than the alternative, which was no narrative at all" (55).

9. The term "atrocious" is derived from Langer's phrase "literature of atrocity." It was coined, to the best of our knowledge, by Kathryn Banks, to whom I am indebted for clarifying this and many other key points in this article (personal correspondence, July 2002).

10. Stewart's starting point is Freud's essay on the uncanny. Freud explores the ambiguity in the German word *"Heimlich,"* which can mean both domestic and secret, and thus merges with its opposite, *"unheimlich"* ("uncanny"); hence Stewart's "un/familiar" (101).

11. Many of these vignettes were first written in an old account book, and later edited and published as *Anne Frank's Tales from the Secret Annex*. Anne copied some of the tales into the b-text of her diary (they are annotated "T" in the *Critical Edition*).

12. "Cady's Life," which appears in *Anne Frank's Tales from the Secret Annex* (74–96) which was one of Anne's favorites, contains the same realization by its eponymous heroine.

13. The term "virtual experience" was coined by Susanne Langer (qtd. in Galda 262).

14. Celan described the Holocaust as "das, was geschah" in a speech accepting the Literature Prize of the City of Bremen (Felstiner, *Selected Poems* 395).

15. The addressee's identity is further complicated because Kitty "might not be her name at all" (*Critical Edition* 387). Van Marxveldt's books have not been translated into English, but it would be interesting to know how Anne's "Kitty" is similar to and different from her literary precedent.

16. See the annotations on p. 718 of the *Critical Edition,* which list the corrections in the manuscripts. There is a different confusion in an a-text entry which she signs "Mary Anne Frank" (559). Mary is the Jewish friend (with a quintessentially Christian name) in "Cady's Life" (*Tales* 74–96) who is deported at the end of this unfinished story. Although Anne laughs off the slip ("mistake! That must be from all the excitement!"), Cady's feelings of guilt towards Mary are similar to Anne's feelings towards Hannelies (436). Anne's full name was Annelies Marie Frank.

17. This raises tricky questions about the ethics of printing and reading the *Critical Edition*. Perhaps one justification would be that this weighty tome is not aimed at the general reader, but at the critical community.

18. In "The Americanization of the Holocaust," Langer heaps criticism on the stage and movie versions of the *Diary* for their message of "mercurial optimism" (17). He acknowledges, however, that this passage (which is absent from the stage play) "at least adds some complexity to her youthful vision" (17).

WORKS CITED

Becker, Elizabeth. "Museum Gives Anne Frank Her Space." *New York Times* 12 June 2003: B1+.

Berryman, John. *The Freedom of the Poet.* New York: Farrar, 1976.

Britton, James. *Language and Learning.* Second Edition. Portsmouth, NH: Boynton/Cook, 1993.

———. "Viewpoints: The Distinction between Participant and Spectator Role Language in Research and Practice." *Research in the Teaching of English* 18 (1984): 320–331.

Chiarello, Barbara. "The Utopian Space of a Nightmare." A Scholarly Look at *The Diary of Anne Frank*. Ed. Harold Bloom. Philadelphia: Chelsea House, 1999. 85–99.

Ergas, Yasmine. "Growing Up Banished: A Reading of Anne Frank and Etty Hillesum." *A Scholarly Look at The Diary of Anne Frank*. Ed. Harold Bloom. Philadelphia: Chelsea House, 1999. 35–44.

Feldhay Brenner, Rachel. "Writing Herself Against History: Anne Frank's Self-Portrait as a Young Artist." *Modern Judaism* 16 (1996): 105–134.

Felstiner, John. *Paul Celan: Poet, Survivor, Jew.* Yale: Yale University Press, 1995.

———, Ed. and Trans. *Selected Poems and Prose of Paul Celan.* New York: Norton, 2001.

Frank, Anne. *Anne Frank: The Diary of a Young Girl.* 1947. Trans. B. M. Mooyart-Doubleday. London: Valentine, Mitchell and New York: Doubleday, 1952.

———. *Anne Frank's Tales from the Secret Annex.* Trans. Ralph Mannheim and Michel Mok. New York: Doubleday, 1984.

———. *The Diary of Anne Frank: The Critical Edition.* Ed. David Barnouw and Gerrold van der Stroom. Trans. Arnold Pomerans and B. M. Mooyart-Doubleday. New York: Doubleday, 1989.

———. *The Diary of a Young Girl: The Definitive Edition.* Ed. Otto Frank and Mirjam Pressler. Trans. Susan Massotty. New York: Bantam, 1995.

Galda, Lee. "A Longitudinal Study of the Spectator Stance as a Function of Age and Genre." *Research in the Teaching of English* 24 (1990): 261–278.

Garber, Zev. *Shoah: The Paradigmatic Genocide.* Lanham, MD: University Press of America, 1994.

Harding, Daniel W. "Psychological Processes in the Reading of Fiction." *Scrutiny* 6 (1962): 247–258.

Hardy, H. J. J. "Document Examination and Handwriting Identification of the Text Known as the Diary of Anne Frank: Summary of Findings." *The Diary of Anne Frank: The Critical Edition.* Ed. David Barnouw and Gerrold van der Stroom. Trans. Arnold Pomerans and B. M. Mooyart-Doubleday. New York: Doubleday, 1989. 102–165.

Iskander, Sylvia P. "Anne Frank's Reading." *Children's Literature Association Quarterly* 13.3 (1988): 137–141.

Kertzer, Adrienne. "'Do you know what "Auschwitz" means?' Children's Literature and the Holocaust." *The Lion and the Unicorn* 23.2 (Apr. 1999): 238–256.

Kosinski, Jerzy. *The Painted Bird.* 2nd ed. New York: Grove Press, 1976.

Langer, Lawrence. "The Americanization of the Holocaust on Stage and Screen." *A Scholarly Look at The Diary of Anne Frank.* Ed. Harold Bloom. Philadelphia: Chelsea House, 1999. 15–34.

———. *The Holocaust and the Literary Imagination.* Yale: Yale University Press, 1975.

Mendelsohn, Daniel. "What Happened to Uncle Schmiel?" *New York Times Magazine* 14 July 2002: 24+.

Ozick, Cynthia. "Who Owns Anne Frank?" *A Scholarly Look at The Diary of Anne Frank.* Ed. Harold Bloom. Philadelphia: Chelsea House, 1999. 102–120.

Pressler, Mirjam. *Anne Frank: A Hidden Life.* New York: Dutton Children's Books, 2000.

———. "Foreword." *The Diary of Anne Frank: The Definitive Edition.* Ed. Otto Frank and Mirjam Pressler. Trans. Susan Massotty. New York: Bantam, 1995. v–viii.

Rosenblatt, Louise. *The Reader, the Text, the Poem: The Transactional Theory of the Literary Work.* Carbondale: Southern Illinois University Press, 1978.

———. "Viewpoints: Transaction versus interaction." *Research in the Teaching of English* 19 (1985): 96–107.

Russell, David L. "Reading the Shards and Fragments: Holocaust Literature for Young Readers." *The Lion and the Unicorn* 21.2 (Apr. 1997): 267–280.

Stewart, Victoria. "Anne Frank and the Uncanny." *Paragraph* 24 (2001): 99–113.

Sullivan, Ed. "Beyond Anne Frank: Recent Holocaust Literature for Young People." *The New Advocate* 15 (2001): 49–55.

van der Stroom, Gerrold. "The Diaries, Het Achterhuis and the Translations." *The Diary of Anne Frank: The Critical Edition*. Ed. David Barnouw and Gerrold van der Stroom. Trans. Arnold Pomerans and B. M. Mooyart-Doubleday. New York: Doubleday, 1989. 59–83.

ACKNOWLEDGMENT

The author would like to thank Lawrence Sipe for his generous help and incisive comments during the rereading and rewriting process.

PASCALE BOS

Reconsidering Anne Frank: Teaching the Diary in Its Historical and Cultural Context

It is said that after the Bible, Anne Frank's diary is the most widely read text in the world. Thirty-one million copies of the diary have been sold, and it has been translated into more than sixty-five languages. In the United States, Anne Frank has been one of the central figures in Holocaust education for at least two generations, as her diary is used in almost all courses (and course sections) dealing with the Holocaust on the elementary and secondary education levels. To support this educational effort, great volumes of teaching materials have been created, suggesting a variety of approaches to teaching the diary. Considering the central presence of Frank, one may wonder what more could be said about the diary's use in the classroom. Quite a lot, in fact: while the use of Frank's diary (or the 1955 screenplay based on her journal) has largely gone undisputed among secondary school educators, the ubiquitous presence—some would argue overuse or misuse—of Frank's journal and her legacy in Holocaust education has led to pronounced discomfort among some cultural critics and academics. For this reason, many college professors would not even consider teaching Frank's diary in a course on Holocaust history or literature. This essay briefly discusses the prolific, varied critiques of the pedagogical uses of Anne Frank's diary and persona that have emerged over the past two decades and suggests an approach that takes into account these objections.

Teaching the Representation of the Holocaust, Eds. Marianne Hirsh and Irene Kacandes (New York: The Modern Language Association, 2004): pp. 348–359. Copyright © 2004 The Modern Language Association.

The numerous critiques of the use of Frank's diary tend to revolve around the following issues: the neglect or even erasure of Anne's Jewishness and/or the specific historical circumstances under which her family lived and died (as German Jewish refugees who hid in Amsterdam and who were betrayed by Dutchmen), the sanctification of her in a way that erases the complexity of her work and her self-representation, the attempt to mitigate the horrors of the Holocaust through an emphasis on her optimism and/or on the family's helpers (while ignoring the family's murder in concentration camps), and a universalizing of her experience of persecution to such a degree that it applies to all kinds of injustices in the world (which positions the Holocaust as less than unique and renders the actual circumstances of her life and death almost irrelevant).

A number of these problematic uses can be attributed to the figure of Anne herself and to the nature of her journal: that she came from an assimilated Jewish background rather than an observant one, for example, explains the less than pronounced Jewishness of her perspective. Her optimism, in contrast, needs to be understood as a result of the fact that she was hidden from the horrors of the Holocaust initially and that the diary ends before she would come to know its ultimate horrors firsthand. In other ways, however, the questionable approaches to her diary may have resulted from misconceptions about people in the age group to which most of the teaching material about her has been directed (eighth to twelfth graders rather than college students) and from the particular pedagogical goals these materials tend to have.

Anne Frank Universalized

In middle school and high school curricula, the Frank text is often used precisely for its potential to serve as a universal example of victimization as the result of racism. While the goal may be to teach about the Holocaust specifically, the larger goal is to have young students understand racial (and other forms of) discrimination, its roots, and its ultimate consequences (mass murder) and to educate them to be vigilant and to be aware of personal choice and responsibility.[1] These curricula thus frequently present the diary without a thorough-enough analysis of the specific national and historical context of which it is a product and only broadly situate it as a Holocaust text (perhaps within the context of a few class hours discussing the background of World War II and National Socialism).

De-emphasizing the diary's historical specificity allows young students to identify with a victim "just like them," a girl who struggles with common adolescent issues: her parents, youthful infatuation, burgeoning sexuality, and a need for independence. In this approach, the drama of the diary (or the stage play or the film versions) stems from Anne's insightful adolescent descriptions of interfamilial conflicts playing themselves out in the pressure cooker of the secret annex while the Nazis terrorize the Jews of Europe on the outside. Through this relatively harmless exercise in identification, it is hoped, students may gain a deeper insight into, and interest in, the experiences of those who were persecuted for their race or belief; it is the empathy they feel for Anne that brings the Holocaust back to a manageable, human scale. Once her diary is covered, many curricula shift from the Holocaust and Jewish persecution to discrimination and (racial) oppression in general, leading to discussions on contemporary conflicts in the United States or on wars and genocide and on broader moral lessons about human behavior and individual choice.

At times, the use of Anne's diary in teaching about the Holocaust also clearly serves to mitigate the horror of the Holocaust. Many of the curricula suggest, for instance, that the diary can be used to introduce even very young students to this difficult topic, for Anne's idealism and her hope in the fundamental goodness of people balance out the bleakness of Holocaust history. While the drama of her life is heightened if students also learn about her death in Bergen-Belsen, their overall impression should be that good ultimately triumphs over evil.

Although it is easy to see how such a broad and general treatment of this text and the Holocaust is problematic and particularly inappropriate for college-age students and although much criticism has indeed been directed toward such generic readings, few critics have suggested what a more useful approach to Frank's diary would look like.

I propose that the text should be brought back to college classes precisely because Frank's persona and diary are already familiar to most American students. Both the journal and the writer, therefore, lend themselves to an analysis that demythologizes what students have learned so far about the book, the persona of its author, and the Holocaust more generally. I suggest an approach that emphasizes the story's very particularity instead of its supposed universality: a study that places in context her assimilated German Jewish background and her life as a member of an upper-middle-class German Jewish refugee family under Nazi occupation in Amsterdam. Students can look at both the German Jewish context and that of the Jews in the Netherlands during the Nazi occupation. A second approach, which can be developed separately or in conjunction with the first, is to examine the wealth of new critical literature on the use and misuse of Anne Frank and to make the adaptation and marketing of this text over the past five decades, and in different national contexts, a topic of investigation. Analyzing how the diary and Anne Frank herself came to have the iconic status they now have can serve as an interesting case study in the power of Holocaust representations.

There are, then, two different ways to recontextualize the text historically and culturally. First, the diary can be used to explore the Frank family's unique predicament as a German Jewish family whose sense of Jewish identity was both historically specific and class-specific, that was unexpectedly confronted with antisemitic persecution (see Blasius and Diner; Kaplan; Moore, *Refugees*; Mosse). By understanding the Franks' German Jewish identity, students can consider Anne's writing as a particular cultural response that was not unique to her or to her family but was indebted to a German Jewish cultural tradition that continued in the family after their emigration to the Netherlands. Students can come to understand this culture by reading passages in the diary that deal with Anne's sense of religious and cultural identity and then gathering relevant background information (Mosse). From this activity students will learn that middle-class and upper-middle-class Jews in Germany were steeped in the nineteenth-century German ideal of *Bildung*—that is, of a culture based on a classically informed humanism rather than on religion or nationality. Anne's awareness of her own experience of persecution—as a human being first, and as a Jew second—can be read as stemming from this cultural tradition, as can her ideas about what may resolve such conflicts in the future. Whereas her views are less religiously or traditionally Jewish than what we as (in particular, American) readers may expect to find in the diary of a persecuted Jewish teenager, they mirror quite faithfully the cultural background in which Anne, as an assimilated German Jew, was raised. Furthermore, the marketing of the diary after the war by Anne's father, Otto, and his choice of cuts and elisions can be understood, from this perspective, as conforming to an ideal of assimilation in which Jewish, Christian, and humanist values informed German Jewish life equally.

Such an explanation thus takes into account the assimilated nature of the Frank family and their relationship to Judaism, which would become contested in the American reception of the diary and the ensuing theater and film production. Understood in historical context, Anne's particular sense of Jewish identity and Otto Frank's postwar choice of editorial cuts and the marketing strategy of his daughter's work and her legacy as a universal (not necessarily Jewish) figure of oppression become comprehensible. Seen this way, the diary clarifies, in turn, the ways in which Anne's life and writing were more traditionally Jewish than those who treat her book as a testimony to universal human suffering wish to suggest but certainly less traditionally Jewish than those who would present her story primarily as one of religious persecution would like to see.

Placing the Franks in their Dutch context, to look at the relatively unfamiliar story of the Dutch Jews and of German Jewish refugees under Nazi occupation in the Netherlands, is revealing as well (see Blom; Colijn and Littell; Hirschfeld; Jong; Moore, *Victims*; Presser). For the Franks' privileged life as prosperous German Jewish emigrants in Amsterdam who would successfully hide as a family in the city for over two years was, in fact, unusual. The story of most Jews in the Netherlands was considerably more grim. The majority of the refugees in the Netherlands were able neither to integrate culturally nor to become stable financially, and they were the first to be caught when the Nazis occupied the country. Furthermore, finding a place to hide was difficult for all Jews, and most were quickly betrayed (only 10% survived in hiding, almost always separated from their families). It is thus important to enhance students' understanding of the diary by providing background reading that shows that it was the Frank family's end—their betrayal, deportation, and death—rather than their life in hiding that was typical of the Dutch experience. Discussing in some detail the Dutch Jewish death rate will be revealing, as this record is astonishing: the Nazis succeeded in deporting over 82% of the Jewish population of the Netherlands, and less than 5% of the deportees survived, resulting in a Jewish death rate of over 75%. Emphasizing that this murder rate of Jews is by far the highest of any Western European country and studying the complex reasons for these numbers will deepen students' interaction with the text.

For readers keeping in mind Anne's diary images—in which she notes the help the family receives; in which Dutch collaborators are scarcely mentioned; and in which the family's eventual betrayal, deportation, and her death cannot be foreseen—the extent of the Dutch Jewish extermination tends to shock and surprise. Discussing the diary as a representation of the Dutch historical experience despite no tradition of antisemitism in the Netherlands, it includes a high collaboration rate, little participation in resistance, and a substantial rate of betrayal of Jews in hiding—allows students to question what role accommodation and collaboration played in the success or failure of Nazi deportations in different European nations and how national war myths as deceptive as that of the Dutch develop.

That the myth of the Dutch as a righteous nation and the Netherlands as a liberal haven emerged and perpetuated itself in relation to Anne's diary is particularly instructive. Some American critics have accused the Dutch of manipulating Frank's image to construct a more favorable image of their role in the war, so that Frank serves as "Holland's unofficial patron saint" (see Miller 95). However, an analysis of the development of this image suggests that it derives from Otto Frank's editorial cuts and more specifically from the American play and film adaptation of Anne's diary, neither of which can be attributed to a deliberate attempt on the part of the Dutch to falsify their own image. Indeed, if Frank's iconization suggests anything, it is that the American investment in the myth of the Dutch as an upstanding people who hid Jews like the Franks and thus resisted the Nazis may be as strong as that of the Dutch.

This observation brings me to the final suggestion for teaching the diary: to discuss Frank's work and its legacy critically, tracing the publication and reception of the diary itself, with its reprints, reedits, and stage and film versions. Such an activity offers insight into the marketing and reception of Holocaust texts and the evolution of a Holocaust literary genre more generally, of which the Frank text is one of the earliest and most popular examples.

It has been well documented that, notwithstanding its later success, Otto Frank initially had great difficulty finding a Dutch publisher for his daughter's diary. Once he did, the diary appeared in a. shortened, edited version. Through an analysis of the original and later editions of the diary (again, use the *Critical Edition* [ed. Barnouw and van der Stroom], in which the different versions and editions of the diary can be found side by side), students can examine the editorial choices Otto Frank and the Dutch publisher made for the first publication of the work, choices that were then repeated, with interesting additional revisions in the German and other translations. Those changes reveal a desire to have Anne portrayed a certain way. By deleting the passages that dealt with her conflicted relationship with her mother, her sexual development, and her anger toward the antisemitism in Dutch and German culture, her father and the original publisher could underplay the more complex aspects of her personality and her Jewish background—facilitating, in turn, her transformation into an idealized, universal figure of martyrdom.

The transformation of the diary became even more dramatic after the American edition was published. Its enormous success led to the creation of a theater version by the Hollywood screenwriters Frances Goodrich and Albert Hackett. The story of the creation of this play is a fascinating one, as it illustrates what occurred in the repackaging of Frank's story for an American audience of the 1950s. The play, first performed in the United States in 1955 and in Europe in 1956, became a huge hit. By 1959, a film had been made of the play (for which the screenplay was itself modified), and Frank's life became even more widely known.

Much has been written on the marketing of Frank that took place by means of these rewritings, and a reading of some of the background material and a student's comparison of the diary in its different versions with the play and the film serve as a good exercise to gain insight into the Americanization of Frank's literature and the Holocaust more broadly. In the 1970s and 1980s, some critics have argued, Anne Frank's legacy in the United States went through a radical transformation once more: while her persona had once been universalized, it was now placed exclusively in a Jewish and Holocaust context. As such, Anne became the quintessential Holocaust victim and the central focus of Holocaust education. An analysis of the transformations provides a framework in which to discuss the larger social and political forces at work in the American literary establishment's early and more recent attempts to represent the Holocaust and the public's attempt to come to terms with it through the persona and diary of Anne Frank.

Finally, to understand more broadly the Anne Frank industry that emerged in the United States as well as in the Netherlands and elsewhere since the initial publication of the diary, one should also examine the various Frank organizations, their histories and philosophies.[2] Looking at the educational initiatives these organizations have developed over time, the books and films they have produced, and in particular the international exhibits they have put on suggests the different contexts in which Anne Frank's legacy is placed and offers insight into the meanings her memory has taken on in the participating nations.

The approaches outlined here thus attempt to take into account most if not all of the critiques directed at the use of the diary. Both the erasure of Anne's Jewishness and the opposite tendency, to make her stand in for all Jewish children murdered in the Holocaust, can be addressed through an analysis of her specific background and experiences as a German Jewish refugee. Furthermore, by looking at the complexity of the Frank family's sense of Jewish identification, we gain insight into the assimilated German Jewish cultural tradition Anne's writing should be seen in, if we are to resist a universalizing of her work. Discussing the Dutch historical context in detail allows for a much needed adjustment of the commonly held, overly positive views of gentile wartime behavior toward the Jews in the Netherlands and elsewhere. The analysis also leads to an awareness of accommodation and collaboration more generally in occupied nations, complicating the story of simple heroism sometimes presented through Frank's diary.

Finally, Frank's work should be discussed not as either typical or exemplary, I believe, but rather as one of the many texts Jews created while living through the Holocaust. It is one, however, that, for a number of specific cultural and historical reasons, managed to exude an unequaled power to engage its audiences. In addressing its popularity, we should first look at Anne's writing itself. After sixty years, it still sparkles, amuses, moves, and engages. When we also look at the various diary editions and in particular at the theater and film adaptations, however, we can see the transformations that led to the author's subsequent iconization. Analyzing these adaptations and her phenomenal, enduring popularity allows us to look at what purpose her persona and her work have served over the past decades and still serve for us now and to evaluate our own goals and motivations in Holocaust education.

NOTES

1. See, for example, the questions that are part of the online Anne Frank Center USA teaching guide. Students are asked to define the terms *stereotype* and

scapegoat and examine how nationalism and national identity have "been used to justify discrimination and war." Students are then encouraged to organize "a campaign to promote racial, religious, cultural understanding in their school" *(Teacher's Guide)*.

2. There are six organizations that officially represent the Frank legacy and propose extensive curricula: Anne Frank House in Amsterdam (Anne Frank Foundation); Anne Frank Center USA (founded in 1977 "to educate people about the causes, instruments and dangers of discrimination and violence through the story of Anne Frank"—see www.annefrank.com); Anne Frank–Fonds in Basel, Switzerland (established in 1963 by Otto Frank, "to promote charitable work and to play a social and cultural role in the spirit of Anne Frank"—see www.annefrank. ch/e); Anne Frank Zentrum in Berlin (the German partner organization of the Anne Frank House in Amsterdam); Anne Frank Educational Trust UK (which aims to "educate against all forms of racism and discrimination by explaining the history of Anne Frank and the Holocaust"—see www.afet.org.uk); and Anne Frank Youth Center, Frankfurt am Main (which presents an exhibition and organizes activities "for the promotion of understanding between different cultures, nations and religions"—see www.jbs-anne-frank.de/indexen.htm).

WORKS CITED

Barnouw, David, and Gerrold van der Stroom, eds. *The Diary of Anne Frank: The Critical Edition.* Prepared by the Netherlands State Inst. for War Documentation. New York: Doubleday, 1989.

Cole, Tim. *Selling the Holocaust, from Auschwitz to Schindler: How History Is Bought, Packaged, and Sold.* New York: Routledge, 1999.

Colijn, Jan G. "Toward a Proper Legacy." Rittner 95–104.

Frank, Anne. The Diary of a Young Girl: *The Definitive Edition.* Ed. Otto Frank and Mirjam Pressler. Trans. Susan Massotty. New York: Doubleday, 1995.

Goodrich, Frances, and Albert Hackett. *The Diary of Anne Frank.* New York: Random, 1956.

Kniesmeyer, Joke. *Anne Frank in the World, 1929–1945.* Amsterdam: Bakker, 1985.

Miller, Judith. *One, by One, by One: Facing the Holocaust.* New York: Simon, 1990.

Morger, Susan. *Teaching the Diary of Anne Frank: An In-depth Resource for Learning about the Holocaust through the Writings of Anne Frank.* New York: Scholastic, 1998.

Rittner, Carol, ed. *Anne Frank in the World: Essays and Reflections.* Armonk: Sharpe, 1998.

Rosner, Hedda. *Understanding Anne Frank's* The Diary of a Young Girl: *A Student Casebook to Issues, Sources, and Historical Documents.* Westport: Greenwood, 1997.

Teacher's Guide to the Exhibit: Anne Frank: A History for Today. Anne Frank Center, USA Online. 2000. 13 Apr. 2004 <http://www.annefrank.com/download/material_guidetoexhibit.doc>.

SUGGESTED READING

Anne Frank in German Jewish Context

Blasius, Dirk, and Dan Diner, eds. *Zerbrochene Geschichte: Leben und Selbstverständnis der Juden in Deutschland [Shattered History: Life and Self-Definition of the Jews in Germany].* Frankfurt: Fischer, 1991.

Kaplan, Marion A. *Between Dignity and Despair: Jewish Life in Nazi Germany.* New York: Oxford University Press, 1998.

Moore, Bob. *Refugees from Nazi Germany in the Netherlands, 1933–1940.* Dordrecht: Nijhoff, 1986.

Morse, George. *German Jews beyond Judaism.* Bloomington: Indiana University Press, 1985.

Anne Frank in Dutch Jewish Context

Blom, J. C. H. "The Persecution of the Jews in the Netherlands in a Comparative International Perspective." *Dutch Jewish History: Proceedings of the Fourth Symposium on the History of the Jews in the Netherlands.* Vol 2. Ed. Jozeph Michman. Assen, Neth.: Van Gorcum, 1989. 273–289.

Colijn, Jan, and Marcia S. Littell, eds. *The Netherlands and Nazi Genocide: Papers of the Twenty-First Annual Scholars' Conference.* Lewiston: Mellen, 1992.

Hirschfeld, Gerhard. *Nazi Rule and Dutch Collaboration: The Netherlands under German Occupation, 1940–1945.* Trans. Louise Willmot. Oxford: Berg, 1988.

Jong, Louis de. *The Netherlands and Nazi Germany.* Erasmus Lectures, 1988. Cambridge: Harvard University Press, 1990.

Moore, Bob. *Victims and Survivors: The Nazi Persecution of the Jews in the Netherlands, 1940–1945.* London: Arnold, 1997.

Presser, Jacques. *The Destruction of the Dutch Jews,* New York: Dutton, 1969.

Young, James. "The Anne Frank House: Holland's Memorial 'Shrine of the Book.'" *The Art of Memory: Holocaust Memorials in History.* Ed. Young. New York: Jewish Museum, with Prestel, 1994. 131–137.

Critical Readings of Anne Frank's Diary and Legacy

Bettelheim, Bruno. "The Ignored Lesson of Anne Frank." *"Surviving" and Other Essays.* New York: Knopf, 1979. 246–257.

Doneson, Judith. "The American History of Anne Frank's Diary." *Holocaust and Genocide Studies* 2.1 (1987): 149–160.

Graver, Lawrence. *An Obsession with Anne Frank: Meyer Levin and the Diary.* Berkeley: University of California Press, 1995.

Langer, Lawrence L. "The Americanization of the Holocaust on Stage and Screen." *From Hester Street to Hollywood: The Jewish-American Stage and Screen.* Ed. Sarah Blacher Cohen. Bloomington: Indiana University Press, 1983. 213–230.

———. "The Uses—and Misuses—of a Young Girl's Diary: 'If Anne Frank Could Return from among the Murdered, She Would Be Appalled.'" *Forward* 17 Mar. 1995: 1, 5.

Melnick, Ralph. *The Stolen Legacy of Anne Frank: Meyer-Levin, Lillian Hellman, and the Staging of the Diary.* New Haven: Yale University Press, 1997.

Ozick, Cynthia. "Who Owns Anne Frank?" *New Yorker* 6 Oct. 1997: 76–87.

Rosenfeld, Alvin H. "Popularization and Memory: The Case of Anne Frank." *Lessons and Legacies: The Meaning of the Holocaust in a Changing World.* Ed. Peter Hayes. Evanston: Northwestern University Press, 1991. 243–278.

AIMEE POZORSKI

How to Tell a True Ghost Story:
The Ghost Writer *and the Case of Anne Frank*

*T*he *Ghost Writer,* Philip Roth's 1979 novel about the young Nathan Zuckerman, examines the role of the Jewish writer and limits of a son's loyalty to his father. The novel opens as twenty-three-year-old Zuckerman prepares to meet E. I. Lonoff, a Jewish novelist Zuckerman admires, and from whom he secretly hopes to gain a compensatory paternal affection after arguing with his own father. Nathan explains that, like "many a *Bildungsroman* hero" before him, he was already thinking about writing his "own massive *Bildungsroman*" (3). With the repetition of "Bildungsroman," or "novel of education," Zuckerman announces that this narrative in which he is the hero will detail his survival through a crisis and eventual recognition of his place in the world.

However, despite these opening metafictional remarks, *The Ghost Writer* is not your typical novel of education. Nathan suffers from a crisis of personal and ethnic identity: He and his father have quarreled about a short story Nathan has written, titled "Higher Education." This story about Jews feuding over money, his father argues, will only provide anti-Semites with ammunition. In response to such a devastating blow, Nathan imagines that he meets the living—surviving!—Anne Frank at Lonoff's. Marrying Anne Frank, Nathan fantasizes, would certainly force his father, and the rest of his family, to understand that Nathan really is a good son, and a good Jew. His

Philip Roth: New Perspectives on an American Author, ed. Derek Parker Poyal (Westport, Conn.: Praeger, 2005) pp. 89–102. Copyright © 2005 Greenwood Press.

"maturation," in other words, derives partly from Nathan's own imagination—and not from lived experience at all.

One problem that has repeatedly vexed critics involves how to understand the relationship between the argument over "Higher Education" and Nathan's fantasy that Anne Frank has survived, if only to marry Nathan Zuckerman. One way to read these two major aspects of the novel is as two approaches to the same conflict—the conflict of idealization versus reality, of separating what happened from what seemed to happen, or what ought to happen, or what we would like to happen. As the novel implies, this tension between ideality and reality has consequences not only for art but for history, particularly the history of the Jews after the devastation of the Holocaust.

Despite Zuckerman's lengthy Anne Frank fantasy and its suspension of any simple reading of *The Ghost Writer* as a bildungsroman, very few critics are willing to classify Philip Roth as a Holocaust novelist. Of those who consider Roth's unique brand of Holocaust representation, Sophia Lehmann proposes that "Roth presents fantasy as a positive force for creatively reimagining the Holocaust in ways that challenge established historical truisms and dogma" (36). Sanford Pinker similarly considers Roth's relationship with the imaginative force of the Holocaust, suggesting that "for all of *The Ghost Writer*'s technical brilliance, the question still nags: how to imagine the Holocaust, or in this case, how to reimagine an Anne Frank?" (231). However, both Lehmann and Pinsker focus their readings on the power of the imagination in confronting historical atrocity, as if reality is perhaps too stark or somehow not enough for the source of a novel. By contrast, Nathan Zuckerman's fantasizing about Anne Frank's "ghost" suggests, as has Cynthia Ozick, that reality is always sacrificed on the altar of communal ideals. In other words, Nathan imagines Anne Frank as alive in order to destroy her as an icon of Jewishness, thereby allowing a truer account of Jewish experience to arise. Although Nathan's family and community criticize him for not considering the history of the Jews and its vexed relation to "Higher Education," Nathan's position, like Ozick's, is actually more historical than the ideal representations of Jews advanced by his father, Doc Zuckerman, and the heartened readers of *The Diary of Anne Frank*.

Initially, *The Ghost Writer* appears as a playful representation of one young writer's deep admiration for another writer, and his journey to meet this mentor at his home in New England. As the novel progresses, however, the cultural weight of the writer's responsibilities become increasingly pronounced. The novel is divided into four sections. Each is narrated by Nathan Zuckerman and takes as its focus a particular crisis of one of the four main characters. "Maestro," the first part, details Zuckerman's obsession with Lonoff, despite the fact that Lonoff de-romanticizes his craft, saying that he turns sentences around for a living (17). The second, "Nathan Dedalus," alludes to James Joyce's character Stephen Dedalus. Like Stephen, Nathan learns that in order to defend "Higher Education," he must turn his back on his family and reject the conventions of his culture. "Femme Fatale," the next section, showcases Zuckerman's fantasy that Amy Bellette is really Anne Frank—the Holocaust's greatest survivor in the living room of his very own mentor. And finally, part four, "Married to Tolstoy," takes the perspective of Lonoff's wife, Hope, as she begs her husband to take Amy as his mistress and to free her from domestic life with this writer. Leo Tolstoy, like Lonoff, was of Russian descent (8, 10, 50). But unlike Lonoff, he believed that all art originates in personal experience and that critics could judge a work of art solely on whether it has been an instrument for progress toward the elimination of cruelty. In fact, that Lonoff is not like Tolstoy is perhaps his wife's greatest complaint. In a fit of despair, she laments that Lonoff's fiction depends upon a kind of failure to actually live in the world (174–175).

With the Holocaust in the novel's immediate background, and the many references to such aesthetes as Joyce, Tolstoy, Franz Kafka, Henry James, and, above all, Amy Bellette/Anne Frank in the novel's foreground, Roth complicates the role of the post-Holocaust writer. As Zuckerman's contentious story and his fantasy of Anne Frank's survival both make clear, writers must continuously negotiate between fact and fiction, self and society, history and individual life. But, no matter which avenue they choose, especially if they are Jewish, the Holocaust looms large as a historical force that both refuses and demands full recognition. Nathan's argument with his father over the consequences of "Higher Education" explicitly invokes the Holocaust and emphasizes the vexed identity politics behind bearing witness to genocide. This intergenerational argument, which is arguably the force driving the novel, offers a double-edged perspective on the legacy of the Holocaust as Nathan's father enacts his worry about the causal relationship between anti-Semitism and genocide.

Nathan's controversial story is about a small incident in the history of the Zuckerman family, a family argument that became a lawsuit over money that was left in a will for the higher education of Nathan's cousins. The dispute occurred between the mother of these cousins, who intended to send her sons to medical school, and her brother Sidney, who rejected such earnestness in favor of hedonism. According to Nathan's story, Sidney refuses to give up such pastimes as womanizing, entertaining shady friends, and pursuing an affair in the name of two more wealthy doctors (81). Doc Zuckerman accuses Nathan of fostering anti-Semitic stereotypes, arguing that Nathan makes everyone in his family seem—in his words—"awfully greedy" (86). And Nathan counters by saying that everyone in his family *did* seem greedy in this particular instance. The conflict, for Nathan, is that what he writes about really did happen in his own family—that for him, this particular instance is "the truth."

But for his father, it is self-loathing at its most pernicious. Doc Zuckerman forcefully argues, sitting with Nathan as the afternoon sun is setting behind them while they await Nathan's bus: "Nathan, your story, as far as Gentiles are concerned, is about one thing and one thing only. [. . .] It is about kikes. Kikes and their love of money. That is all our good Christian friends will see, I guarantee you" (94). For Doc Zuckerman, there is a distinct division between "kikes" and "Christians," "Jews" and "Gentiles." Although he wants those whom he ironically calls "good Christians" to see accomplished and sacrificing Jews in Nathan's story, he is sure that, for such readers, the category of "Jew" permanently excludes positive characteristics such as accomplishment and self-sacrifice. Nathan admits that anti-Semitism is real and that it had effects in Nazi Germany, but he refuses to change his story: for him, Sidney *really* existed and it is in this story that Nathan has located the qualities of good fiction.

Nathan's father counters with the claim that, as a Jewish writer, Nathan has a responsibility to tell "the *whole* story" about his family in order to balance the unsympathetic character of Sidney with the many likable and well-respected Jews in his family (87). As such, this debate between father and son over a writer's responsibilities ventriloquizes a fight Roth has been having with his readership for several decades. In 1963, for example, Roth wrote an essay entitled "Writing About Jews" in order to respond to criticism that he unfairly and unsympathetically renders Jewish characters, despite his status as a Jewish writer. Here, Roth explains, "though moral complexities are not exclusively a Jew's, I never for a moment considered that the characters in the story should be anything other than Jews. Someone else might have written a story embodying the same themes, and similar events perhaps, and had at its center Negroes or Irishmen; for me there was no choice" (157). Roth argues here that he writes about Jews living in America because it is something about which he has intense and immediate knowledge.

Because of Roth's interest in the quandaries of humankind and the everyday lives of Jews, Aharon Appelfeld calls Roth a true "Jewish" writer. Appelfeld emphasizes that Roth remains true to Jewish life as he knows it by portraying the complexity of Jewish characters and upheavals of their lives. As a result, he says, Roth "knows about both the recognisable and the hidden movements of his characters. Whenever possible, he observes them with scrutinizing attention and without interfering with their lives. He has never idealized a Jew" (13–14). Nathan Zuckerman is perhaps the same kind of Jewish writer. Truly, he has not idealized his cousin Sidney. Through the conversation between Nathan and his father, in other words, we see the mounting tension between Roth and his own critics. However, Roth does not make choosing sides so easy; for him, the terms of the debate are not simply black and white. Doc Zuckerman, for instance, persuasively defends his position by alluding to Nathan's relative naïveté: "I happen to know what ordinary people will think when they read something like this story. And you don't. You can't. You have been sheltered from it all of your life. [. . .] People don't read art—they read about *people*. And they judge them as such. And how do you think they will judge the people in your story, what conclusions do you think they will reach?" (91–92). The distinction between "art" and "people" here fully captures the differences in values between Nathan and his father. In the same manner that the literary "ghosts" who haunt the novel, (among them, Amy Bellette, Henry James, James Joyce, and Franz Kafka) value aesthetics over a literal-minded version of realism, so too does Nathan expect that people will read his story for "art's sake." However, as his father recognizes, aesthetics and realism go hand in hand, and often people suffer because of it. Ironically, even though Nathan argues on the side of "art," he must defend his story based upon fact. And even though Nathan's father emphasizes that the story is about "real people," it really is about stereotypes. In his worry about the story's effects as a chronicler of Jewish people and Jewish stereotypes, Nathan's father also introduces the language of the courtroom and of ethics, repeating the word "judge" twice in his response to Nathan.

In fact, the idea of judgment does not end with this private conversation between father and son. Nathan's father brings in a third party to settle the dispute: Judge Leopold Wapter, a well-respected Jewish community leader who writes a letter to Nathan asking him to defend himself. The Judge asks, referring to the origins of thought that accelerated into genocide, "Can you honestly say that there is anything in your short story that would not warm the heart of a Julius Streicher or a Joseph Goebbels?" (104). Of course, the joke is that one cannot possibly imagine *anything* warming the heart of cold-hearted, anti-Semitic killers: Julius Streicher used anti-Semitic teachings for twenty-five years to foster the German hatred of Jews that eventually led to persecution and extermination; Joseph Goebbels was, of course, in charge of propaganda for the Nazi regime. Putting Nathan in the company of these two Nazis as an attack against him is hyperbolic at best. Although he fails to distinguish between anti-Jewish propaganda and a short story about a Jew-ish family's conflict, between anti-Semitism with intent and the naïveté of a young writer, the Judge in fact succeeds in reminding Nathan of the reality of the Holocaust. However, Nathan already knows about the effects of the Ho-locaust and the dangers of idealizing such historical figures as Anne Frank. Although the account is humorous in typical Roth fashion, the remnants of traumatic memory still linger—and the accusation has more bite than the joke lets on.

Perhaps the raw-nerve quality of the Judge's "judgment" comes from a real-life experience that Roth had with a rabbi who assumed that no Gentile would read Roth's stories correctly, and that all Gentiles hate Jews. What critics like the rabbi, and characters like Judge Wapter, fail to realize, according to Roth, is that "deliberately keeping Jews out of the imagination of Gentiles, for fear of the bigots and their stereotyping minds, is really to invite the invention of stereotypical ideas" ("Writing About Jews" 166). Like Nathan, Roth, too, has been criticized for advancing the anti-Semitic attitudes that produced the Holocaust. By staging the debate between Nathan and his father, and between Nathan and Judge Wapter, Roth both mocks anti-Semitic attitudes and places diverse Jewish characters in the imaginations of all readers—Jewish and Gentile alike.

Although she sides with her husband, Zuckerman's mother also adds fuel to his fire—drawing out, perhaps, Nathan's most lacerating rejection of his belated role in the emergence of the Holocaust. His mother defends Judge Wapter's exaggerated questioning by explaining that "he only meant that what happened to the Jews" to which Nathan answers, "In Europe—not in Newark! We are not the wretched of Belsen!" (106). Nathan goes on to deprecate the comparison of his writing's effect with the events of Nazi Germany by shouting that physical violence done to Jews in Newark can instead be found at the plastic surgeon's office where girls go to get nose jobs (106). When his mother says that everyone is reacting so strongly against his story because of the shock it produced in them, Nathan counters with, "Oh, maybe then you all shock a little too easily. Jews are heirs to greater shocks than I can possibly deliver with a story that has a sharpie in it like Sidney" (107). Nathan's frustration may seem warranted in some ways. For example, Murray Baumgarten and Barbara Gottfried suggest that, in the dialogues with his parents, Nathan encounters "the paranoia of twentieth-century Jewry" and he "emphasizes the differences between America and Eastern Europe, present and past, in order to disentangle himself from the folkfear and the limited vision on which it feeds" (166). Negotiating not only the liminal space between America and Eastern Europe, these discussions also interject a complicated temporal quality that the novel never resolves. Characters like Doc Zuckerman and Judge Wapter speak as if Nathan is a contemporary of Streicher and Goebbels, promoting anti-Semitic treatises in the 1930s. In pointing out that "Jews are heirs to greater shocks than I can possibly deliver," Nathan alludes here to an entire history of displacement and genocide—one that culminates with the Holocaust but that nevertheless points out the importance of representing Jewish life in all its complexity.

This first critical moment in *The Ghost Writer* emphasizes the complicated nature of the relationship between fathers and their children. As the feud over "Higher Education" with his father makes clear, Nathan is expected to write as a representative of the Jews, putting a positive gloss on their pasts and daily lives as would a typical ghostwriter. Instead, however, Nathan writes the ghosts—both the ghosts of stereotypes haunting Jews in America as well as the ghosts of the Holocaust past. After being denounced by his own father for drawing on the ghosts of Jewry's past in his story, Zuckerman seeks the paternal affirmation of E. I. Lonoff. But shortly after he arrives at the Lonoff home, Zuckerman fantasizes about the past of the mysterious woman he glimpses there, thinking particularly of "the triumph it would be to kiss that face" and how exciting it would be if she reciprocated (24).

However, as one would expect from Roth, this is not your typical day-dream. Zuckerman does not simply imagine seducing Amy Bellette, the young woman assisting Lonoff with his papers; he also comes to believe that she has a different identity completely. He recreates her into a resurrected, or—more precisely—a surviving Anne Frank, a woman he can take home to his family and introduce as his wife in order to convince them that he is a good Jewish son after all. "Oh, marry me, Anne Frank," Zuckerman secretly pines, "exonerate me before my outraged elders of this idiotic indictment! Heedless of Jewish feeling? Indifferent to Jewish survival? Brutish about their well-being? Who dares to accuse of such unthinking crimes the husband of Anne Frank?" (170–171). Here, using such words as "exonerate," "indictment," "accuse," and "crimes," Zuckerman speaks as a true war criminal, anticipating how the televised Eichmann Trial will so deeply affect the Zuckerman family in the rest of the trilogy during the 1960s. On the one hand, this passage mocks the young writer for appropriating global and cataclysmic history for the mere purpose of conciliating a family affair—an affair that is a relatively small misfortune compared with the total human suffering Zuckerman invokes in his Amy Bellette/Anne Frank fantasy. Yet, on the other hand, the passage reveals the very real presence of the Holocaust in the minds of survivors and bystanders alike.

By invoking Anne Frank in what on the surface seems sacrilegious, Zuckerman writes the ghost of Anne Frank in order to tell the "the truth" not simply about the Holocaust, but also about living as a Jew in America in the 1950s when the novel is set. If what Tim O'Brien says about war in *The Things They Carried* is true—if "what *seems* to happen becomes its own happening and has to be told that way" (78)—then Zuckerman is to be taken seriously, if only for the implications of *his* ghost story: It *is* difficult to separate the facts of history from the fiction of life—both of which need equally to be told in their own way. There is, in fact, more than one ghost in Roth's novel, and there is more than one writer. As such, the odd intermingling of the lives and art of Anne Frank and Nathan Zuckerman detail the ways in which the Holocaust haunts cultural memory and raises troubling questions about representation in its wake.

In particular, Nathan resurrects the ghost of Anne Frank by rewriting her past, in part to bring her back as a possible wife for him. However, if he brings her back, she is no longer a martyr—but just another young woman who happens to be Jewish. The ambivalence around the idea of the ghost writer—what it means to be a ghost writer, a writer of "ghost" stories—mirrors the ambivalence of the novel about the life of Anne Frank. If she is secretly alive, then Nathan can be a good Jew by marrying her, but he also kills her as a martyr, which would render her life and death no longer celebratory.

Nathan reports early that he wanted desperately to make his father proud, and when the disagreement over "Higher Education" peaks, Nathan feels both devastated and rebellious. This ambivalence gives way to a second critical moment, one in which Zuckerman seeks paternal approval with Lonoff but finds his answer in Anne Frank instead. The match seems perfect at first glance: Nathan harbors hurt feelings about a strained relationship with his father and seeks validation for his controversial story; Anne Frank, in "surviving" chooses a life of independence rather than informing her father of her survival while also remaining the quintessential Jewish writer. And while Nathan's Jewishness turns his factual fiction into artillery for Christians, Anne Frank obscures her Jewishness, making her an all-American teen.

Given these issues of survival and hidden identities, Nathan not only writes a ghost, but also underscores the importance of an actual ghostwriter. The traditional meaning of a ghostwriter is someone who writes a book, story, article, or speech based on another person's experience, as if he *were* that other person. In other words, a ghostwriter is a writer who helps a nonwriter tell a story or make a point and presents the work as written by the nonwriter—often a celebrity. In this sense, Nathan appears to need a ghostwriter—someone anonymous who could extract the fact of Nathan's ethnic identity from the content of his story: a bitter dispute over money that, as it stands, seems inextricably bound up with the Jewish heritage. Such anonymity would ultimately free him to write about that which he thinks makes good "fiction." However, a ghostwriter also puts a positive gloss on another person's story—such a writer does not necessarily lie but rather withholds potentially damning evidence and anecdotes. In this sense, Doc Zuckerman expects his son *to be* a ghostwriter—using his art only for the most flattering, the ideal, representation of Jews. Instead, however, Nathan writes the ghosts—he uncovers and rehashes old stereotypes as well as romanticizes Anne Frank in a way that even the most naïve readers of her diary have avoided.

By emphasizing the role of the ghost writer and the relationship between reality and fiction, "Higher Education" refers not simply to medical school, but also to what Nathan learns regarding his family's attitudes toward anti-Semitism as well as the potential of the imagination in re-presenting the Holocaust. In the process of his education, Nathan tries to find a way to negotiate his family's discontent over his creative impulses by fantasizing that he marries Anne Frank. After all, Anne Frank is one of the most respected

Jewish writers of all time, a writer who also became "famous" by telling the truth about her experience as a Jew.

It is this very paradox that has led R. Clifton Spargo to suggest that "Roth traces the debt of Nathan's extravagant fiction to the particulars of the 1950s cultural memory of Anne Frank as it was shaped by the Broadway and Hollywood representations of her story. [...] *The Ghost Writer* employs parodic memory to call attention to these cultural layerings, it also explores the give and take between history and cultural memory" (89). For Michael Rothberg, "[t]he coming together of Roth's self-consciousness about representation in general and his tragic-comic recognition of the inevitable contamination of representing the Holocaust can be glimpsed throughout much of his fiction" (190). Although Spargo's analysis of Roth's "parodic memory" and Rothberg's analysis of Roth's "tragic-comic recognition" both seem entirely appropriate, these readings might be extended to account for the traumatic memory pervading the text. Both the parodic memory and tragic-comic recognition in the novel give way to traumatic memory that affects an entire culture—not only the culture of Jews living in the United States in the 1950s but also the global landscape as a whole. In fact, the omnipresence of the Holocaust in *The Ghost Writer* illustrates that this moment in history is so difficult to process in conscious thought that it becomes manifest in other artistic venues. In 1979, as Spargo illustrates, *The Ghost Writer* took on the Holocaust in its fiction but also in its allusions to the glossy productions of *The Diary of Anne Frank* for both stage and film in the 1950s. We as a culture, it seems, were not—indeed, *are* not—ready fully to comprehend the enormity of the event. As such, the Holocaust *keeps coming back,* in movies, in staged productions, and in novels.

An embodiment of traumatic memory, the invocation of the Holocaust, in contrast with the intra-Zuckerman feud, points to something much more serious than a typical Nathan Zuckerman whimsy. The Anne Frank fantasy recalls not just Anne Frank and her family in hiding but also the concentration camps, death by typhus, and the genocide of six million Jews. The first ghost that *The Ghost Writer* "conjures," in other words, is the ghost of Anne Frank and the inassimilable experience she represents. In so doing, the novel claims, Anne Frank is not the ideal Jewish girl we have inherited from her diary and revised through the decades. This darker side of Zuckerman's imaginings reveals that even for a comic writer like Roth, the Holocaust still consumes Jewish Americans—and, indeed, all of us—living relatively safe lives in the United States.

In part, Nathan's representation of the living Anne Frank has sexual origins; he falls in love with Amy Bellette's dark eyes and foreign accent the moment he sees her. Primarily, however, Nathan "writes" the ghost of Anne Frank in an attempt to prove that he is not anti-Semitic; he uses Anne Frank as a projection for all of his hopes and fears. Similarly, millions of Americans

idealized Anne Frank as a way to assuage their passivity during the Holocaust. Ironically, Nathan thinks that if he stays within the borders his father
has constructed for him, he will be considered "the good son" again. And yet,
Anne Frank may have been so easily embraced as a Jewish victim of the Holocaust because, in fact, she was not identified as a loyal Jew. As Zuckerman
points out, it is she, and not her sister Margot, who wrote: "the time will come
when we are people again, and not just the Jews" (142).

In fact, this question of Anne Frank's ethnic identity emerges often
in her diary. On December 24, 1943, Anne reflects: "I sometimes wonder
if anyone will ever understand what I mean, if anyone will ever overlook
my ingratitude and not worry about whether or not I'm Jewish and merely
see me as a teenager badly in need of some good plain fun" (154). The
popularization of Anne Frank, due in part because of Anne's self-con-
sciously crafted writing persona as merely a teenager and not a victim of
the Holocaust—along with the concomitant dangers of both romanticiz-
ing and distorting the world she describes in her diary—are issues that
have been passionately taken up by current Holocaust scholars. Alvin H.
Rosenfeld, for example, recognizes that readers of Anne Frank's diary see
her "as a young, innocent, vivacious girl, full of life and blessed with an
optimistic spirit that enabled her never to lose hope in humanity, even as
its worst representatives were intent on hunting her down and murdering
her" (248). Anne Frank's optimism, Rosenfeld emphasizes, dulls the painful awareness of history at its worst, and effaces the fact of Anne's death in
a concentration camp.

Cynthia Ozick's analysis of the appropriation of Anne Frank for Hollywood and Broadway, and the general consumption of her forgiveness of humankind, is much less forgiving than Rosenfeld's. According to Ozick, "any
projection of Anne Frank as a contemporary figure is an unholy speculation;
it tampers with history, with reality, with deadly truth" (76). She raises legitimate concerns about how *The Diary of a Young Girl* has been misinterpreted
in the past; one such example involves Frances Goodrich and Albert Hackett,
who wrote the famous play, which ultimately provides unfounded comfort
and hope in a post-Holocaust world. Ozick claims that:

> the diary in itself, richly crammed though it is with incident and
> passion, cannot count as Anne Frank's story. A story may not be
> said to be a story if the end is missing. And because the end is
> missing, the story of Anne Frank in the fifty years since "The
> Diary of a Young Girl" was first published has been bowdlerized,
> distorted, transmuted, traduced, reduced; it has been infantilized,
> Americanized, homogenized, sentimentalized; falsified, kitschified,
> and, in fact, blatantly and arrogantly denied. (78)

Here, Ozick asserts that *The Diary of a Young Girl* should not be read for Anne's endearing and comforting proclamation that, "it's a wonder I haven't abandoned all my ideals, they seem so absurd and impractical. Yet I cling to them because I still believe, in spite of everything, that people are truly good at heart" (Frank 332). Ultimately, Ozick envisions for the famous diary a more "salvational outcome": that Anne Frank's diary was "burned, vanished, lost—saved from a world that made of it all things" (87). Ozick's argument is paradoxical, however: although she seems to want to deny Frank's diary any salvational value at all, even she cannot overcome the desire for such an outcome. *The Ghost Writer* stages such an ambivalence. Judge Wapter closes his scathing letter of critique to Nathan with an unexpected "P.S.: If you have not yet seen the Broadway production of *The Diary of Anne Frank*, I strongly advise that you do so" (102). As presented by Wapter, seeing the melodramatic, although happily ending, play can serve as some kind of corrective to Nathan's crime against Jews. But, as Amy/Anne laments, all of the woman "crying over her" from their safe positions in the theatre actually takes away from the horror she endured (123).

In fact, the "real" Anne Frank was not a simple, one-dimensional martyr. Her response to the persecution of the Jews was as complex as the intricate structure of the Nazi genocidal machine. In one of the most desperate moments in her diary, Anne expresses both fear and anger as she laments: "We've been strongly reminded of the fact that we're Jews in chains, chained to one spot, without any rights, but with a thousand obligations. [. . .] One day this terrible war will be over. The time will come when we'll be people again and not just Jews" (261). Frank's strength of feeling here, both with regard to her fate as a Jew as well as the entrapment she feels, undercuts the more typical view of the forgiving girl, the girl who believes that everyone really is good and kind.

Ozick's scathing *New Yorker* article about the public consumption of Anne Frank is aptly entitled, "Who Owns Anne Frank?"—a title that alludes not only to the feeling of enslavement Frank depicts in her journal, but also to the commercialized value of her words since her death. Perhaps Zuckerman is just as guilty as the Broadway and Hollywood appropriators—creating a fictional Anne to suit his wants and needs. Certainly, he has no right to "own" Anne Frank. However, Zuckerman's fantasy is more complex than a simple idealization of the famous belletrist. For, in Zuckerman's fantasy, Anne Frank is not the perfect martyr. She is a girl who, when asked by her history teacher why Jews have been hated for centuries, angrily responds: "Don't ask me that! [. . .] ask the madmen who hate us!" (131). And in English class, she earns praise for writing about Jewish oppression because she has a "great subject" (136).

With the surprising turn to Anne Frank's story—both lived and imagined—*The Ghost Writer* raises questions it refuses to answer regarding the role and responsibility of the Jewish writer: What makes a writer Jewish? When does the label of ethnic background matter? Not insignificantly, Anne Frank's status of Jew matters profoundly but is ultimately obscured in her journal. Conversely, for Zuckerman, being Jewish is not central to "Higher Education" but nonetheless gets superimposed by his suspicious family and "good Christian" readers.

These questions gesture beyond Roth's lived experience as a writer and a Jew and look to historical atrocity and its haunting affects on a generation of Americans following the Holocaust. Many critics tend to read Roth's earlier fiction as generally solipsistic or too narrowly focused within the realm of his own lived experience. Ken Gordon, for example, praises Roth's most recent American Trilogy, asking, "What happened? The new books seem to recognize the existence of *other people*. Or, rather, the fact that other people can be as endlessly fascinating and unknowable as Nathan Zuckerman" (2). However, as *The Ghost Writer* emphasizes, Nathan Zuckerman believes that he is not the only (ghost) writer of import in American letters. Staging the debate between realism and idealism, Zuckerman's defense of "Higher Education" and creation of a jaded Anne Frank gestures away from the imagination to return to Jews in history and politics. This interest in historical atrocity is evident in both Roth's content and style. According to Steven Milowitz, Roth "employs a style that inverts the conditions of the Holocaust world. The world of anxiety, of choicelessness and fear, of ideology and judgment, of unambiguous language and definitive truth is rewritten to become a world where choice is reborn, where ideology is indefensible, where language thrives in rich play of meaning, and where truth remains elusive" (53). His ambiguous and playful style, in other words, is a continuous counter to the rigidity and fixed universe of fascism that authored the Holocaust.

In its emphases on familial relations, elusive truths, and the traumatic facts of history, *The Ghost Writer* anticipates some of Roth's best novels, among them *Patrimony* (1991), *Operation Shylock* (1993), and *American Pastoral* (1997). However, *The Ghost Writer* has also carved out a category of second-generation authors writing about the Holocaust that extends far beyond the Roth canon. Such compelling works as Art Spiegelman's *Maus* (1986), Carl Friedman's *Nightfather* (1991), and Thane Rosenbaum's *Second Hand Smoke* (1999) write the ghosts of the Holocaust with both the humor and insight forged by Roth decades before them. As Steven Milowitz has so powerfully articulated, "Roth's work begins and ends in the tragedy of history, in the post-pastoral universe inherited from the fact of concentration camps" (xi). It is within this universe that—to return to O'Brien—"the angles of vision are skewed. [. . .] You tend to miss a lot" (78). To be sure, we would miss a lot if it were not for Roth's ghosts: those writers of history, of tragedy, and—above all—of humanity.

Works Cited

Appelfeld, Aharon. "The Artist as Jewish Writer." *Reading Philip Roth.* Ed. Asher Z. Milbauer and Donald G. Watson. New York: St. Martin's Press, 1988. 13–16.

Baumgarten, Murray, and Barbara Gottfried. *Understanding Philip Roth.* Columbia: University of South Carolina Press, 1990.

Frank, Anne. *The Diary of a Young Girl.* Trans. Susan Massotty. Ed. Otto H. Frank and Mirjam Pressler. New York: Doubleday, 1995.

Gordon, Ken. "Philip Roth: The Zuckerman Books." *Salon.com* 26 March 2003. 3 January 2004. <http://www.salon.com/ent/masterpiece/2002/03/26/zuckerman/index.html.>

Lehmann, Sophia. "'And Here [Their] Troubles Began': The Legacy of the Holocaust in the Writing of Cynthia Ozick, Art Spiegelman, and Philip Roth." *CLIO.* 28.1 (1998): 29–52.

Milowitz, Steven. *Philip Roth Considered: The Concentrationary Universe of the American Writer.* New York: Garland, 2000.

O'Brien, Tim. *The Things They Carried.* New York: Penguin, 1990.

Ozick, Cynthia. "Who Owns Anne Frank?" *New Yorker.* Oct. 1997: 76–87.

Pinsker, Sanford. "Jewish-American Literature's Lost-And-Found Department: How Philip Roth and Cynthia Ozick Reimagine Their Significant Dead." *Modern Fiction Studies.* 35.2 (1989): 223–235.

Rosenfeld, Alvin H. "Popularization and Memory. The Case of Anne Frank." *Lessons and Legacies. The Meaning of the Holocaust in a Changing World.* Ed. Peter Hayes. Evanston: Northwestern University Press, 1991. 243–278.

Roth, Philip. *The Ghost Writer.* New York: Farrar, Straus and Giroux, 1979.

——— . "Writing About Jews." *Reading Myself and Others.* New York: Farrar, Straus and Giroux, 1975. 149–170.

Rothberg, Michael. "Reading Jewish: Philip Roth, Art Spiegelman, and Holocaust Postmemory." *Traumatic Realism: The Demands of Holocaust Representation.* Minneapolis: University of Minnesota Press, 2000.

Spargo, R. Clifton. "To Invent as Presumptuously as Real Life: Parody and the Cultural Memory of Anne Frank in Roth's *The Ghost Writer.*" *Representations.* 76 (2001): 88–119.

WAYNE HOWKINS

Finding Meaning in the Diaries of Anne Frank

The Limitations of Author-based Readings

In *The Death of the Author,* an essay he wrote in 1968, Roland Barthes asserts that:

> The image of literature to be found in ordinary culture is tyrannically centred on the author . . . The *explanation* of a work is always sought in the man or woman who produces it, as if it were always, in the end, through the more or less transparent allegory of the fiction, the voice of a single person, the *author* 'confiding' in us. (1977: 143)

Leaving aside for a moment the question of whether a search for author-based explanations of literature is as natural and as fallacious as Barthes suggests, such a search would indeed be particularly comprehensible in the case of Anne Frank's diary. There are several reasons why this might be the case. Primarily, and most obviously, the diary is a first-person account, centred on the period of the writer's life during which it was written. Thus its generic form inevitably puts the author in the foreground of any consideration of the text, in that it is ostensibly 'about' her. A further consideration in this regard is that the text was not <u>published</u> by its author. Consequently it is assumed to be a private diary rather than, for example, a memoir or autobiography,

Journal of Children's Literature Studies, Volume 4, Number 3 (July 2007): pp. 113–132.
Copyright © 2007 Pied Piper Publishing.

though whether this was its author's intention is a more complex matter. It was written by an adolescent girl who is still perceived as (to pick up Barthes' term) 'confiding' in the pages of the document itself and only by virtue of the contingency of its having been published, in us as readers.

Secondly, the circumstances of the author's life are, in themselves, remarkable. They are quite different from the experiences of the vast majority of the diary's modern readers, particularly those in politically stable and economically developed areas such as America, central Europe and Japan—places where the diary is enormously popular. In this sense, the assumed characteristics and life of the author are not easily overlooked in any reading of the diary.

Thirdly, the specific circumstances of the author's life **and death** provide a ready-made reading of the text. We read the diary in the light of the outcome of Anne's life, and it is a short, arguably uncomplicated and easily-accessible life-story—a definable 'text' in itself, complementary to the written text.

In this paper I want to consider how the implicit assumption about the role of the author In explaining text emerges throughout conventional writings about—and, therefore, readings of—Anne's diary. Beyond that, discuss what I understand to be alternative ways of reading text that deliberately de-emphasise authorial intention and serve to question the status and explanatory power of the author-text relationship. Finally, offer my own reading of the diary, reflecting various approaches but tied to none.

A Disconnection Between the Diary's Reader and the Text?

A prior issue here is whether Barthes has in mind texts such as Anne Frank's diary when he challenges us so radically to rethink our approach. Barthes is referring to a work of fiction, Balzac's *Sarrasine*, both in the essay from which I have quoted and, in a systematic analysis of the text, in his book *S/Z*. But in *The Death of the Author*, he makes the point that:

> As soon as a fact is *narrated* no longer with a view to acting directly on reality but intransitively, that is to say, finally outside of any function other than that of the very practice of the symbol itself, this disconnection occurs, the voice loses its origin, the author enters into his own death, writing begins. (1977: 142)

I wonder if this 'disconnection' between writer and text-product is as clear-cut as Barthes suggests. The distance in space and time between writer and reader has developed historically. Did, say, sixteenth century manuscripts disconnect their authors from the narrow group of friends and associates among whom they were circulated in the same way that universally available texts disconnect today's author and reader? We know that Anne exchanged parts of her diary with her sister, Margot (Netherlands Institute for War Documentation [NIWD], 2001: 298, 543). Elements of what she wrote would have had inter-personal goals in mind, and would have 'functioned' on this level, if only in that they had a dynamic effect on her thinking and her spoken engagement with her family and the others in hiding. Essential to the special character of the diaries is that they serve many different purposes, as I shall show later. Certainly, however, I would suggest that there is enough in them that we can regard as 'intransitive' and 'narrative' to fall within Barthes' concept and tempt us to question whether Anne Frank is, indeed, a dependable source of meaning in any reading of her diaries.

We seem in our attempts to explain and interpret the diary, then, predisposed towards a search for Anne herself. And, conversely, when we try to explain Anne as a person, as we inevitably do, we look to her diary.

The Textual History of the Diary

In order to make intelligible my discussion of a range of examples from Anne's writing, a necessary preliminary is to account very briefly for its complex textual history. Anne had begun a diary on her thirteenth birthday in June 1942, less than a month before the family moved into the secret annexe. It was a red and white checked autograph album—a birthday present, in fact. This volume survived and is referred to by students and critics, most notably the Netherlands Institute for War Documentation, which established key terms of reference in its Critical Edition, as Diary 1 of Version 'a'. Entries in this first diary ran until it was more or less filled on December 5th, 1942. The assumption is that at this point Anne continued her entries in a second book. Though it almost certainly existed, however, this book has not survived: it was not in the pile of notebooks and papers that were rescued from the annexe by Miep Gies, one of the Franks' devoted helpers, when the family was arrested in August 1944. It was, therefore, missing when those materials were passed by her to Otto Frank a year later, two months after his return from Auschwitz. There is, thus, a gap of slightly more than a year, since on December 22nd, 1943 Anne began her entry in what is referred to as Diary 2 of Version 'a': 'Daddy has tracked down another new diary for me' (NIWD, 2001: 447). There was one more book after this, which Anne was still using at the time of the arrest at the start of August 1944, and these three collectively constitute the 'a' texts. In late March, 1944, Anne records in her diary the announcement of Gerrit Bolkestein, the Arts and Education Minister for the London-based Dutch government, that after the war the government would bring together 'vast quantities of . . . simple, everyday [documentary] material' to build up a picture of the struggle of the Dutch people during the occupation (NIWD,

2001: 59). Shortly after this, she began to revise her diary—in effect to begin again—and she worked on the revision, whilst at the same time continuing the original 'a' diary until the arrest. The revision is assumed to be partially based on the missing 'a' text book covering most of 1943 and it reaches the period of the announcement itself, some four months before the end came. This rewritten diary is known as Version 'b', though, because of the material on which it was written, it is also referred to as the 'loose sheets.' Version 'c' is the amalgam of 'a' and 'b' that constitutes the text as it has become known to readers over the years—certainly until the Critical and Definitive editions of 1986 and 1991 respectively. It emerged from a series of typescripts made initially by Otto Frank and later by his friend Isa Cauvern in the months immediately after Otto read Anne's manuscripts. These typewritten versions were the basis of the first edition, published in Dutch in 1947, and subsequently for the translated German and French editions (1950) and the UK/USA edition (1952).

In his analysis of the diary, rare for being one that attempts a detailed comparison of the 'a' and 'b' texts, Nigel Caplan (2004) considers the impact of Bolkestein's announcement on Anne's thinking and, in turn, on the diary itself. He methodically explains features of the 'b' text—and, indeed, the post-Bolkestein 'a' text—as arising from Anne's newly-conceived intentions for the diary: for example, her more dramatic, sometimes *in medias res*, style, her reordering of events and her effective removal of the romance with Peter van Pels, the son of the family with whom the Franks were living in hiding. Certainly, Anne acknowledges only a week after the Bolkestein announcement, 'I must work, so as not to be a fool, to get on, to become a journalist . . . I know that I can write' (NIWD 2001: 608). It is impossible to ignore this personal ambition in any reading of the diary as it has come down to us—that is, in its largely 'b' version.

Reading the Diary

I want to return later to a consideration of the significance of the textual changes, but the primary, albeit implicit, assumption is clear and of great importance: that the intentions of the author as a person significantly explain to us the nature of the text—that in our natural inclination as readers to construct some kind of meaning from or, in Barthes' term, 'explanation' of this text, an imperative lies before us to make sense of its author and how she responded to her predicament. Countless other interpretations of the diary, though they might differ from Caplan's in many other ways, are based on this same assumption.

Carol Ann Lee's biography of Otto Frank (2002) skilfully draws the reader into attempts to answer the major unresolved questions of Otto's life. One question, predictably, is that of who betrayed the Franks. Of even greater significance seems to be the very different question of how Otto, and by implication we, as readers, should interpret Anne's diary. My own eagerness as a reader grew the closer I came to the point in the story where Otto 'began to read slowly, only a few pages each day' his daughter's diary (Lee, 2002: 166). (It might be noted here that he had kept the diary, unread, for four months.) When I reflect on why I was so eager to reach Otto's first act of engagement with the diary, I realise it is because I intuitively made the same assumption about author and text that is at issue: the closest I can get to an understanding of this text, my habit of mind told me, is through Otto Frank, since Otto was the person closest to its author. A part of me looked to Otto, in lieu of Anne, to demystify and explain the text.

I return later to how these two particular sources of 'evidence'—Caplan's analysis and Lee's biography of Otto—have influenced my own reading of the diaries, but my simple point at this stage is that as a reader in what Barthes would see as an 'ordinary culture' of readers, my instinct is to put the author at the very centre of the meaning I construct around the text. Whether my notion of the author as an explanatory source is misguided or not, I certainly find it difficult to resist its power as a key to explaining the text.

Interpreting the Author through the Text

As I suggested earlier, interpretations of author through text are as common and implicit as those of text through author. Some appear obvious and uncontroversial. In his book, *The Past in Hiding* (2000), Mark Roseman describes the lives of many, Jews in particular, who were forced to conceal themselves from the Nazis in occupied Europe: any such life, he says, was 'a life of frustration'; Anne Frank's, we are told, was an 'intense inner life' (2000: 15). The assessments or judgments revealed in other interpretations might be seen as more contentious. In Aidan Chambers' novel, *Postcards from No Man's Land* (1999), the main character, a young Englishman called Jacob, is befriended by an elderly Dutch lady after his pockets are picked on a visit to the Anne Frank house in Amsterdam. She asks him what he loves most of all about Anne. He thinks about his answer, before confidently replying, 'Her honesty. About herself. About everybody' (1999: 49). It seems that we are curious observers of human nature, just as we are curious readers: when we want to know who or what the *person* behind the text is, we scrutinise the text itself—seek to gain advantage in our search for the author in yet closer, more informed, analysis of his or her writing.

There is, indeed, a point at which it actually becomes difficult to disentangle text from author in considering response to and analysis of the diary. Hanno Loewy, in his detailed article about the 'universalization' of Anne Frank, points to the contradiction—one of many—between Anne's 'childish narcissism' and her 'merciless self-scrutiny' (Loewy, 1999). But are these descriptions of the girl, or of what she writes in her diary? We are tempted, of course, to say that they are both, since author and writing appear to merge into a single entity. It is possible that all that is happening in such observations as Loewy's is that a single state of mind, rather than a trait or an entire persona, is being inferred from the text and the text is seen as simply a representation of that state of mind. In any case, the construction of the author in whole or part is seen as a necessary key to the text: the text explains the author, who in turn explains the text.

Alternative Readings

Among the possible alternatives to this process are readings that route the reader beyond the author to realities, many of which are social in origin, in which the author is situated and which function *through* the author to emerge in the text. After looking at these, I move the focus to what I assume to be the other side of Barthes' 'disconnect' in the process of reading, namely to the reader and the nature of the reader's response. There is, of course, a third area to which we might look for our explanation of text, namely the formal features of the text itself. In this case, a major concern is whether what we have can be regarded as a **diary** in the conventional sense, especially given its multi-text form. This is a matter to which I turn in the final section of this essay, where I outline some of the key features of my own reading.

Authors might, then, for a number of reasons, be unaware of the meaning they bring to their writing; other meanings may emerge from what they write that would seem to be beyond the intentions that they have. Authors are thus, potentially, at least, vehicles for meanings whose sources lie beyond them, and it is to these origins that we must look in any informed reading. One such source would be the social environments of language and ideology from which the author emerges.

Another origin might be the author's subconscious mind; perhaps, in Jung's account, a mind that draws heavily upon the archetypes of a collective—that is, again, a socially constructed, or at least socially experienced—unconscious. A further account is that the meaning of a text can be understood in relation to other texts of which the author is aware: it is, as Barthes suggests, 'a tissue of quotations' (1977: 146). A 'text' here may be understood as any 'chunk of meaning' (Hartman, 1995), however small, that has significance to the author. I see all these possible accounts as implying both that a more meaningful explanation of text can be gained from, in a sense, bypassing the author and that meanings with a broader significance can be found by doing this. It is, I think, from many passages we regard as carrying at least some discernible meaning that we assemble our major interpretations of texts. If we arrive at such a global sense of meaning in respect of Anne's diary, or in relation to any other work of literature, it is via these multiple chunks of meaning constructed during the process of our reading.

The passages about menstruation

Anne's account of her menstruation can be used as an example which allows us some scope to consider how the meanings we might find in the diaries many have origins beyond her conscious attempts to mean. As early as 4th October, 1942, Anne expresses her eagerness to start her periods. The onset of her menstruation about a year later is described as a 'sweet secret' (NIWD, 2001: 462) and is an obvious source of self-esteem. Leaving aside concerns about her intended audience, it seems that the author's words bring the reader directly, even exclusively, to an intentional and joyous reflection on the changes occurring within her body. Yet the notion that what is intentional on the author's part—that over which she has conscious control—is a sufficient basis for a reading of the diary here immediately gives way with Aidan Chambers' suggestion that Anne's periods were 'a monthly flow of blood [that] released a tidal flow of words.' Indeed, by Chambers' account, we can read the entire diary as divided by the onset of menstruation, a 'pivotal' point after which 'the change is palpable' and there is 'a surge of energy, a new sense of purpose, an astonishing clarity' (2001: 18). It is an energy, biologically grounded, that clearly guides the reader well beyond the intentional presence of an author in her text. In the revised 'b' version of the diary, Anne entirely omits both the references to her menstruation I cite above, so that we might read the statements as primarily expressing her *im*maturity—the confession of things about which she would later 'blush with shame' (NIWD, 2001: 324). Alternatively, and if we allow ourselves corroboration from other parts of the text, we can see in her original words the absence not of sexual maturity but of literary artfulness (or journalistic, Bolkestein-oriented, focus) at this relatively early stage in her life/writing. Elsewhere in the diary we see her asserting in powerful terms her admiration for and pride in the female gender: the 'strength', 'courage', 'endurance' and 'beauty' of women in society (NIWD 2001: 623, 700). Thus, that she celebrates her passage into womanhood might 'mean' her nascent feminism. Or when she writes about her periods she may have been influenced by the experiential texts of her own sexual maturation and the possibilities opening up for her of adult relationships. Access to romantic fiction, of varying degrees of explicitness, and its suitability for boys or girls of different ages, was a long-standing background issue in the annexe. Sex and romance were subjects that undoubtedly preoccupied Anne and about which she was 'extremely curious' (Lee, 2002: 69): the diary often reflects her own interest in boys—largely, but not exclusively Peter—and her speculations about her parents' and others' marriages.

But issues concerning the meaning in religious terms of Anne's writing about her periods are also difficult to ignore and are perhaps worthy of special consideration. Such issues are at the centre of the contest for the interpretation of the diaries that was to emerge after their publication. Her family were not Orthodox in their outlook and lifestyle. Certainly, their circle of friends and acquaintances went well beyond the Amsterdam Jewish community. More important, however, is the fact that, whilst her mother, whose own upbringing had been an Orthodox one, sometimes attended synagogue with Anne's sister, Margot, Otto's visits were very rare. Anne, who was 'crazy about her father' (Metselaar, 1998) and, as the 'a' text, in particular, reveals, alienated from her mother, unsurprisingly exercised the right afforded her to stay away from the synagogue, just as, unlike Margot, she chose to attend school on the Jewish Sabbath. Orthodox Jewish attitudes towards menstruation are not homogenous. The laws that forbid sex (or any physical contact) during menstruation are sometimes interpreted to suggest that a woman is unclean, but are rejected by others as being based upon a mistranslation of the Hebrew 'tuma', which is ritualised as the loss from the world of a potential soul rather than the outward sign of women's impurity. Alternatively, some authorities view menstruation as among the signifiers of humanity's Fallen state, rather than a cause for celebration. Thus, in Anne's writing on this subject, the absence of any such considerations and, indeed, the presence instead of her excited, celebratory tone in 'a' and her confident openness in later passages, can easily be construed along religious lines as expressing her assimilationist background: one where, in the mix of ideas determining her sense of who she was, traditional Jewish attitudes had little place alongside secular, independent ones.[1]

In themselves, the words Anne writes about menstruation might seem to have little significance, but, as I suggest, earlier the global reading of a text comprises multiple 'chunks' of meaning, and certainly in the religious (and ideological) context, the wider reading those words slip into has attracted enormous controversy concerned with whether Anne ultimately 'emerges as a member of the *human* community [or] . . . as one who identified herself as part of a collective *Jewish* tragedy' (Brenner, 1996: 107).

This issue became a prominent feature of Otto's later life through his protracted conflict with Meyer Levin, whose script for the stage adaptation of the diary he had rejected, essentially for being too 'Judaised'. Until his own death, Otto asserted the 'universal' message that he believed his daughter sought to convey through her diary. Though Anne wrote movingly about the horrors that were being perpetrated against her race and 'this hatred of the Jews' (NIWD, 2001: 678) that drove the persecution, her views on anti-Semitism —partly as a result of Otto's editing of key passages—and indeed her Jewishness itself are not seen as prominent features of the diary. In Japan, for example, where the book has become enormously successful, it is promoted 'as a protest against the great misfortunes brought by war' (Lee, 2002: 190); interestingly it is associated by its largely young readership with openness about menstruation.

Meanings carried by Anne's words

I would argue, then, that when we return to the central question, 'What does the diary (or any part of it) mean?' we are compelled to go beyond Anne Frank's intentions and move towards, 'What meaning do her words carry?: what do they imply about the features of which she is an embodiment or against the background of which she wrote?' Among, no doubt, many other potential sources of meaning, they might show us the author as a female; an assimilated or 'liberal' Jew; a German citizen (though living in Holland—someone who certainly saw herself as Dutch); a diarist (as distinct from a memoirist); a member of a relatively privileged, certainly educated, social class; a child—or rather a teenager and adolescent; someone in hiding (arguably in 'resistance' against persecution). And from this wider accommodation of meanings, we are inevitably led to the question, 'What do the words mean to specific readers?'

In *The Death of the Author,* Barthes is asserting that attempts such as the one in which I have been engaged, namely, to find in, or affix to, a text some meaning by analysing its author—whether her conscious intentions or what influences her from beyond such intentions—are ultimately futile. We shall never know' (1977: 143), Barthes tells us, as he ponders on Balzac's meaning in respect of a particular passage in *Sarrasine.* Whatever the author's words may be a response to, this response is made in terms of other responses that are already prefigured by language—a 'structure' or 'thread' of meanings which can only ever be 'disentangled' but never 'deciphered' to reveal something stable and ultimately explanatory beneath. Thus, even if we allow that it was from, say, her sense of what it is to be female that Anne wrote about her menstruation, we must acknowledge that this was itself rooted in other texts—her mother's pronouncements, perhaps, or her interpretation of Paul de Kruif's book *The Fight for Life* (NIWD, 2001: 700), which she had read and which clearly influenced her views in this area. In turn, these 'texts' were themselves products of other texts, arising from yet other texts, and so on. Anne's involvement is merely the accident of being captured in this particular matrix of meaning, pen in hand, as it were, expressing a text with another text. And because of the nature of language, the words of the text are 'only explainable through other words, and so on indefinitely', in the 'tissue of quotations' placed before the reader (Barthes, 1977: 146). Thus it is that Barthes considers the death of the author, who is not merely unreachable but does not exist as a consistent, recognisable presence, to be the price we should willingly pay for 'the birth of the reader.' However, hardly are the readers born in Barthes' radical account than they are consigned to the same oblivion as he reserves for the author. For, Barthes tells us as he concludes his essay, 'the reader is without history, biography, psychology,' but is merely the destination for the 'traces' of the written text—the 'someone who holds [them] together' at the point of reading (1977: 148). What is evident here to me is that Barthes' theory has little to do with how we can and should engage with text on a practical level. It seems, rather, to attest to the impossibility of finding a 'centred' self at the heart of *any* human activity, than to show us something specific to the reading process.

The 'reader response' theories of Stanley Fish seem, at first, more promising. For Fish (1980), all readers belong to an 'interpretive community' that gives them a perspective on the text and a set of 'interpretive strategies' as they read. This ethnic, gendered, historically and ideologically formed perspective is so pervasive that it *constitutes* the very text—is the 'shape' of the reading itself. We are thus drawn in our understanding of Anne's diary to the interpretive activities of its readers and the communally-based rationales that engender them—to the revisionists who question its authenticity, for example, or the survivors of the Holocaust or the Japanese teenagers. But on such accounts, no reader can access the interpretive community of any other, nor that of the author herself, so the text has no effective existence outside of its realisation in a given reader's mind: a text *is* merely what a text *does* in producing 'the developing responses of the reader in relation to the words as they succeed one another in time' (Fish, 1980: 27).

Louise Rosenblatt sees reading as a 'transaction' between reader and text. Reading itself becomes an 'event', but one during which the reader's understanding of language continues to be affected historically by the text and the text itself continues to be perceived according to the associations 'stirred up' in the reader's 'linguistic-experiential reservoir' (1988). Such an account recognises the essential role of the reader and the place of the reader's response in any search for 'meaning', but, she tells us, 'a full understanding of literature requires both a consciousness of the reader's own 'angle of refraction' and any information that can illuminate the assumptions implicit in the text' (1994: 115). Rosenblatt, unlike Fish or Barthes, seems to accept and find interesting the fact that the same orders of meaning, with their disparate and diverse origins, are immanent in authors and readers of text alike, and that, in an important sense, the two parties are separated by the mere contingency of the writing act itself. The second half of the Otto Frank biography to which I earlier referred is littered with examples of the language of competing reader responses to the diary, and often its claims to understand Anne's background and psyche, as well as her intentions, are central to them. Meaning is 'interpreted', 'reconstructed', protected from 'falsification';

it becomes 'property', a 'legacy', a 'mission'. We cannot ignore these readings of Anne Frank's diaries, nor reader-response to, or transaction with, texts generally. They illuminate, potentially, the fullness of text, its *significance,* and, thus, the extent of its meaning.

My Own Reading

To account for my own reading of the diaries I begin with an extract from the memoirs of Michel Mielnicki, a Polish Jew who survived four death and concentration camps. He writes here of his two encounters with Dr Josef Mengele in Auschwitz:

> I have never forgotten the scene: I come up, click my naked heels, stand straight, and salute, 'Herr Oberst, number 98040.' Mengele, elegant and aloof in his immaculate, starched, white doctor's coat and beautiful, shiny, knee-high black boots, casts a critical eye over my thin body with its blonde fuzz and asks, 'Bist du Deutscher?' I reply, 'Nein, Herr Oberst. Ich bin Jude.' 'What a pity,' he says, then smiles, 'go to this side.'

> The second time I came before Mengele was a few weeks later. Same procedure. I was as skinny as the first time. I raised my arm in salute, and said in effect, 'Yes, Sir, here I am at your service.' He looked at me, and responded, 'You are here again? Good for you. Go.' (Ravvin, 2006)

We are inured to the reality of the cultural and ideological emplacement of language and text, and yet at the same time, I believe, we still allow the possibility that text can be almost *un*authored—that it has the potential to route the reader to an absolute reality that lies beyond itself, or at least beyond any rhetorical intentions of the author. Barthes, particularly through his 1957 collection of essays, *Mythologies,* was an early educator of readers to the realities of advertising and other mass communications: to the creation of new 'signifieds', to the intelligence and articulatedness of much of the text to which we are commonly exposed. In radical contrast, the extract above from Mielnicki's memoirs seems to be free from such contamination. The 'prone'-ness[2] of the man himself, standing before Mengele, seems to merge with the proneness of the writing before the truth. It is tempting to see both life and text as contingencies. Thus, Mielnicki's life predicament is contingent upon the inexorability of genocide, his fate upon the whim (or racial fastidiousness) of a sadistic killer. The text waits upon, if not 'truth', then the truth of the experience and on the seeming impossibility of rendering it in any alternative way. Both individual and text appear to have meanings given to or placed in them; they are meanings that can only take the forms they take, prone as they are to a teleology—the Shoah or, perhaps more deeply, some archetype of oppression—that is outside of them. Yet it is something of which they are inherently a part, which tells itself through them—through the story, as through the actual meetings with Mengele.

As I read Anne Frank's diaries I am acutely aware that, perhaps with the reader's instinct I described earlier in this essay and that Barthes disparages so much, I am searching for a quality in the *author*—in this case, an introvertedness befitting someone writing a private diary—of which the writing itself is merely a necessary expression. To attest to it I look for its textual equivalent and extension. It is a 'proneness', as I have described it, in the substance of the writing that I see in Mielnicki's memoir: a sense that, though the work of its author, the text is primarily subject to and an inevitable consequence of the events it describes, transparently revealing itself as no more than their product. Perhaps I am simply in search of the 'honesty' that Chambers identifies as so important a feature of her Anne's writing. But from the course of my reading of previous readings and interpretations of the diary I am also searching for, or am at least sensitive to, evidence of *writing*—that is, of control and rhetorical purposefulness—and for the person behind *that* approach. So that, as well as Anne the introverted diarist, I am as liable to find Anne the writer. Here I want to consider whether either figure is present in the text and whether it can bring me to a better understanding of both diarist and writer.

Anne as Introverted Diarist and as Writer

The first two entries of Anne's diary, on the 12th and 14th June, 1942, seem neatly prototypical of the introvert and the writer who will both feature throughout the entries to follow. On the 12th she begins, 'I hope I shall be able to confide in you completely.' Whilst the tone is eager and suggests an optimism about the act of writing itself, it reveals a purpose that is clearly concerned with self-examination, a process in which she asks for the diary's 'support and comfort.' By the second sentence of the following entry, on the 14th, she is embarking upon what is to be the first of countless 'stories' in the diary: 'I'll start with the moment I got you . . . ' (NIWD, 2001: 197). What follows is a largely narrativised account of her birthday and how she acquired the diary. The impact of the Bolkestein announcement, which obviously came much later but which prompted a revision affecting all but the last four months of the diary, is an obviously relevant factor here as I try to gauge how much the diary discloses about Anne as a person looking inwards and how much about a writer looking out to an audience. It is of great importance, however, that we understand in detail its effect upon Anne's writing and its operation upon tendencies already present before Anne became aware of it.

Nigel Caplan has written that, 'A close comparison of the ['a' and 'b'] texts reveals that the differences are not factual, occasionally substantial and . . . mostly strategic' (2004: 79). This is quite a misleading and somewhat surprising statement. Book 1 of version 'a' is substantially different from the revised 'b' version covering the same six month period. In the 'a' version only, for example, does Anne address her entries to other Cissy van Marxveldt characters (from this author's *Joop ter Heul* stories) besides Kitty and the content of her writing to their imaginary affairs. In 'b', her approach to the events of the period is much more informative and deliberately attempts a psychologically continuous account of *a*—as opposed to *her*—life in hiding. And this same version omits entirely several lengthy entries that Anne clearly regarded as of little reader-interest when she reviewed them. In the context of the totality of the diary, however, the amount of change is not substantial since this is not only a relatively short period but also by far the most sparsely covered. Arguably, the omission of Peter from much later parts is both more substantial and more clearly symptomatic of Anne the writer. When the Bolksetein announcement came, Anne's immediate reaction was to envisage the diary as a collection of tales about *Het Achterhuis* ('behind the house')—a fictionalised account. It was only when she considered the matter 'seriously' (NIWD, 2001: 600) that she saw a documentary form for the diary as more appropriate. The news thus partially validated a feature that had been present in the diary from the start: the telling of tales, of which an episode concerning Mrs van Pels's false modesty and one concerning Peter and a forbidden book, are early examples.

What lies behind Anne's story-telling is fundamental to my understanding of her diary. It appears to have sprung from a deeply innate tendency to narrativise life, especially her own. One of the most obvious demonstrations is her account of her father's unhappy past: his lost love—a girl to whom he was engaged but whose identity has never been firmly established—and his acquiescence in marriage to Anne's mother, Edith, a woman he never loved. It is a story upon which, as she writes on 8th February, 1944, Anne was happy to embroider: '. . . what I don't know, I've made up' (NIWD, 2001: 503). In *Cady's Life*, Anne's unfinished novel, she adopts the story for Cady—or rather, as she explains in her diary, a version of her father's life was what lay ahead for Cady beyond the point in the novel she had reached, as she had sketched it out in her mind. Moreover, Cady deliberately represents Anne herself as she was at the time the story was written: a girl who believed herself misunderstood by an emotionally distant mother and was constantly 'longing . . . for trust [and] love' (NIWD, 2001: 325), and searching for guidance from her relationships with others. Thus Cady becomes attached to the nurse who cares for her after a near-fatal car accident and to a young man she meets on one of her convalescent rambles, who becomes the equivalent to the lost love of her father's life. *Cady's Life* is, as Anne says, both 'the story of Father's life' (NIWD, 2001: 669) and a partial storying of her own. In these narrative threads and in other overtly creative writing found with the diaries—writing that she returned and added to again and again during her period in hiding—we see Anne trying to understand by representation in characters and events who she was and what had happened/ was happening/ would happen to her. Her own reading, particularly of the van Marxveldt books, was obviously connected with this process. It seems to me that the tendency I describe here is also apparent from the very terms in which Anne perceived people, including herself, particularly her habit of making 'types' (NIWD, 2001: 214) of the people around her. Her characterisations, her storying of the people she knew, seem to be so facile and habitual it is as if they reflect a 'life-story' of her own that goes back well beyond her actual experience; the people she encounters quickly become absorbed as characters in her story. As the period in hiding begins and continues, we also see emerge a story of the war. It is a text perhaps largely supplied by the BBC, but Anne readily scripts it herself around such characters as 'Windston Churchil' [sic], 'Gandi' [sic], and the members of the Dutch royal family about whose life-stories she loved to learn. Bolkestein's announcement had minimal impact on the diary as narrative. More embellished stories were written than had previously existed or might have been written, but the rendering of life as narrative simply continued. What is important, I believe, is that these stories did not come into existence because of an audience and are not a product of Anne as a 'writer.' Rather, they were the externalisation of a personal need to make sense of her experience—the human tendency that Sartre describes in *Nausea:* to live life as if recounting it.

However, that Anne was also inclined to go beyond mere story-telling is not in doubt. Bolkestein's announcement reinvigorated the nascent writer in her and with that a wish to engage and influence an audience by writing a diary 'that speaks' (NIWD, 2001: 608). The desire took many forms; it would have been apparent in the occasional readings from the diary that so entertained the others and motivated her attempts to widen the scope of the diary and make it acceptable for publication. It produced a variety of writing styles and registers of address to the reader, sometimes leading her far away from narrative. The diary is, in this sense, an expression of her confusion about its exact purpose: would it be a collection of tales—humorous or otherwise—or a documentation of the war or of a single wartime life? Did she imagine it at times as a monument to a life well-lived—her own—as might be suggested by her famous words, 'I want to go on living after my death' (NIWD, 2001: 609)? This multi-purposed, multi-textual aspect of the diary is, again, something that must be a feature of our reading of it: all readers, I believe, should be aware of both 'a' and 'b' texts.

The 'b' text provides considerable evidence for the presence of Anne, the writer. Whilst the changes for the period of the first 'a' text book are small in the wider context of the whole diary, they are a part of a more considerable revision that reflects her aspirations and does not merely reflect an embarrassment about things that were 'put . . . down so bluntly' before (NIWD, 2001: 324). Whole passages or sometimes just an odd word reflect her attempts to anticipate and control the reactions of a notional readership existing somewhere in the unstable mix of imagination and forbidding realism that must have informed each session of her writing. Her collection of *Tales from the Secret Annex*, the forty one deliberately extended versions of incidents to be found originally scattered throughout the diary entries themselves, is the most substantial display of this endeavour to reach and please an audience. The intention to use the diary to hone her writing skills must be inferred from her comments immediately after the Bolkestein announcement, to which I have already referred (NIWD, 2001: 608).

In shifting my attention, finally, to the presence of the other Anne, Anne the confiding diarist—a presence which in my own reading of the text find extraordinarily moving—I want to return to Otto's first encounter with his daughter's diaries in 1945:

> I began to read slowly, only a few pages each day, more would have been impossible as I was overwhelmed by painful memories. For me it was a revelation. Here was revealed a completely different Anne to the child that I had lost. I had no idea of the depths of her thoughts and feelings . . . (Lee, 2002: 166.)

When I read the diary, it is very often the **lack** of writerly control, and, in its place, a 'proneness', as I have described it, to events and to one's own 'thoughts and feelings', that so often claims my attention. In my view this is the *de facto* priority of Anne Frank's diary: an expression of the basic human need to respond to, and find meaning in, life. The diary was the one reliable means of meeting this need at her disposal and her dependence on it grew to be an established part of her life during her time in hiding.

Often Anne's use of the diary takes the form of deliberate attempts to address the central issues: the 'contradiction', of which she is so acutely aware, between the self-indulgent and contemplative sides of her nature, but also and crucially, her longing to have an imperative or at least a message of some kind for the world. This latter, I believe, is ultimately the purpose for which she sees writing in general: it is 'the finest thing I have' (NIWD, 2001: 519). Her final entry, seen in its full textual context, is perhaps the best demonstration of her explicit engagement with these twin issues. Anne's final words in the diary are taken to be:

> . . . and finally I twist my heart round again, so that the bad is
> on the outside and the good is on the inside and keep on trying
> to find a way of becoming what I would so like to be and what I
> could be, if . . . there weren't any other people living in the world.
> (NIWD, 2001: 721)

However, what are usually not read—and, sadly, are absent from the *Definitive Edition*—are the absolutely final words of the diary, 'Soit gentil et tiens courage', which she wrote on the inside of the back cover of 'a' text (Book 3 NIWD, 2001: 721).

At other times Anne is aware of the problems and responsibilities she has, but is less able or willing to explore them fully. Thus, for example, she writes of the effects of a misguided letter she wrote to her father at the height of her feelings of alienation: about her guilt and longing for a friend who she knew had been deported to a camp, and even about not wishing to kiss her mother goodnight. Similarly she tries to rationalise the audaciousness of her affair with Peter and later her 'disappointment' that he is less than she had hoped. Most often, however, it is entirely through the author's writing that we see the contradictions and frustrated aspirations that she addresses directly in the more contemplative passages. Sometimes, far from displaying the self-awareness often attributed to her, the diary strikingly lacks such a quality. For example, we read of Anne's pleasure in the exchange of notes with her sister Margot, but not long afterwards Anne says, 'I don't tell her a single thing.' Margot has 'long ceased to count in my feelings' she tells us one minute, but is a 'darling' the next (NIWD, 2001: 562, 338, 548). The same inconsistencies are in evidence as far as all of Anne's relationships are concerned—even with her mother. The romance with Peter provides many instances of this seemingly 'unauthored' writing. Here is a description of their first kiss:

> How I suddenly made the right move, I don't know, but before we
> went downstairs he kissed me, through my hair, half on my left
> cheek, half on my ear; I tore downstairs without looking around,
> and am simply longing for today. (NIWD, 2001: 629)

Elsewhere she writes, 'Is there anything more beautiful in the world . . . than to have a darling boy in your arms?', having told her diary only a day earlier: 'I don't get any satisfaction out of lying in each other's arms' (NIWD, 2001: 635, 636). The writing seems as transparent to the experience as it is possible to be. But the experiences themselves must, for all that, be prone to our glare, or rather, as is our readerly instinct, we turn that glare upon the author who lies beyond: who does not take a view of Anne Frank on reading her diary?

The messy inconsistency of Anne's writing sometimes points to quite profound truths but without, it seems, any intention to do so. The poignant beauty of her entry of June 16th, 1944, where she recounts how 'the dark, rainy evening, the gale, the scudding clouds held me entirely in their power' lies in the fact that a newly-revived fear of detection meant she could only recall the experience, not describe it at first hand. The ambitiousness of her reasoning in the remainder of the entry is extraordinary (NIWD, 2001: 698–699). What really strikes me here, though, is that her following entry is utterly domestic in content and utterly prosaic as writing. I am reminded of how often Shakespeare shocks us with the contiguity of opposites—of life and death, good and evil or the beautiful and the grotesque. But Shakespeare, knew what he was doing as a writer, whereas very often Anne Frank did not.

In my reading of Anne's diaries I take account of them in many different ways: they are, for example, undeniably the products of an adolescent girl's mind; they represent a variety of textual enterprises; they appeal to my needs and strike chords with my intertextuality as a reader; I have, like all readers, a unique focus and a unique 'reservoir' of experience to bring to them. The 'tyranny'—whether in the 'ordinary culture of readers' or within any other, more specialised readership—would seem to me not that of the author but, rather, the tyranny of the imperative to locate, verify and elevate a single meaning or a single type of meaning which is to be perceived as the essential product of our reading. To pursue such a unitary response, whether based upon authorial intention, biographical background, ideology, psychology, textual form or reader response, appears misguided. It wastes the potential of other responses and the perspectives implicit within them to shed light, not only on the text and how it came to be what it is, but also on the nature of our own and others' encounters with it, and, potentially, on aspects of our lives beyond it. All of these are fitting domains for the construction of meaning in our engagement with text.

Notes

1. Information about Jewish attitudes here has been derived from http:www.beingjewish.com/kresell-facts.html.

2. In the sense of 'having a natural inclination or tendency to something: inclined, disposed, apt, liable' (*Shorter Oxford Dictionary*, 1973, p. 1685), rather than of the primary listed meaning there.

Works Cited

Printed sources

Barthes, R (1977) *Image-Music-Text*. Glasgow: Collins

Brenner, R F (1996) 'Writing Herself Against History: Anne Frank's Self-Portrait as a Young Artist' in *Modern Judaism*, Vol. 16, pp105–134

Caplan, N A (2004) 'Revisiting the Diary: Rereading Anne Frank's Rewriting' in *The Lion and the Unicorn*, Vol. 28.1, pp77–95

Chambers, A (1999) *Postcards from No Man's Land*. London: Random House

Chambers, A (2001) *Reading Talk*. Stroud: The Thimble Press

Fish, S (1980) *Is There a Text in This Class?: The Authority of Interpretive Communities*. Cambridge (Mass.): Harvard University Press

Frank, A (1991) *The Diary of a Young Girl*. Harmondsworth: Penguin

Hartman, D (1995) 'Eight readers reading: The intertextual links of proficient readers reading multiple passages' in *Reading Research Quarterly*, Vol. 30, No. 3, pp520–561

Holliday, L (1995) *Children's Wartime Diaries*. London: Piatkus

Lee, C A (2002) *The Hidden Life of Otto Frank*. London: Penguin

Netherlands Institute for War Documentation (2001) *The Diary of Anne Frank: the Revised Critical Edition*. New York: Random House

Roseman, M (2000) *The Past in Hiding*. Harmondsworth: Penguin

Rosenblatt, L (1994) *The Reader, The Text, The Poem: the Transaction Theory of the Literary Work*. Carbondale, Illinois: Southern Illinois Press

Electronic sources {Accessed July 2006}

Loewy, H (1999) *Saving the Child: The Universalization of Anne Frank* http://www.cine-holocaust.de/mat/fbw001473emat.html

Metselaar, M (1998) *Anne Frank Magazine* http://www.annefrank.org/contest.asp?PID=483&LID=2

Ravvin, N (2006) *Wartime Memories* http://www.canlit.ca/review-177/281_Ravvin.html

Rosenblatt, L (1988) *Writing and Reading: the Transactional Theory* http://www.writingproject.org.downloads/csw/TR13.pdf

http://www.beingjewish.com/kresel/facts.html

MARK M. ANDERSON

The Child Victim as Witness to the Holocaust: An American Story?

In the steadily growing body of literature about the Holocaust, the murder of more than one million children has not gone unnoticed. Indeed, their fate constitutes one of the most powerful indictments of Nazi criminality and the most heart-rending evidence of the victims' loss. Nonetheless, despite the wealth of memoirs, memorials, and academic studies devoted to this topic, the role that children have played in *representing* the Holocaust as a whole, especially in the United States, is still poorly understood. In the early stages of American Holocaust awareness—from *The Diary of Anne Frank* to the child narrator of Elie Wiesel's *Night*, from the famous picture of the boy with upraised arms in the Warsaw ghetto to the artwork and poetry of young prisoners in Theresienstadt—children have consistently proved to be the most moving and believable witnesses. Since the late 1970s, with American interest in the Jewish genocide on the rise, this leading role for children has continued, especially in popular, mass-audience representations such as Steven Spielberg's *Schindler's List* and the U.S. Holocaust Memorial Museum in Washington, D.C. What accounts for this iconic role of the child victim in representing the totality of Holocaust loss? What are the aesthetic and affective implications of what is, after all, a rhetorical figure—synecdoche, in which a part represents the whole? Is it a legitimate figure? Does it

Jewish Social Studies: History, Culture, and Society, Volume 14, Number 1 (Fall 2007): pp. 1–22. Copyright © 2007 Indiana University Press.

simplify or distort the actual historical event? Most of all, what does it tell us about the American reception of the Holocaust?

As recent commentators have pointed out, Holocaust awareness in the United States was extremely limited in the 1950s and 1960s. Eager to put the war behind them, most non-Jewish Americans showed little willingness to grapple with the full dimensions of a complex historical event that had taken place far from American shores. Camp survivors and European Jews who had found refuge in the United States were largely unwelcome reminders of the past in a society focused on Cold War issues of nuclear proliferation and the spread of communism. This marginalization of the Holocaust began to reverse course in the late 1970s, culminating in a veritable flood of memoirs, academic studies, and popular representations in the next two decades. NBC's nine-hour docudrama *Holocaust* (1978), which portrayed the fictional story of a German-Jewish family during the Hitler period and was seen by tens of millions of viewers, reflected a clear change in national attitude. On May 1 of that year, two weeks after the program had aired on national television, President Jimmy Carter stood in the Rose Garden with the Israeli ambassador to mark the thirtieth anniversary of the founding of the State of Israel and announced plans for a Holocaust memorial to commemorate the death of six million Jews. Whereas in 1964 the parks commissioner of New York City had rejected plans for a memorial to the victims of the Warsaw ghetto because city monuments must "be limited to events of American history,"[1] Carter's plan, which was supported by all three subsequent presidents, led to the creation of the Holocaust Museum in Washington in 1993. The museum is now one of the capital's most popular tourist venues, adjacent to the Mall and in symbolic proximity to the Lincoln Memorial and the Washington Monument.

The surprising aspect of this popular response is how willingly mainstream, non-Jewish audiences with no prior connection to the Holocaust have accepted this historical event as "an American memory" and helped weave it into the nation's institutional fabric. As historian Peter Novick points out,

> In a growing number of states the teaching of the Holocaust in public schools is legislatively mandated. Instructions for conducting "Days of Remembrance" are distributed throughout the American military establishment, and commemorative ceremonies are held annually in the Capital Rotunda. . . . In Boston, the New England Holocaust Memorial is located on the Freedom Trail, along with Paul Revere's house and the Bunker Hill Monument. Public officials throughout the country told Americans that seeing *Schindler's List* was their civic duty.[2]

"How did this European event come to loom so large in American consciousness?" Novick asks. The answer he provides dovetails with Edward Linenthal's absorbing account of the creation of the Holocaust Museum in Washington and Alan Mintz's judicious survey of the Holocaust in American popular culture.[3] Although their perspectives and conclusions vary, these writers agree on the importance of international politics, specifically Israel's endangered status after the wars in 1967 and 1973, which altered the American Jewish community's relation to Israel and affected American foreign policy as well. However, politics alone cannot explain why so many Americans, most of them non-Jews with slight interest in foreign policy and no personal commitment to Israel, have responded to this particular human tragedy as if it had touched them personally.

As this article will attempt to show, a key enabling factor has been the focus on families and especially on child victims of the Nazis. For many Americans with little knowledge of European history, who are often baffled or bored when confronted with the maze of geographic locales, statistics, and confusing political ideologies inherent in this complex event, the figure of the persecuted child turns the Holocaust into a moving and accessible story with religious and mythic associations. Transcending history even as it affirms the most dreadful historical reality, it appeals to our own memories of childhood, our identities as parents, sisters, brothers: it speaks to us in existential and moral terms, and only secondarily in historical or political ones. This is the source of the Holocaust's power as *narrative*—for novelists, playwrights, filmmakers, and, of course, politicians. But it is also the source of its potential exploitation.

* * *

It all started, of course, with *The Diary of Anne Frank*, first published in English translation in 1952 and then turned into a successful Broadway play (1955) and Hollywood film (1959). "The power of the diary," writes Mintz, "lay in its ability to . . . create a bridge of empathic connection, even identification between the fate of European Jewry and ordinary American readers who had no ethnic or religious link to the victims and often no knowledge whatsoever of the event itself."[4] Anne's identity as a child or adolescent (she was 10 when the war broke out, 12 when she and her family went into hiding in the "secret annex," 15 at her death) was crucial for the transmission of the event to mainstream American audiences. Purged of much of her developing sexuality in the diary's first editions as well as in the Broadway and film versions, Anne personalized the events leading up to the Holocaust through her perspective as a naïve and innocent child. Mintz and other commentators have stressed that Anne Frank's assimilated Jewish background made it easier for American audiences to identify with her at a time when antisemitic prejudice was still wide-spread.[5] True enough, but this claim misses the real point: Anne's identity as a child muted her Jewishness from the very beginning. Unformed, still developing, and then suddenly and tragically dead—Anne could be a Jew to Jewish audiences or simply a courageous girl whose Judaism posed no real obstacle to those who wanted to identify with her "existentially." It was *because* she was a child that even latently antisemitic American audiences of the 1950s could welcome her into their hearts while continuing to frequent restricted hotels and country clubs. If a bearded Polish rabbi or a wealthy German-Jewish businessman had written a comparable memoir (and many did), would big-name publishers, Broadway producers, and Hollywood moguls have rushed to make their stories known?

For much of the 1950s, Anne Frank's story was virtually the only Holocaust narrative that mainstream American audiences were familiar with, either through the written text itself or through its popular theatrical and cinematic renditions. The young narrator in Elie Wiesel's memoir, *Night,* was a second important guide, taking readers on a much more demanding emotional journey from a largely religiously traditional Jewish village in Transylvania into the death camps themselves. First published in 1958 in French while Wiesel was working as a journalist in Paris, the memoir appeared in English translation two years later and quickly assumed an importance comparable only to that of the Anne Frank story. But despite the challenges Night posed for a popular reception—its depiction of Hasidism was foreign to many readers, and its account of camp atrocities was shockingly raw at the time—Wiesel's simply narrated tale of a child and his family caught up in the death machinery of Auschwitz proved irresistibly powerful.

The authorial perspective of this "child" witness is so natural, corresponding with Wiesel's own biography, that one can easily overlook its constructed nature. Although he was almost 16 when he entered Auschwitz (and told the German doctors he was 18 to avoid selection for the furnaces), Wiesel repeatedly refers to himself not as an adolescent or youth but as a "child," an *"enfant"*—a choice in vocabulary that brings out his symbolic defenselessness. Wiesel wrote *Night* at the age of 30 and could have adopted this adult perspective to narrate the events that had taken place some 10 to 15 years earlier. But apart from two brief passages, none of this mature perspective appears in *Night.* The story begins with Wiesel living as a boy in his Transylvanian village and ends with him in the "children's block" of the hospital at Buchenwald just after its liberation. The adult author has disappeared, leaving only the child's "pure" vision of the events as they unfold.

To be sure, Wiesel may have wished to preserve the perspective of his original experience. Still, there is an important difference between Anne Frank's diary, composed day by day in immediate response to the situation she was in, and a starkly revised memoir written with full knowledge of the outcome of the war, the extent of Jewish suffering, and of course the author's own survival. And yet Wiesel's memoir unfolds *as if* he were experiencing his ordeal as immediately, as naïvely, as the Dutch girl in Amsterdam. The suppression of the adult survivor is one of the reasons the narrative is so powerful—it offers itself in a simple, almost ahistorical manner expressive of the young protagonist's vision of reality. A Talmud student who spends much of his time praying, he has little conception of an outside world, of history or politics. When he is brought to Auschwitz in the summer of 1944, one of the prisoners asks him incredulously: "Didn't you know what was in store for you at Auschwitz? Haven't you heard about it? In 1944?" Wiesel ruefully admits that he and others from his town "had no idea." This political ignorance turns them into metaphorical children before the reality of a world whose true horror is only now being revealed to them.[6]

Central to this story of the "children" of Sighet is the destruction of Wiesel's own family and his identity as a son. After witnessing the invasion and destruction of their home and village, Wiesel's family is wrenched apart at the selection ramp at Auschwitz, the mother and sisters going immediately to the gas chambers whereas the son and father are assigned to a work detail. During their imprisonment, the roles of father and son are prematurely and perversely reversed: the father regresses to an enfeebled, defenseless child while the son is thrust into the role of adult caretaker. "I too had become a completely different person. The student of the Talmud, the child that I was, had been consumed in the flames."[7] Wiesel survives Auschwitz physically, but the believing child within himself, his innocence and purity, have been murdered.

On a metaphysical level, the death of Wiesel's father corresponds to the death of God the Father and the narrator's loss of belief in a divinely ordered universe. This spiritual loss crystallizes in what is perhaps the book's most emotionally taxing—and unforgettable—scene, which narrates the brutal murder of another child. Accused of stashing weapons in the barracks, a beloved little "boy" with the refined and beautiful face of a "sad angel" is tortured and then hanged from the gallows in front of the other prisoners. "'Where is God now?'" one man asks. Wiesel then hears a voice deep within himself responding: "Where is he? Here he is—He is hanging here on this gallows."[8] Evoking Christ's crucifixion even as it denies the existence of God, Wiesel's account of Auschwitz turns it into a religious drama accessible to all readers, Jews and Christians. It becomes a moral tale about the sanctity of "angelic" children rather than a historical meditation on Nazi crimes and gentile complicity.

The mythic, child-centered dimension of Wiesel's French text becomes all the more apparent when compared with the versions that preceded it: the

800-page Yiddish manuscript he wrote on a boat to Brazil right after the war, and the 250-page Yiddish account he published in 1956 in Buenos Aires. Entitled *Un di velt hot geshvign* (And the World Kept Silent), it is narrated by an adult who knows very well what the Nazis have done and who denounces not God but the European nations whose collaboration made Hitler's genocidal program possible. Though parallel to *Night* in many respects, the shorter of the two Yiddish narratives departs from it in key passages. As Naomi Seidman points out, Wiesel's French version (and the English translation) describes the newly liberated inmates as having no thoughts of revenge, whereas the Yiddish text concludes: "Early the next day Jewish boys ran off to Weimar to steal clothing and potatoes. And to rape German girls *[un tsu fargvaldikn daytshe shikses]*."[9] Here the Jewish "boys" appear as thieving and sexually aggressive adults, whose actions go hand in hand with a desire for revenge against the gentile world. By contrast, Wiesel's French text relinquishes the stance of the angry adult Jewish survivor to take on the innocent, uncomprehending, nonjudgmental voice of the child victim. By fashioning a "timeless" narrative of innocent children led to slaughter, and by accusing God rather than the European nations of abandoning the Jews, Wiesel moved his narrative from the contested realm of history and politics to an existential plane where Catholic and Jew could meet. And though steeped in the author's talmudic tradition, *Night* relies on the essentially Christian symbolism of an innocent child hanging from a cross as its central figure for Jewish suffering.

* * *

NBC's 1978 docudrama *Holocaust* marked the crucial turning point in American awareness of the Jewish genocide precisely because it knew how to appeal to mainstream American families. Subtitled "The Story of the Family Weiss," it adroitly sets up a mirror relationship between subject and audience. Piano lessons and sports, not ritual prayer and dietary restrictions, characterize the assimilated Weiss family's life in Berlin. The millions of religious Jews in Eastern Europe who were murdered serve as a distant backdrop to this "story" of an affluent, cultured German family with its three likable and talented children. Speaking in familiar American accents, Jewish in name only, they are indistinguishable from the characters in any other prime-time American television show, or from the millions of American viewers who watched them. Even the "synagogue" that burns during the movie's opening credits looks American: a wooden, two-story house with a front porch, it sits in an empty field like the proverbial "home on the prairie."

Holocaust also subtly connects Nazi violence to the growing American concern with victims of sexual abuse, especially children, who in the mid-1970s were increasingly referred to as "survivors" in medical and popular literature.[10] Although several members of the Weiss family die in the gas chambers, the only violence that is directly shown takes place when the youngest daughter foolishly leaves her hiding place and goes out alone on the city streets. In one of the film's most disturbing scenes, she is raped by three drunken Germans, two of them in Nazi uniform. We see the powerful hand at her throat and her open, pleading mouth as she is violated. Traumatized by the rape, she becomes catatonic and is brought to a sanatorium for the mentally ill. Although isolated rapes like this one undoubtedly occurred under the Nazi regime, they had little to do with the actual methods of genocide. But the rape of the Weiss girl was the kind of crime that American families of the 1970s could relate to: the violence of cities, the abusiveness of drunken men, the vulnerability of adolescent girls.

To be sure, *Holocaust* also shows powerful scenes of naked adults being gunned down, and its plot follows the major historical developments of Nazi persecution and mass slaughter. But these victims remain anonymous and are quickly passed over to follow the fictional story of the Weiss family, who seem to provide an archetype of all the victims as family members. When large numbers of Jews are deported from the Warsaw ghetto, the action is described as involving "whole families, mothers with kids, old people." A major portion of *Holocaust* is devoted to the heroic actions of son Karl's attempt to smuggle children's artwork out of Theresienstadt (a topic first made familiar to American audiences in 1964 through the popular exhibition of children's poems and drawings).[11] In the end, the "true" Nazi crime—according to the NBC series—is the murder of children, as one of the chief perpetrators confesses somewhat illogically after his capture: "The Jews had to be dealt with. Their money and influence would destroy Germany. We had to liquidate children. The children, we had to kill the children." And although *Holocaust* can hardly be accused of providing a happy end, its closing scene depicts the youngest Weiss son teaching little boys to play soccer. His young wife murdered, he will devote himself to smuggling Greek-Jewish orphans into Palestine, the future State of Israel. The implied message of this quintessentially American view of the genocide thus seems to be: the children, we have to save the children.

* * *

One of the most perceptive viewers of *Holocaust* was the young filmmaker Steven Spielberg, an avowed champion of children and their unique perspective on reality. Among the major reasons why his films are popular is their appeal to children—and to the "inner child" in many adults. So it is not surprising that he recognized the cinematic potential in the Holocaust, which he began exploiting well before *Schindler's List* in the three "Indiana Jones" adventure movies starring Harrison Ford. At a time when political considerations had put most American groups off-limits as cinematic "bad guys" (Native Americans would have provided the natural opponent for

Spielberg's cowboy hero a generation earlier), in the 1980s the Nazis could still be used as credible villains: undeniably evil, historically real, and still capable of providing the audience with a *frisson* of fear. It is interesting to note that Spielberg makes his most serious foray into Holocaust territory in the second Indiana Jones movie, *The Temple of Doom* (1984), which apparently has nothing to do with Nazis and Jews. Set far from Hitler's Germany in an exotic Indian locale, it comes complete with jungle, primitive village, and a giant palace covering a gloomy, subterranean temple. Evil people have taken control of a local tribe by stealing its magic stones, the source of the community's spiritual strength. But the real crime, the one that arouses Indiana Jones's outrage and spurs him into a daredevil rescue mission, is the violation of the village children, who have been magically seduced to the palace and forced to work as slaves in a gruesome underground torture chamber. The conditions of their confinement directly recall those of Nazi labor camps. Thin, half-naked children in chains toil away in dark, airless caverns at difficult and seemingly pointless physical tasks while sadistic guards stand over them with whips. Those who falter are mercilessly beaten or boiled alive in lava. Two railway tracks run through their work area, and we see children struggling to push heavy metal containers along the tracks—imagery that unmistakably recalls the transports and railways leading to the crematoria.

Few contemporary viewers of *Temple of Doom* realized that Spielberg had smuggled the Holocaust into his entertaining "adventure" flick and, indeed, a much darker view of it than popular representations of the period dared to portray. Yet history bends before the fantasies of Hollywood and its need for a happy end. The leader of the villains, the Maharajah, is a child transformed by an evil spell into a sexually depraved, sadistic ruler who has forgotten his original goodness and solidarity with the other children. With the aid of his young sidekick, Indiana Jones manages to snap the child monarch out of his "adult" spell and win his assistance in liberating the young prisoners. The scene of the joyful children throwing off their chains and storming out of the work camp, accompanied by a rousing John Williams soundtrack, brings the movie to its emotional highpoint—and looks for all the world like a rescue fantasy of the murdered children of Auschwitz.

Schindler's List initially struck many fans as an unlikely venue for Spielberg's particular brand of optimistic, wide-eyed adventure. The movie is not primarily about children, and Spielberg's choice of this "adult" subject was praised by critics as a momentous shift in his artistic career as he left behind the "juvenile" fantasy worlds of the Indiana Jones movies, *E.T.*, and *Jurassic Park*. However, anyone who has watched the movie knows that Spielberg did not abandon his commitment to children or their unique perspective. As in many of his films, his placement of the camera low to the ground encourages spectators to adopt a child's point of view. Oskar Schindler is first seen in a close-up shot from waist level while getting dressed for a night of revelry in which he bribes his way into the Nazis' good graces. We see his hands, his tie, his cufflinks, the front of his dress shirt, his Nazi pin, but not his face—a camera angle that implicitly suggests the intimate and fragmented view a child might have of his or her father at home. Throughout the movie, strategically selected camera angles encourage us to "look up" to Schindler or, alternatively, to look "down" on the world when taking his perspective. It makes the hero big, larger than mere mortals, a symbolic father and moral authority, and it subtly turns the audience into symbolic children.

Most of the controversy surrounding Spielberg's film has centered on the appropriateness of making a non-Jewish German the heroic rescuer of Jews. Though based on a true story, commentators point out, the actions of "righteous gentiles" are a statistically marginal part of the Holocaust. But Spielberg's pseudo-documentary film about Germans and Jews actually depends on a deeper narrative of children, marital fidelity, and the importance of family. Consider the one spot of color in the black-and-white Holocaust sequences: the little red coat worn by a small girl who wanders alone through the streets of the Kraków ghetto as it is being razed. Her orphaned journey serves as the film's visual and emotional leitmotif for the essential inhumanity of the Holocaust. Schindler's heroic transformation from opportunistic, womanizing businessman to heroic savior begins with his vision of the little girl, whom he first sees while sitting on horseback, his mistress at his side, watching the destruction from a bluff overlooking the city. In a brutal scene where Nazis are shown burning corpses on giant bonfires, he sees the girl's body with its tattered red coat being carried past him; he holds a handkerchief to his mouth and then lowers it, staring in disbelief. This vision is the turning point of his moral rehabilitation, a change that eventually allows him to assume the role of symbolic father—he has no children of his own—to "his" Jews.

Not surprisingly, Spielberg cannily gives Schindler's transformation a sexual dimension, brushing up against the genre of "Nazi porn" that Italian cinema had developed two decades earlier (in films like Visconti's "Twilight of the Gods," Liliana Cavani's "Night Porter," and a host of lesser, much seedier products). In the film's early stages, Schindler is repeatedly shown as sexually wayward. When his wife comes to visit, she discovers him in bed with his mistress; she asks him to give up his philandering, and he quickly sends her packing. His depraved counterpart in this respect is the camp commandant, Amon Goeth, whose sexuality is explicitly linked to his enjoyment of wanton killing. In one scene he gets up from having sex and goes out on his villa's terrace where, still bare-chested, he takes his rifle and begins shooting randomly at prisoners. Like the child Maharajah in *Temple of Doom*, Goeth is depicted as a perverted and spoiled child. When he goes back inside his bedroom and jokingly takes aim at his naked mistress, she yells out "Amon, you're such a damn fucking child"; he mockingly replies "Wocky, wocky," then goes to the bathroom and is shown urinating.

The linking of perverse sexuality and sadism also appears in Goeth's choice of a young and beautiful Jewish prisoner named Helen Hirsch as his maid, whom he terrorizes by alternately beating and threatening to use as sexual prey. Schindler's womanizing, by contrast, is never tied to violence and becomes increasingly paternal. He reassures Helen that Goeth will not kill her, stroking her hair and planting a chaste kiss on her forehead. Later he wrests Helen from Goeth's employ by "winning" her in a card game and including her among the factory workers he will save. He gives a further sign of his moral transformation when he goes to his wife while she is praying in a church and pledges his fidelity, which in the film he appears to maintain. (In fact, the historical Schindler kept his mistress to the very end, fleeing the Nazis with her and his wife in the same car.) The dramatic highpoint of Schindler's rescue actions takes place near the end of the movie, when the train carrying women and children to work in his factory in Czechoslovakia is mistakenly sent back to Auschwitz. Schindler immediately goes there to rescue them from certain death, insisting on the children's "special" talents to an incredulous Nazi guard. "These are mine," he roars to the German. "They're skilled munitions workers. They are essential, essential girls." Then, taking the hand of a little girl and thrusting it into the guard's face, he explains: "Their fingers polish the insides of shell metal casings. How else am I to polish the inside of a 45 millimeter shell casing? You tell me." (Note that Schindler saves these girls by professionalizing them, insisting on their adult skills—the exact opposite of Nazi policies that deprofessionalized and infantilized grownups.) Although the number of children among the actual *Schindlerjuden* was tiny, the presentation of these "little hands" is one of the emotional climaxes of the movie, directly preceding the escape of Schindler's Jews from Poland to the safety of his factory and, surely not coincidentally, his birthplace in Czechoslovakia. The final scene in the historical drama takes place here, when Schindler, reunited with his wife, is honored by the rescued Jews with a gold ring they have made for him. He falls to the ground, weeping for the Jews he did not save, as his "children" gather around to comfort him.

The point of this scene and of the movie in general is not that a "good German" has rescued Jews but that this particular individual has transcended the very national and ethnic identities with which Nazis targeted Jews in the first place—transcended them to become the good father who has sacrificed himself for children in need. Symbolically, Schindler's apotheosis as good husband and father effectively resolves the moral quandary posed by the film's opening, when an implied child spectator watches Schindler getting dressed for a night of drunkenness, shady deals with the Nazis, and sexual debauchery. The abandoned child has finally found his (or rather *her*) father; the fragmented family has been made whole.[12]

* * *

That children and their unique perspective have played a large role in the popular dissemination of Holocaust awareness in America, particularly in television and movie entertainment, may not be all that surprising. After all, we should not expect Hollywood to give us reliable history lessons, even if the success of pseudo-documentary films like *Schindler's List* depends precisely on their historical link to reality. What is surprising is to find the same emphasis in venues that purport to give an authoritative, objective account of the Holocaust as a whole. But in school curricula, documentary films, memorials, and museum exhibitions, "objective" history often gives way to gripping, visually enhanced "stories," while a careful contextualization of German antisemitism and European Jews is replaced by an ethics lesson on religious tolerance and respect for "otherness." Running through all these educational efforts is the theme of children and families, which provides the basis for an emotional, spontaneous response from audiences of various ethnic and cultural backgrounds.

The Holocaust Museum in Washington provides a striking example of this tendency. In their commitment to create an exhibition that would serve as historical evidence against Holocaust deniers and revisionists, the museum's planners admitted to "an almost fanatic commitment to historical truth."[13] The slightest doubt about the accuracy of any fact or the authenticity of any artifact led to its immediate disqualification, since "any mistakes would have left the museum open to critical attacks against its historical reliability"—a claim that has become even more pertinent since the museum and its official website are now widely considered the nation's official source of truth about the Holocaust.[14] However, this notion of an "objective" account of a historical event as complex and massive as the Holocaust is not only theoretically naïve but also in direct conflict with the planners' stated intention of creating a "living" or "narrative" museum whose principal task is "to affect and change the mental and moral attitudes of [its] visitors."[15] Unlike traditional museums that present a collection of artifacts, the Holocaust Museum was deliberately organized around a "story" or "plot" that requires the visitors to identify with the victims emotionally. "The emotional effect of the narrative in the museum exhibition is comparable to that of the narrative in novels, plays, or motion pictures. Being gripped by the plot, projecting ourselves into it, *identifying with its heroes and developing resentment towards its villains,* we get emotionally involved. This emotional involvement opens us to educational influence," museum planners explain. Visitors are not free to choose their own way through the museum, "just as they are not free to choose their own way between the scenes of a play or a film."[16]

But how could the museum tell a "story" of such unmitigated atrocity and still be able to draw a broad audience? "The museum's mission was to teach people about the Holocaust and bring about civic transformation; yet, since the public had to *desire* to visit, the museum felt the need to find a balance between the tolerable and the intolerable."[17] Martin Smith, director of the exhibition department, felt that the museum needed "to scald people" with its documentation and that any attempt to soften the story would prevent them from "taking it on in some profound way."[18] Others, including museum director Jeshajahu Weinberg, insisted on toning down the horror so that it could still "play" for visitors from middle America—often referred to in internal discussions as the "Iowa farm family." The operative word was "family"—what could adult visitors be expected to tolerate in the presence of their children? Curator Raye Farr initially supported the "hard-core" presentation of a color picture of naked cadavers in Buchenwald, but she changed her mind when her daughter told her the image was too strong for the beginning of the exhibit.[19]

Children visitors thus posed a special dilemma for the Holocaust Museum, but they also provided a brilliant solution. The large number of child visitors not only justified the museum's choice of a toned-down version of historical events but also supplied the "hot" story that Weinberg was looking for: the story of innocent child victims and evil adult Nazis.[20] This theme begins with the ground-floor exhibition specifically designed for children, entitled "Remember the Children: Daniel's Story." Mobilizing a darkened theme-park interior with movie clips and recorded voices, this exhibition narrates the plight of a "typical" German-Jewish family through the various stages of persecution and murder. The story is told by a fictional 11-year-old boy, "Daniel," in terms that all children can relate to: "Have you ever been punished for something you didn't do?" he asks. "We were." At the end of the itinerary through domestic interiors that reassuringly call to mind American rather than German households, visitors hear Daniel's voice again: "Over one and a half million kids died. That's like a whole school disappearing every day for eight years. Millions of grown-ups died too. People like you and me. That's why they call it the Holocaust. Remember the children. Remember my story."

Whereas the ground-floor exhibit reduces the Holocaust to a children's tale largely unencumbered by external political events (there is no mention of World War II, for example), and where adults serve as incidental extras to the main stars ("grown-ups died too"), the permanent exhibition on the upper floors makes a serious effort to document and contextualize the historical reality of Nazi Germany. Still, the children's version carries over into the adult exhibition in a number of crucial ways. The first presentation of the victims is provided by a bank of video monitors showing clips of Jews throughout the world. A few Jewish men with beards appear, but in all the other clips children constitute the overwhelming majority of visible subjects. Often a camera will show a close-up of a child's face, then pull back to reveal the child surrounded by a group of adults. A short film on antisemitism at the beginning of the exhibition closes with the words: "six million Jews—these are some of them." Then viewers see a series of 11 photos, *all* of children.

This imbalance continues throughout the main exhibition. We see two fearful brothers about eight years old boarding a transport train; schoolteachers leading children to the gas chambers; an old woman cradling an infant she has taken from its mother; the head of a naked little girl being measured by a doctor to support Nazi theories about racial physiognomy. The actual affidavit signed by Auschwitz commandant Rudolf Hoess stating that his camp gassed two million inmates is attached to a photo of three adults walking hurriedly with eight children. Although this imbalance would be perfectly justifiable for situations in which children were disproportionately targeted (as in the selection process at Auschwitz, where children too weak to work went straight to the gas chambers), children are also conspicuously foregrounded in groups where they formed a minority of victims. In the section on the Roma and Sinti, for instance, there is not a single picture of an adult, only children. And though "authentic" artifacts like a woman's dress or a lone fiddle on a wooden cart effectively conjure up an eerie absence, they also keep the adult owners of these objects out of sight. The section on the Nazi euthanasia program, which killed some 85,000 mentally and physically handicapped people, also shows only children (two heart-rending photographs of a naked boy and girl who, incidentally, do not look handicapped at all); yet children represented less than 6 percent of the total victims in this group.[21] The brief section on Hitler's homosexual victims, who could not easily be fitted into the narrative of children and families, provides a striking but isolated counterexample. One of the final corridors displays colorful artwork and pictures of the children of Theresienstadt under the heading "The Children of the Holocaust." On the facing wall, we see a row of photos entitled simply "The Killers"—black-and-white images of impassive Nazi officials on trial.

One of the most effective and celebrated parts of the exhibition is the so-called "Tower of Faces" through which visitors must leave the museum: thousands of photographs of a single village in Poland before its destruction. Collected by Holocaust survivor and Jewish Studies scholar Yaffa Eliach after the war, these images speak all the more eloquently through their intimate, domestic appearance. They are "family photographs," noted one museum planner, "with scalloped edges . . . cut in the shape of hearts to become part of cards, birthday cards and greeting cards . . . stained edges . . . that had been colored and pasted down. We wanted to preserve that character."[22] As they exit the museum, visitors are left with the impression that they have witnessed the personal lives of an entire village that has tragically disappeared. But so have the victims' political and professional identities. There is no attempt to depict, say, the political views of many of these villagers. Communists, socialists, anarchists, Zionists have become fathers and mothers, grandparents and children, human beings in their family identities: "people just like us."[23]

* * *

In the above examples, I have focused on key moments in the history of American Holocaust awareness, almost all of which have significantly employed the figure of the child victim as narrator and witness. Since September 11, 2001, and the ensuing war on terrorism, the popular media's fascination with the Holocaust seems to have abated somewhat. But the recent documentary feature *Paper Clips* (released by Miramax in November 2004) suggests that the Holocaust continues to exert a strong hold on the mainstream American imagination and that it does so precisely because of the "exemplary" tale it can tell about—and for—children. Described in promotional materials as the "moving story about [American] students and their emotional journey [through] the horrors and tragedies of the Holocaust," the "Paper Clip Project" began in 1998 when a group of middle-school children and teachers from Whitwell, Tennessee, set out to confront the prejudices and lack of diversity in their own community.[24] The small town had no Jews, Muslims, or even Catholics, and it had only a handful of African-American families. However, "if we studied about the Holocaust," the school's white-haired, matronly principal explains, "we could learn a whole lot about evil, about [a] whole other culture." But the children quickly abandoned the study of religious and cultural difference in an effort to "experience" the enormity of the Jewish victims by collecting six million paper clips (chosen because Norwegians had purportedly fastened paper clips to their lapels during the war to protest the Nazi occupation). They began writing letters to friends, relatives, politicians, and celebrities, and within a year they had received donations of several hundred thousand clips.

Here the project might have come to a halt. But two German journalists got wind of the children's initiative and began publicizing it in Germany and in the United States. In April 2001 a celebratory article appeared in the *Washington Post*, a story on NBC and CNN followed, and soon Whitwell was submerged with journalists and camera crews. Politicians and celebrities, including former presidents George Bush and Bill Clinton, Tom Hanks, Bill Cosby, and Steven Spielberg, got into the act, and before long so many paper clips were coming in that the local post office was overwhelmed and the school did not know where to put them. Eventually the students collected almost 30 million clips, 11 million of which were placed in an "authentic" boxcar from Germany that had been used for Jewish transports, thus creating a memorial museum complete with a walkway of cheerful butterfly drawings and statues.[25] The museum was inaugurated on November 9, 2001, the anniversary of Kristallnacht. Jewish children were brought in from Atlanta to say kaddish while Christian children sang inspirational hymns.

From the beginning, participants and filmmakers understood the significance of this project in terms of a multicultural celebration of difference and tolerance. Orthodox Jewish backers for the project were moved by the fact that Christian children had started the project "with no other agenda but to do good. You can't help but be touched by it." As Matthew Hiltzik, a senior vice president at Miramax explained in the promotional materials, the "beauty of the film is that it isn't just a memorial to those who died in the Holocaust. It's a celebration of tolerance, respect, pride, commitment, the public school system—everything that's good about America that you don't hear enough about." In one emotional scene in *Paper Clips*, teacher David Smith admits to his father having used racial slurs about blacks that he unthinkingly adopted. The Paper Clip Project has changed him, he says haltingly, and he pledges never to transmit prejudice to his own sons. In another scene, the inhabitants of Whitwell listen in rapt attention to the stories and words of wisdom from Holocaust survivors who have been flown in from New York for the occasion; afterward, the local children and adults embrace them tearfully. Hiltzik recalls his stay in Whitwell for the movie's premiere as one of the "most meaningful experiences" of his life. "I was the only Jew in the room, and yet I felt completely comfortable and welcome." At the end of the film, a 95-year-old Holocaust survivor tells us (through the Yiddish-accented voice of a professional actress) that the children of Whitwell signify the dawning of "a new age . . . an age of responsibility, of kindness."

Even before its commercial release, the film garnered a number of impressive awards, receiving "Audience Favorite" award for "Best Documentary Feature" at the Palm Springs International Film Festival, the Atlanta Jewish Film Festival, and FilmFest DC. Benefiting from strong German support from the beginning—Germans contributed many of the paper clips, and the two German journalists found the Nazi boxcar and had it shipped to the United States—the project went on tour in Germany, visiting 17 schools in the Berlin area to great acclaim. "I've never made a film like this before," says filmmaker Joe Fab. "It changed the way I think about my wife, my kids, my grandkids." Teacher David Smith agrees: "The filmmakers were around us all the time; they came to our homes and we ate together. They're like our family now."

The problem with this celebration of tolerance and family values is that it is based on what might be called "no-cost multiculturalism." It provides the illusion of diversity without requiring that anything or anyone actually change. It is one thing for the conservative Southern Baptists in Whitwell to share an emotional moment with elderly Holocaust survivors, or to work for a few months with Jewish filmmakers and producers. But what would happen if they had to live side by side with a sizable community of Jews, some of whom might have supported gun control and the right to abortion, or opposed the teaching of creationism in public schools? Identifying with Jews who died 60 years ago in a foreign country is safe: no living Jewish community threatens Whitwell's religious and ethnic homogeneity. In this regard one cannot help asking why, if the project was meant to address the school's lack of diversity, the students did not choose to study the Ku Klux Klan (which was founded a short distance from Whitwell) rather than the Holocaust, or why the film-makers did not interview a single one of the five black students about their perception of racism and prejudice today.

No-cost multiculturalism goes hand in hand with an almost complete lack of historical perspective. After all the efforts of Holocaust historians and contemporary witnesses to *restore* the identities of victims whom the Nazis had reduced to faceless numbers and statistics, the Paper Clip Project turns these lives back into a mass of identical office objects that are piled up in bins and crates, which inevitably calls to mind the piles of ownerless shoes and eyeglasses amassed in the death camps. It seems hard to imagine that none of the participants questioned the appropriateness of stuffing these paper-clip tokens of Jewish life into an "authentic" German railcar that had actually been used for deportations to the death camps. But the students were focused only on themselves; the identities of the actual victims disappeared when the students meticulously recorded the names of the paper clip *donors*, ensuring that the memory of *their* largesse would endure. Even the name of this project suggests its lack of historical awareness. If the students—or for that matter the filmmakers—had done more research, they might have discovered that CIA operatives smuggled high-ranking Nazi scientists into the United States during the Cold War under the code name "Operation Paper Clip."

Like many popular Holocaust representations, the Whitwell children's memorial ultimately is more about American values and American children than about the Jewish victims. One student says the memorial "made me realize the next time I say the Pledge of Allegiance, I'll think how glad I am it's a free country and I have the right to do and say what I feel." In her opening sentence at the memorial's inauguration, the school principal tells us how grateful she is "to live in the United States of America. I love this town, the children." Add to this patriotic encomium a Christian allegory of rebirth through loving children, and the film's message is complete. The murdered Jews never received proper burial in Germany or Austria, we learn in the closing sequence, but "now they have come home," they have found a resting place "in Tennessee, among loving children." This is the film's rather appalling subtext, so innocently symbolized by the brightly colored butterflies adorning the memorial walkway: American Baptist children have finally redeemed the murdered Jews of Europe.

* * *

With the degradation of Holocaust memory represented by *Paper Clips* and other self-absorbed commemorative projects, it is all too easy to forget the horrific atrocity that stands out about the Nazi genocide: the cold-blooded, systematic murder of more than a million children. Nothing that is written here is meant to lessen or relativize that crime or the suffering it caused. The question raised here concerns, rather, the reception of this historical event in postwar America. Why have the breakthrough moments in Holocaust awareness been so consistently associated with the special plight of children and families? To be sure, counterexamples like the Adolf Eichmann trial in 1961, together with Hannah Arendt's coverage of the proceedings for *The New Yorker* and her controversial book on the "banality of evil," are not lacking in the 60-year history of this reception. But, though it was undoubtedly a watershed event for Jewish America's awareness of the Holocaust, the Eichmann affair remained a political, legal, and intellectual matter that never touched a majority of Americans in the personal way that Anne Frank's *Diary* or Steven Spielberg's *Schindler's List* did. And whereas one would be hard pressed to name other breakthrough events besides the Eichmann trial that do not involve children or families, the examples discussed in this article could easily be expanded to include the exhibition of poetry and artwork by children inmates in Theresienstadt, which touched millions of viewers in the early 1960s, or the large number of books and documentaries concerning the *Kindertransporte* from Nazi Germany to England, or the growing body of children's literature that is used to teach the Holocaust in secondary and elementary schools. I make no claim to have covered all major aspects of Holocaust memory of the past 60 years, only to have pointed out a salient feature of those "canonical" representations that have become so familiar that we risk forgetting how and why they achieved this status.

The questions are why, and whether it is a good thing. If the personalized child narratives of Anne Frank and Elie Wiesel had the undeniable merit of winning the hearts of mainstream, non-Jewish audiences in the 1950s and 1960s when "mere" documentary presentations did not, they also set the terms for an Americanization of Holocaust memory that privatized and sentimentalized the historical event and all too often effaced the memory of actual victims for the sake of an effective dramatization. However legitimate the end, however well intentioned the motive, the invocation of young victims easily leads to rhetorical and ideological distortion. Wiesel himself protested against the exploitation of the Holocaust as early as the mid-1970s, but his own strategic mobilization of the child narrator in *Night* cut both ways. It allowed for mainstream, Christian identification with the Jewish victims, thus facilitating a crucial breakthrough in public recognition of the Jewish tragedy. But it also depoliticized and sacralized the Holocaust, filed off the rough edges of the Jewish protagonists, and sought reconciliation rather than confrontation with the gentile world that had assisted Hitler's genocidal plan by remaining silent.

This tendency becomes all too apparent in subsequent popular American representations: made-for-television docudramas like NBC's *Holocaust*, big-budget Hollywood movies like *Schindler's List*, and memorial museums like the Holocaust Museum in Washington. Here, too, the foregrounding of child victimhood cuts both ways, allowing for a previously unimaginable emotional response from broad segments of the population but also systematically skewing and effacing crucial aspects of the historical event. These "true" or "living" stories become another form of entertainment that provides American audiences with the "thrill of the real," with the *impression* of bumping up against an authentic historical tragedy, when in fact they offer a simplified narrative of good and evil that does not necessarily lead to greater historical knowledge, critical awareness, or political commitment. As the particularly self-absorbed Paper Clip Project indicates, the mobilization of "loving children" can have more to do with conservative American notions of family values and Christian spirituality than with any real encounter with past or present politics; it can neutralize historical understanding while claiming to celebrate "memory." Sixty years after the end of the war, as the living memory of the Holocaust recedes further into the distance, the commercial and dramatic exploitation of the child victims should seem less and less tolerable.

Notes

1. As quoted by James Young in Hilene Flanzbaum, *The Americanization of the Holocaust* (Baltimore, Md., 1999), 70; the original source stems from *The New York Times*, Feb. 11, 1965, p. 1.

2. Peter Novick, *The Holocaust in American Life* (Boston, 1999), 207.

3. Edward T. Linenthal, *Preserving Memory: The Struggle to Create America's Holocaust Museum* (New York, 1995); Alan Mintz, *Popular Culture and the Shaping of Holocaust Memory in America* (Seattle, 2001). Flanzbaum, *Americanization of the Holocaust*, provides an anthology of contrasting and generally moderate views. For extremely polemical accounts, see Norman G. Finkelstein, *The Holocaust Industry: Reflections on the Exploitation of Jewish Suffering* (London, 2000), and Tim Cole, *Selling the Holocaust: From Auschwitz to Schindler. How History Is Bought, Packaged, and Sold* (New York, 1999).

4. Mintz, *Popular Culture*, 17.

5. From the very beginning, the *Diary* had been subject to competing attempts to claim her for this or that group, with novelist and playwright Meyer Levin famously charging the original publishers and Broadway producers (many of them Jews themselves) with a conspiracy to minimize the Jewish content of Anne's story in favor of a "universal" message of courage and hope. See Ralph Melnick, *The Stolen Legacy of Anne Frank* (New Haven, Conn., 1997), and Lawrence Graver, *An Obsession with Anne Frank* (Berkeley, 1995). Cynthia Ozick's incisive *New Yorker* essay "Who Owns Anne Frank?" has been reprinted in *Quarrel and Quandary* (New York, 2000), 74–102.

6. Naomi Seidman makes the point that in the original Yiddish version of Wiesel's experience, first published in Mark Turov's series in Buenos Aires in 1956, the naïveté of the Sighet villagers was unusual. "None of the readers of Turkov's series on Polish Jewry would have taken it as representative." See Naomi Seidman, "Elie Wiesel and the Scandal of Jewish Rage," *Jewish Social Studies* n.s. 3, no. 1 (Fall 1996): 1–19.

7. Elie Wiesel, *Night* (New York, 1960), 34.

8. Ibid., 62.

9. Wiesel as quoted in Seidman, "Scandal," 3.

10. The national foundation Prevent Child Abuse America was set up in 1972, and the U.S. Congress established the National Clearinghouse on Child Abuse and Neglect Information in 1974, the very years in which Holocaust memory began its dramatic rise in American popular culture. Curiously, Novick devotes a major portion of his study to the American culture of victimization but fails to note the special prominence of children in this discourse; see Novick, *American Life*, 8–11, 189–203.

11. The full title of the exhibition was . . . *I never saw another butterfly . . . Children's Drawings and Poems from Terezin Concentration Camp, 1942–1944*. First published in Czech in 1959 and in English in 1964, the anthology was a huge popular success in the United States and a milestone in mainstream acceptance of the Holocaust. Since then, millions of people worldwide have seen exhibitions of this material. A permanent exhibition has been mounted in Prague, and the U.S. Holocaust Museum in Washington, D.C., has also incorporated part of this material into its permanent exhibition and helped republish the original catalogue in 1993.

12. Although they never meet in the film, the orphaned girl in red is surely Schindler's symbolic child. The cover illustration for the video and DVD versions shows a strong adult hand grasping a child's hand, the cuff of her red coat just visible below it.

13. Jeshajahu Weinberg and Rina Elieli, *The Holocaust Museum in Washington* (New York, 1995), 153.

14. While allowing that "there is no such thing as objective historiography" and that Holocaust scholars still disagree on many issues, the planners insist that "the actual course of events has now been largely established. . . . [A]t most there is marginal controversy about the exact number of victims." German historian Hans Mommsen, quoted in Weinberg and Elieli, *Museum*, 155.

15. Ibid., 50.

16. Ibid., 51.

17. Linenthal, *Preserving Memory*, 198.

18. Ibid.

19. Ibid., 194.

20. Having worked previously as a theater director in Tel Aviv and as the creator of two "story telling" museums in Israel, Weinberg wanted the museum to be a "primer on the Holocaust," a "hot" museum that would "trigger in the visitor's heart feelings of emotional identification with the victims," leading him or her to consider the "moral implications" of the historical materials on display (ibid., 142). To this end, he eschewed traditional curators in favor of documentary filmmaker Martin Smith and material culture expert Ralph Appelbaum (who had helped create the Living History Center at Independence Hall in Philadelphia), both of whom "saw the world the same way . . . visually, pictorially . . . as storytellers" (ibid., 145).

21. Henry Friedlander estimates that some 80,000 adults and 5,000 children were killed in this program. See his *The Origins of the Nazi Genocide: From Euthanasia to the Final Solution* (Chapel Hill, N.C., 1995), 61.

22. Linenthal, *Preserving Memory*, 180–181.

23. Despite the planners' stated objective to include "all the victims" of the Holocaust, there is no mention of communists or socialists in the museum catalogue, only "political dissidents."

24. "Paper Clips Press Notes," Miramax Films, 12 pages, no date or place of publication given.

25. The butterflies derive from the well-known poem by a child inmate of Theresienstadt, "The Butterfly," which provided the title for the above-mentioned exhibition of children's artwork and poetry, "I Never Saw Another Butterfly." But the religious implications of the butterfly should not be missed.

Chronology

1929	Anneliese Marie (Anne) Frank born June 12 in Frankfurt am Main, the daughter of Otto Frank and Edith Hollander Frank. Her older sister, Margot Betti, was born February 16, 1926.
1933	Summer: After the Nazis win municipal elections in Frankfurt, Otto Frank decides to immigrate with his family to the Netherlands, a neutral country, where he opens a branch of his brother's company, the Dutch Opekta Company, in Amsterdam. Edith and Margot join him in December; the family resides in an apartment at 378 Merwedeplein. Anne remains in Aachen, Germany, with her maternal grandmother, joining her family in March 1934.
1939	Grandmother Rosa Stern Hollander flees Aachen and joins the family in Amsterdam.
1940	May: Germany invades the Netherlands and occupation begins. October 22: Nazis issue "Aryanization" decree that no Jew may own a business; Otto Frank cedes legal control of business interest to trusted employees and friends Jan Gies and Victor Kugler.
1941	September: Anne and other Jewish children no longer allowed to attend school with non-Jews. Anti-Jewish decrees increase and freedom of movement becomes increasingly restricted.

1942   January: Otto Frank tries to obtain emigration papers for the family; Grandmother Hollander dies. May: All Dutch Jews, age six and older, required to wear a yellow Star of David sewn to their clothing; mass arrests of Jews and mandatory service in German work camps becomes routine. Frank family prepares to go into hiding in annex of rooms above Otto Frank's office at 263 Prinsengracht; members of Opekta Company staff agree to help them. June 12: Anne celebrates thirteenth birthday; receives a notebook with a red and white checked cover; she begins the first of two extant diaries, dated June 12 to December 5, 1942. July 5: Margot receives notice that she will be deported to a Nazi work camp. July 6: Otto, Edith, Margot, and Anne move into the annex. July 13: Otto Frank's business associate, Herman Van Pels, moves into the annex with his wife and son, Peter. Anne will call them the van Daans in her diary. November 16: Friedrich Pfeffer, a dentist, moves into the annex. Anne will write about him as Mr. Dussel.

1943   December 22: Anne begins a new volume of her diaries, the first entry since December 5, 1942, indicating that one diary has been lost.

1944   March 28: An exiled Minister of the Dutch government in London, in a radio broadcast, asks for documents and accounts of the Dutch war experience; Anne confides to her diary, on May 11, that she will become a journalist and writer: "In any case, I want to publish a book entitled *Het Achterhuis* after the war. Whether I shall succeed or not, I cannot say, but my diary will be a great help." March 29: Last recorded entry, made on loose sheets of paper of notes and stories for *Het Achterhuis;* other versions lost. May 20: Begins writing *Het Achterhuis* ("the house behind" or "the secret annex"). August 4, 10:00 a.m: After an anonymous call, Nazi police and Dutch collaborators arrest the residents of the annex; remove all in a covered truck to Central Office for Jewish Emigration, then to Weteringschans Prison. Miep Gies retrieves Anne's papers and diaries from the annex and hides them. August 8: Frank family, the Van Pels family, and Pfeffer removed to Westerbork transit camp. September 3: On what will be the last Auschwitz-bound train from Westerbork, all transported to Auschwitz death camp in Poland, arriving September 5; Herman Van Pels put to death. October 30: Anne and

Margot transported from Auschwitz to Bergen-Belsen, near Hanover, Germany, where thousands die from starvation and epidemics. December: Friedrich Pfeffer dies at Neuengamme concentration camp, Germany.

1945   January 6: Edith Frank dies of starvation at Auschwitz. January 27: Russian troops liberate Auschwitz. March (?): Margot dies of typhus at Bergen-Belsen. April (?): Anne, age 15, dies of typhus at Bergen-Belsen. April 15, 1945: British troops liberate Bergen-Belsen. May: The Netherlands is liberated; the war in Europe ends. Peter Van Pels survives SS "death march" from Auschwitz but dies May 2 (?) at Mauthausen concentration camp, Austria, three days before it is liberated. June 3: Otto Frank, the only survivor of the annex, returns to Amsterdam, hoping to find his daughters; Miep Gies gives him Anne's papers. Otto Frank copies and edits the diaries and papers, revising them to "the essentials," omitting what he believes offensive to the living, unkind to the dead, or of no interest. Because of the intimate nature of the diary, shocking at that time for Anne's comments upon politics, sexuality, and adults, no publisher will accept it. Otto Frank continues to seek a publisher in order to fulfill Anne's wish to be remembered as a writer.

1946   Jan Romein, Dutch historian and editor of the journal *De Nieuwe Stem*, reads Otto Frank's transcription of the diary and publishes an article praising it, "A Child's Voice," in *Het Parool*, April 3, 1946. "Fragments from the Diary of Anne Frank," heavily edited by Otto Frank at the request of the publishing house, appears in the summer issue of *De Nieuwe Stem*.

1947   Diary published in Dutch as *Het Achterhuis*. 150,000 copies soon followed by second printing.

1950   *Journal de Anne Frank* published in France. *Das Tagebuch der Anne Frank* published in Germany.

1952   *The Diary of a Young Girl, by Anne Frank*, published in England and the United States, where it had previously been rejected by ten publishers.

1955   October 5: *The Diary of Anne Frank*, produced for theater, premiers on Broadway; wins 1955 Pulitzer Prize in drama.

1956   October 1: *The Diary of Anne Frank* performed in Germany;
                November 27, in The Netherlands.

1957   *The Diary of Anne Frank* produced for film. Anne Frank
                Foundation established to preserve the annex and to implement
                "the ideals bequeathed to the world in the *Diary of Anne
                Frank.*"

1960   May 3: Anne Frank House opens as a museum and cultural
                center at 263 Prinsengracht, Amsterdam.

1977   Anne Frank Center U.S.A. opens in New York.

1980   August 19: Otto Frank dies in Basel, Switzerland, at age 91.

1997   December 4: *The Diary of Anne Frank,* a play by Wendy
                Kesselman, opens on Broadway. Anne Frank Zentrum (Center)
                opens in Berlin. More than twenty-four million copies of the
                diary have been sold, and it has been translated into fifty-five
                languages.

Contributors

HAROLD BLOOM is Sterling Professor of the Humanities at Yale University. He is the author of 30 books, including *Shelley's Mythmaking* (1959), *The Visionary Company* (1961), *Blake's Apocalypse* (1963), *Yeats* (1970), *A Map of Misreading* (1975), *Kabbalah and Criticism* (1975), *Agon: Toward a Theory of Revisionism* (1982), *The American Religion* (1992), *The Western Canon* (1994), and *Omens of Millennium: The Gnosis of Angels, Dreams, and Resurrection* (1996). *The Anxiety of Influence* (1973) sets forth Professor Bloom's provocative theory of the literary relationships between the great writers and their predecessors. His most recent books include *Shakespeare: The Invention of the Human* (1998), a 1998 National Book Award finalist; *How to Read and Why* (2000); *Genius: A Mosaic of One Hundred Exemplary Creative Minds* (2002); *Hamlet: Poem Unlimited* (2003); *Where Shall Wisdom Be Found?* (2004); and *Jesus and Yahweh: The Names Divine* (2005). In 1999, Professor Bloom received the prestigious American Academy of Arts and Letters Gold Medal for Criticism. He has also received the International Prize of Catalonia, the Alfonso Reyes Prize of Mexico, and the Hans Christian Andersen Bicentennial Prize of Denmark.

DAVID BARNOUW is a historical researcher for the Netherlands Institute for War Documentation. He is coeditor of *The Diary of Anne Frank: The Critical Edition* (1989). He has published several articles and books about Anne Frank and lectures about her.

DEBORAH E. LIPSTADT is Dorot Professor of Modern Jewish History and Holocaust Studies at Emory University. She has written about those who deny the Holocaust, notably in *History on Trial: My Day in Court with David Irving* (2005) and *Denying the Holocaust: The Growing Assault on Truth and Memory* (1993). From 1996 through 1999 she served as a member of the United States State Department Advisory Committee on Religious Freedom Abroad.

SHELBY MYERS-VERHAGE is assistant professor of English at Kirkwood Community College in Cedar Rapids, Iowa.

RACHEL FELDHAY BRENNER is Max and Frieda Weinstein-Bascom Professor of Jewish Studies and Professor of Modern Hebrew Literature at the Department of Hebrew Studies,University of Wisconsin-Madison. She has published widely on responses to the Holocaust in Jewish Diaspora literature, Israeli literature, and Polish Literature. Among her publications are *Writing as Resistance: Four Women Confronting the Holocaust: Edith Stein, Simone Weil, Anne Frank, and Etty Hillesum* (1997) and *Inextricably Bonded—Israeli Jewish and Arab Writers Re-Visioning Culture* (2003).

JUDITH GOLDSTEIN is the founder and executive director of Humanity in Action, a foundation that sponsors educational programs for university students in Europe and the United States.

NIGEL A. CAPLAN is a second-language specialist at the University of North Carolina at Chapel Hill.

PASCAL BOS is associate professor of comparative literature in the Center for European Studies at the University of Texas, Austin. He wrote *German-Jewish Literature in the Wake of the Holocaust: Grete Weil, Ruth Kluger, and the Politics of Address* (2005).

AIMEE POZORSKI is assistant professor of English at Central Connecticut State University, where she teaches contemporary literature and American fiction.

WAYNE HOWKINS taught at Redmoor High School, Hinckley, England.

MARK M. ANDERSON is professor of comparative literature at Columbia University, where he specializes in German modernism, contemporary Austrian literature and the theory and practice of translation. He wrote *Hitler's Exiles: Personal Stories of the Flight from Nazi Germany to America* (1998).

Bibliography

Adler, David. *Picture Book of Anne Frank*. New York: Holiday House, 1993.

Anderson, Mark M. "The Child Victim as Witness to the Holocaust: An American Story?" *Jewish Social Studies: History, Culture, and Society*, Volume 14, Number 1 (Fall 2007): pp. 1–22.

Barnes, Ian. "Anne Frank Forty Years On," *History Today*, (March 1985): pp. 48–50.

Bunkers, Suzanne L. "Whose Diary Is It, Anyway? Issues of Agency, Authority, Ownership." *A/B: Auto/Biography Studies*, Volume 17, Number 1 (Summer 2002): pp. 11–27.

Chapkis, Wendy. "The Uncensored Anne Frank," *Ms.*, (October 1986): pp. 79–80.

Cohen, Steven A. *Anne Frank in the World*. Amsterdam: Anne Frank Foundation, 1985.

Frank, Anne. *Dagboek Van Anne Frank: Het Achterhuis*. Amsterdam, The Netherlands: Contact, 1968.

———. *The Works of Anne Frank*. New York: Doubleday, 1959.

———. *Tales from the House Behind*. New York: Bantam, 1966. Paperback edition, New York: Washington Square Press, 1984.

———. *The Diary of a Young Girl*. New York: Simon & Schuster, 1972. (This edited version of the diary includes a Reader's Supplement.)

———. *The Diary of a Young Girl: The Definitive Edition*. New York: Doubleday, 1995. (This unedited version of the diary contains versions [a] and [b].)

———. *Anne Frank's Tales from the Secret Annex*. Garden City, N. Y. Doubleday, 1983. (Contains short stories, essays, memoirs, and an unfinished novel; some previously published.)

Gies, Miep. *Anne Frank Remembered: The Story of the Woman Who Helped to Hide the Frank Family*. New York: Simon & Schuster, 1982.

Goldstein, Judith. "Anne Frank: The Redemptive Myth." *Partisan Review*, Volume 70, Number 1 (Winter 2003): pp. 16–23.

Goodrich, Frances, and Albert Hackett. *The Diary of Anne Frank* (play). New York: Random House, 1956.

Graver, Lawrence. *An Obsession with Anne Frank: Meyer Levin and the Diary*. Berkeley: University of California Press, 1995.

Hurwitz, Johanna. *Anne Frank: Life in Hiding*. Philadephia: Jewish Publication Society, 1989.

Kopf, Hedda Rosner. *Understanding Anne Frank's* The Diary of a Young Girl: *A Student Casebook to Issues, Sources, and Historical Documents*. Westport, Conn.: Greenwood Press, 1997.

Larson, Thomas. "'In Spite of Everything': The Definitive Indefinite Anne Frank." *Antioch Review*, Volume 58, Number 1 (Winter 2000): pp. 40–44.

Lindwer, Willy. *The Last Seven Months of Anne Frank*. New York: Pantheon, 1991.

Manheim, Ralph, and Michel Mok, trans. *Anne Frank's Tales from the Secret Annex*. New York: Doubleday, 1984.

Melnick, Ralph. *The Stolen Legacy of Anne Frank: Meyer Levin, Lillian Hellman, and the Staging of the Diary*. New Haven: Yale University Press, 1997.

Pinsker, Sanford. "Marrying Anne Frank: Modernist Art, the Holocaust, and Mr. Philip Roth," *Holocaust Studies Annual*, Volume 3 (1985): pp. 43–58.

Pratt, Jane. "The Anne Frank We Remember," *McCall's*, (January 1986): p. 72.

Pommer, Henry E. "The Legend and Art of Anne Frank," *Judaism*, Volume 9 (1960): pp. 36–46.

Schnabel, Ernst. *Anne Frank: A Portrait in Courage*. New York: Harcourt, Brace, 1958.

Small, Michael. "Miep Gies, Who Hid Anne Frank, Adds a Coda to the Famous Diary," *People Weekly*, Volume 29, Number 15 (April 18, 1988): p. 123.

Solotaroff-Enzer, Sandra, ed. *Anne Frank: Reflections on Her Life and Legacy*. Urbana: University of Illinois Press, 2000.

Steenmeiher, Anna G., ed., with Otto Frank, and Henri van Praag. *A Tribute to Anne Frank*. Garden City, N. Y.: Doubleday, 1971.

Tebbutt, Susan. "Reverberations of the Anne Frank Diaries in Contemporary German and British Children's Literature: Prepared under the Auspices of the International Research Society for Children's Literature," in *The Presence of the Past in Children's Literature*. Ed. Ann Lawson Lucas. Westport, Conn.: Praeger, 2003, pp. 133–142.

van der Rol, Ruud, and Rian Verhoeven. *Anne Frank: Beyond the Diary: A Photographic Remembrance*. New York: Puffin, 1993.

van Galen Last, Dick. *Anne Frank and After.* Amsterdam: Amsterdam University Press, 1996.

Van Maarsen, Jackqueline. *My Friend Anne Frank.* New York: Vantage, 1996.

Western, Richard D. "The Case for Anne Frank: *The Diary of a Young Girl,*" in *Celebrating Censored Books.* Eds. Nicholas J. Karolides and Lee Burress. ERIC, 1985, pp. 12–14.

Wiebe, Philip. "Anne Frank," *Welt der Arbeit* (World of Work April 29, 1955): p. 3.

Wiesenthal, Simon. "Epilogue to Anne Frank's Diary," in *The Murderers Among Us: The Simon Wiesenthal Memoirs.* Ed. Joseph Wechsberg. New York: McGraw-Hill, 1967, pp. 171–183.

Wilson, Matthew. "The Ghost Writer: Kafka, Het Achterhuis, and History," *Studies in American Jewish Literature,* Volume 10, Number 1 (Spring 1991): pp. 44–53.

Other Media:

Anne Frank Remembered (Videocassette). Sony Pictures Classics, 1995.

The Attic: The Hiding of Anne Frank (Videocassette). Great Britain: Yorkshire Television Enterprises, 1988.

Avenue of the Just (Videocassette). New York: Anti-Defamation League.

The Man Who Hid Anne Frank (Videocassette). Canadian Broadcasting System, 1980.

The World of Anne Frank (Videocassette).Teaneck, N. J.: Ergo Media, Inc., 1987.

Acknowledgments

David Barnouw. "The Authenticity of the Diary." in *The Diary of Anne Frank: The Critical Edition,* edited by David Barnouw and Gerrold van der Stroom, translated by Arnold J. Pomerans and B. M. Mooyaart (London: Viking, 1989): pp. 84–101. Copyright © 1989 David Barnouw. Reprinted by permission of the publisher.

Deborah E. Lipstadt. "Twisting the Truth: *The Diary of Anne Frank.*" From *Denying the Holocaust: The Growing Assault on Truth and Memory* (New York: Free Press, 1993): pp. 229–235, 270–271. Copyright © 1993 Deborah E. Lipstadt. Reprinted by permission of the author.

Shelby Myers-Verhage. "Postmarked from Amsterdam: Anne Frank and Her Iowa Pen Pal." *Palimpsest,* Volume 76, Number 4 (Winter 1995): pp. 152–159. Copyright © 1995 University of Colorado. Reprinted by permission of the publisher.

Rachel Feldhay Brenner. "Writing Herself Against History: Anne Frank's Self-Portrait as a Young Artist." *Modern Judaism,* Volume 16, Number 2 (May 1996): pp. 105–134. Copyright © 1996 Rachel Feldhay Brenner. Reprinted by permission of the author.

Judith Goldstein. "Anne Frank: The Redemptive Myth." *Partisan Review,* Volume 70, Number 1 (December 2003): pp. 16–23. Copyright © 2003 Judith Goldstein. Reprinted by permission of the author.

Nigel A. Caplan. "Revisiting the *Diary:* Rereading Anne Frank's Rewriting." *The Lion and the Unicorn,* Volume 28, Number 1 (January 2004): pp. 77–95. Copyright © 2004 The Johns Hopkins University Press. Reprinted by permission of the publisher.

Pascale Bos. "Reconsidering Anne Frank: Teaching the Diary in Its Historical and Cultural Context." In Hirsh, Marianne and Irene Kacandes, eds., *Teaching the Representation of the Holocaust* (New York: The Modern Language Association, 2004): pp. 348–359. Copyright © 2004 The Modern Language Association. Reprinted by permission of the publisher.

Aimee Pozorski. "How to Tell a True Ghost Story: *The Ghost Writer* and the Case of Anne Frank." In Royal, Derek Parker, ed. *Philip Roth: New Perspectives on an American Author* (Westport, Conn.: Praeger, 2005): pp. 89–102. Copyright © 2005 Greenwood Press. Reprinted by permission of the publisher.

Wayne Howkins. "Finding Meaning in the Diaries of Anne Frank." *Journal of Children's Literature Studies,* Volume 4, Number 3 (July 2007): pp. 113–132. Copyright © 2007 Pied Piper Publishing. Reprinted by permission of the publisher.

Mark M. Anderson. "The Child Victim as Witness to the Holocaust: An American Story?" *Jewish Social Studies: History, Culture, and Society,* Volume 14, Number 1 (Fall 2007): pp. 1–22. Copyright © 2007 Indiana University Press. Reprinted by permission of the publisher.

Index

Adorno, Theodor, 83
Aleichem, Sholom, 61, 63
American Mercury, 14, 16, 31
American Pastoral, 122
Anne Frank: A Hidden Life, 93
Anne Frank Diary—A Hoax?, 16
Anne Frank Foundation, 15, 24
Anne Frank House, 81
Anne Frank Remembered, 78
Anne Frank School (Frankfurt), 22
Anne Frank School (Nuremberg),
　22
*Anne Franks Tagebuch—der grosse
　Schwindel (Anne Frank's Diary—
　The Big Fraud)*, 17
*Anne Franks Tagebuch—eine
　Fälschung (Anne Frank's Diary—A
　Forgery)*, 17
anti-Semitism, 17, 23, 105, 113, 118,
　132, 153, 155
Appelfeld, Aharon, 114
Arendt, Hannah, 67, 159
Aristotelian precepts, 58
Atlanta Jewish Film Festival, 157
Augustine, St., 48
Auschwitz, 30, 41, 47, 75, 78–79, 83,
　127, 135, 147, 150, 152, 155
Austria, 31, 77
　Vienna, 5, 14
Authenticity, 5–25
Babylon, 77

Balzac, Honore de, 126, 133
Barthes, Roland, 125, 128, 130,
　133–136
Baschwitz, 8
Baumgarten, Murray, 116
Becker, Minna, 9, 11, 24
Belgium, 39, 44
Bellette, Amy (character), 113, 115,
　117, 119
Bergen-Belsen, 41, 56, 75, 79, 103,
　116
Bergson, Henri, 60
Berryman, John, 48–49, 88
Bettelheim, Bruno, 47
Bible, 54, 101
Bible Researcher, 16
Bloomgarden, Kermit, 30
Bolkestein, 127, 131, 136, 138–139
Bolkstein, Gerit, 84, 87, 90
Braun, Eva, 6
Brazil
　Buenos Aires, 148
British National Front, 15
Britton, James, 92
Broadway, 42, 120–121, 145
Buchenwald, 146, 154
Buddeberg, Heinrich, 6, 12–13
Bundesgerichtshof (Federal High
　Court), 22

Bundeskriminalamt (the BKA, or
    Federal Criminal Investigation
    Bureau), 23, 33
Bunker Hill Monument, 144
Burlington Hawkeye Gazette, 40–41
Burma, Ian, 76
Bush, George, 156
Buskes, J. J., 8
Butz, Arthur R., 15, 21, 32

Cady (character), 137
Cady's Life, 137
California, 42
    Los Angeles, 42
    Torrance, 16
California Un-American Activities
    Committee, 11
Caplan, Nigel, 128, 137
Carter, Jimmy, 144
Carto, Willis, 16
Cauvern, Isa, 128
Cauvern, Ruth, 8–9
Cavani, Liliana, 151
Celan, Paul, 83, 86, 88
Chambers, Aidan, 129, 131
Chiarello, Barbara, 85, 92
children, 151–152, 159
    as Holocaust victims, 143
"Children of the Holocaust, The",
    155
Chomsky, Noam, 21
Churchill, Windston [sic], 138
CIA, 158
Clinton, Bill, 156
CNN, 156
Cold War, 144, 158
Colorado State University, 38
Columbia University, 38
communism, 144
concentration camps, 97
    memoirs of, 45
Conrad, Joseph, 87
Cosby, Bill, 156

Creation-Apocalypse paradigm, 55
Critical Edition of the Diary, The, 46,
    48
Czechoslovakia, 152

D-Day, 90
Danville Community School (Iowa),
    37
Danville Congregational Church
    (Iowa), 43
Danville Enterprise, 38
Das Tagebuch der Anne Frank, 8–12
*Das Tagebuch der Anne Frank—
    Wahrheit oder Fälschung? (The
    Diary of Anne Frank—Truth or
    Forgery?)*, 18
Days of Remembrance, 144
Death of the Author, The, 33, 125
Dedalus, Nathan (character), 112
Dedalus, Stephen (character), 113
de Jong, Louis, 14
Denmark, 39, 78
Der Spiegel, 8, 21, 24, 33
Des Moines County News, 40
De Telegraaf, 5
*Deutsch-Amerikanische Bürger-
    Zeitung*, 6
Deutsche Reichspartei, 5–6, 8
Deutsche Stimme, 22
De Volkskrant, 22
Diary of Anne Frank, The, 42, 75,
    119, 143, 145
Diary of a Young Girl, The, 37, 120
*Did Six Million Really Die? The
    Truth at Last*, 15, 23, 31
"Die Posaunenstelle" (The Shofar
    Place), 83
Doneson, Judith, 46
Doubleday, 30
Dussel (character), 20
Dutch Republic, 76
Dutch State Forensic Science
    Laboratory, 11, 25, 84

E.T., 150
Eastern Europe, 75
Economic Council Letter, 14
Eichmann, Adolf, 117, 159
England, 30, 159
London, 77
Ergas, 92
Europa Korrespondenz, 5, 14
Europe, 38, 75
euthanasia, 155
Ezrahi, Sidra, 46

Fab, Joe, 157
Farley, Margaret, 64
Farr, Raye, 154
Faurisson, Robert, 18, 20–21, 32
Felderer, Ditlieb, 16, 32
feminism, 131
Fight for Life, The, 133
FilmFest DC, 157
Final Solution, 15, 45, 51, 54–55, 63–64, 71
Fish, Stanley, 134
Flesch, A., 7
Folg og Land, 5
Ford, Harrison, 149
France, 18, 30, 39, 44
Paris, 21, 146
Frank, Annelies Marie (Anne Frank), 5–7, 13–14, 20, 23, 29, 31–32, 41–43, 45–72, 75, 79, 81, 85, 101, 111, 115, 117, 121–122, 145–146, 159
handwriting of, 9
iconization of, 105
pen pal of, 37
Frank, Edith, 54, 91, 137
Frank, Margot Betti, 39–44, 69, 79, 88, 127, 132
Frank, Otto, 6–9, 12–13, 15, 17, 20, 22, 24, 30–32, 39–40, 42, 47, 71, 75, 77, 79, 81, 84, 93, 97, 104–105, 127–128, 132, 134, 139

Frankfurter Allgemeine Zeitung, 10
Freedom Trail, 144
Freud, Sigmund, 49
Fria Ord, 5, 14
Friedman, Carl, 122

Gandi, *[sic]* 138
gas chambers, 21, 147, 149
Geiss, Edgar, 23
genocide, 113, 119, 148–149, 159
Georgia
Atlanta, 157
German Department of Justice, 17
Germany, 17, 30, 39, 44, 75, 77, 79, 149–150, 156, 159
Berlin, 77, 157
Bochum, 17
Bonn, 7
Frankfurt, 17–18, 22
Hamburg, 23
Kiel, 10
Lübeck, 6, 12, 18
Munich, 9
Nuremberg, 22
Odenhausen, 17
Schleswig-Holstein, 6
Stuttgart, 22
Wiesbaden, 23
Woltersdorf uber Buchen, 7
Gestapo, 62
Ghost Writer, The, 47, 111, 116, 119, 121–122
Gides, André, 69
Gies, Henk, 79
Gies, Jan, 9
Gies, Miep, 8–9, 53, 75, 78–80, 84, 127
Gilman, Sandor, 46
God, 147
Goebbels, Joseph, 115
Goeth, Amon (character), 151
Gomperts, Hans, 12
Goodrich, Frances, 106, 120
Gordon, Ken, 122

Gottfried, Barbara, 116
Graver, Lawrence, 46
Great Depression, 43
Gregor (character), 50
Gusdorf, Georges, 63

Hackett, Albert, 7, 11, 106, 120
Hague, The, 77
Hamburg University, 9
Hanks, Tom, 156
Hannelies, 91, 95
Harding, Daniel, 92
Harwood, Richard (pseudonym), 15,
    17, 21, 23
Hasidism, 146
Hawaii
    Pearl Harbor, 40
Hellman, Lillian, 31
Hendry, Teressa, 14, 16, 31
Het Achterhuis (The Secret Annexe),
    14, 20, 50, 56, 85, 87, 92, 96–97,
    137
*Het Dagboek van Anne Frank—een
    vervalsing (The Diary of Anne
    Frank—a Forgery),* 18
Hiltzik, Matthew, 157
Hirsch, Helen (character), 152
historical revisionism, 16
Hitler, Adolf, 77, 90, 144, 148, 150,
    155
Hitler und seine Feldherren (Hitler
    and His Generals), 15
Hitler Youth, 6, 22, 31
Hoax of the Twentieth Century, The,
    15
Hoess, Rudolf, 155
Holland, 30, 89, 133
    Amsterdam, 7, 14, 30, 39, 41, 43,
        75–76, 81, 102, 129, 147
    Ijmuiden, 51
    Rotterdam, 79
Hollandse Schouwburg, 81

Hollywood, 106, 121, 145, 150, 153,
    160
Holocaust, 15, 29, 32, 45, 50, 62,
    69, 71, 76, 81, 86, 112–113, 115,
    119–120, 122, 134, 143, 145, 151,
    154, 156, 158–160
    Americanization of, 106
    awareness of in America, 143
    deniers, 5–25, 29, 47, 153
    education about, 101
    marginalization of, 144
    universalization of, 46
Holocaust, 144, 148, 160
Holocaust Museum, 153, 160
    child visitors to, 154
homosexuals
    Holocaust victims, 155
Hübner, Annemarie, 9–11
humanism, 104

Illinois, 42
In Search, 5
Institute for Historical Review, 16
Institut für Zeitgeschichte, 9
Iowa
    Burlington, 39, 41
    Cedar Falls, 38
    Danville, 37, 40–41, 43
    Des Moines County, 37
    Middletown, 40
Iowa State Department of
    Education, 38
Iowa State Teachers College, 38
Iron Curtain, 80
Irving, David, 15, 17, 24, 33
Iskander, Sylvia, 92
Israel, 80, 144, 149

James, Henry, 113, 115
Japan, 132
Jerusalem, 77
Jesus Christ, 76, 147
Jewish Americans, 144
Jews, 37, 102, 114

European, 144, 153
Orthodox, 157
Joan of Arc, 76
Jones, Indiana (character), 149
Joop ter Heul, 93–94, 137
Journal of Historical Review, 16
Journal of the Association of Former Students, 8
Joyce, James, 113, 115
Judaism, 104
Jurassic Park, 150

Kafka, Franz, 49, 113, 115
Kagle, Steven, 65
Kampfbund Deutscher Soldaten (Combat League of German Soldiers), 22
Kermode, Frank, 54
Kertzer, Adrienne, 86, 95
Kindertransporte, 159
Kitty (character), 51, 58, 62, 67, 85, 93, 137
Kitty, 93
Kosinski, Jerzy, 89
Kreisbauernführer (District Farmers Leader), 7
Kristallnacht, 157
Kronemeijer, Matthijs, 80
Kruif, Paul de, 133
Kuhnt, Werner, 22
Ku Klux Klan, 158

labor camps, 150
Langer, Lawrence, 83, 88, 95
Ledermann, Susanne, 42
Lee, Carol Ann, 128
Lehmann, Sophia, 112
Le Journal d'Anne Frank—est-il authentique? (The Diary of Anne Frank—Is It Authentic?), 18
Levi, Primo, 46, 86
Levin, Meyer, 5–6, 9, 14, 16, 22–23, 30–31, 46, 132

Lewinska, Pelagia, 46
liberalism, 46
Liberal Jewish Synagogue (Amsterdam), 81
Liberty Lobby, 16
Lincoln Memorial, 144
Linenthal, Edward, 145
Loewy, Hanno, 129
Lonoff, E. I. (character), 111, 117
Lübecker Nachrichten, 6

Maarsen, Jacqueline van, 94
Maharajah (character), 150–151
Marxveldt, Cissy van, 93–94, 137–138
Massachusetts
    Boston, 144
Mathews, Birdie, 38, 40, 42
Maus, 122
McCarthy era, 46
Mémoire en défense, 21
Menco, Frieda, 79
Mengele, Josef, 135
"Metamorphosis," 49
MGM, 31
Mielnicki, Michel, 135–136
Milowitz, Steven, 122
Mintz, Alan, 145
Miramax, 156–157
Montessori, 41
multiculturalism, 157
Mythologies, 135

Native Americans, 149
Nausea, 138
Nazi Germany, 16, 116, 154, 159
Nazi Party (NSDAP), 6, 8
Nazis (National Socialism), 13, 16, 29, 37, 40, 51, 77, 80, 97, 103, 143, 145, 147–148, 158
NBC, 144, 149, 156, 160
neo-Nazism, 17
Netherlands, 37, 40, 75, 77–80, 104

Jews in, 105
Rijswijk, 25
Netherlands State Institute for War
    Documentation, 14, 33, 47, 84,
    127
Neue Ordnung, 17
New England, 112
New England Holocaust Memorial,
    144
New Jersey
    Newark, 116
New York, 38, 42
    New York City, 144
    Supreme Court, 31
New Yorker, The, 121, 159
New York Times Book Review, 30
Nielsen, Harald, 5
Night, 143, 146, 148, 160
Nightfather, 122
Night Porter, 151
Noack and Noack, 10–12
Noontide Press, 16
Norway, 5, 31, 39, 156
Novick, Peter, 144
nuclear proliferation, 144

Oberschule zum Dom, 6
O'Brien, Tim, 117, 122
Ockelmann, Dorothea, 9, 11
Operation Shylock, 122
Ozick, Cynthia, 76, 92, 112, 120–
    121

Painted Bird, The, 89
Palestine, 149
Palm Springs International Film
    Festival, 157
Paper Clip Project, 156, 158, 160
    Operation Paper Clip, 158
Paper Clips, 156, 159
Patrimony, 122
Pels, Peter van, 86
Pfeffer, Fritz, 41

Pinker, Sanford, 112
Plank Road School (Iowa), 38
poetry, 83
Poland, 152
    Krakow, 151
    underground, 41
    Warsaw, 143, 149
Postcards from No Man's Land, 129
Pressler, Mirjam, 85, 93
Pulitzer Prize, 31

racism, 102
Radio Oranje, 84
Reader's Digest, 14
*Reichsruf, Wochenzeitung für das
    nationale Deutschland*, 5
Rembrandt, 76
"Remember the Children: Daniel's
    Story", 154
Revere, Paul, 144
Revisionist Conference, 16
Ricoeur, Paul, 45, 49, 54, 72
Righteous Gentiles, 80
Roma, 155
Romania
    Sighet, 147
Romein, Jan, 46
Römer, Ernst, 23–24
Roseman, Mark, 129
Rosenbaum, Thane, 122
Rosenblatt, Louise, 87, 134
Rosenfeld, Alvin, 45, 47, 49, 120
Rosenwald, Lawrence, 60
Roth, Heinz, 13, 17–18, 21, 32
Roth, Philip, 47, 111, 116, 119, 122
Rothberg, Michael, 119
Russell, David, 86

S/Z, 126
SA (storm troopers), 6
sadism, 152
Sarrasine, 126, 133
Sartre, Jean-Paul, 138

Schama, Simon, 76
Schindler, Oskar, 151–152
Schindler's List, 143, 149–150, 153,
    159
Schönborn, E., 22
screenplay, 101
Second Hand Smoke, 122
Seidman, Naomi, 148
Sense of Ending, 54
sexuality
    perverse, 152
Seyss-Inquart, Arthur, 77
Shoah, 136
Sieburg, Friedrich, 10–12
Simon Wiesenthal Center, 42
Sinti, 155
Smith, David, 157
Smith, Martin, 154
Sobihor, 78
Social Democrats, 6
Socialism, 102
Southern Baptists, 158
Spargo, R. Clifton, 119
Spiegelman, Art, 122
Spielberg, Steven, 143, 149, 156, 159
Spotlight, The, 16
SS Viking Division, 5
Star of David, 40
State University of Iowa, 38
Steiner, George, 83
Stewart, Victoria, 89
Stielau, Lothar, 6, 8, 10, 12–13
Streicher, Julius, 115
Stroom, Gerrold van der, 85
Sullivan, Ed, 88
Sweden, 5, 16, 31, 78
Switzerland, 39–40
    Basel, 9, 18, 44

Tales From the Secret Annex, 30, 139
Talmud, 147
Temple of Doom, The, 150–151
Tennessee

Whitwell, 156
Teshima, Darren, 80
Theresienstadt, 143, 155, 159
Things They Carried, The, 117
Third Reich, 39, 55
Tillich, Paul, 59
Todorov, Tzvetan, 49
Tolstoy, Leo, 113
*Tom Sawyers grosses Abenteuer (The
    Adventures of Tom Sawyer)*, 6
"Tower of Faces," 155
Transylvania, 146
Tri-County Institutes, 38
Twilight of the Gods, 151
Typescript II, 9

U.S. Holocaust Memorial Museum,
    80, 84, 143
Un di velt hot geshvign (And the
    World Kept Silent), 148
United States, 30
    refuge for Jews, 144
University of Iowa, 43
University of Lyons, 18
Ursula (saint), 76

van Daan, Mr., 20
van Daan, Mrs., 19, 53, 67
van Daan, Peter, 20
Van Pels, Herman, 41
van Pels, Margot, 140
van Pels, Mrs., 137
van Pels, Peter, 41, 66–67, 91, 94,
    128, 137, 140
Verlag, Fischer, 6
Verrall, Richard, 15
victimization, 102
Vietnam, 21
Visconti, Luchino, 151
Volksverhetzung (incitement of the
    people), 22
Voskuijl, Bep, 9
Vrij Nederland, 13

Wagner, Betty Ann, 39–40, 42–43
Wagner, Juanita, 37, 40, 43
Wappen Verlag, 17
Wapter, Leopold (character), 115–
    116, 121
war on terrorism, 156
"Was Anne Frank's Diary a Hoax?,"
    15, 31
Washington, D.C., 80, 143, 153, 160
Washington Monument, 144
Washington Post, 156
Weinberg, Jeshajahu, 154
Weiss, Karl (character), 149
Weiss family (characters), 148
Weltanschauung, 46, 64
Westerbork, 51, 75
West Germany, 31, 32
*What Do You Think of the Modern
    Young Girl?*, 95
"Who Owns Anne Frank?," 121
Wiesel, Elie, 46, 86, 143, 146–147,
    159
Williams, John, 150
World War I, 16

World War II, 16, 37, 42, 102,
    154
"Writing About Jews," 114

Yad Vashem, 80
Young, James, 47

*Zeitschrift der Vereinigung ehemaliger
    Schüler und der Freunde der
    Oberschule zum Dom e.V. Lübeck*
    (Journal of the Association of
    Former Students and Friends of
    the Lübeck *Oberschule zum Dom*),
    6
Zentralrat der Juden in Deutschland
    (Central Council of German
    Jews), 6
Zionism: The Hidden Tyranny, 16
Zuckerman, Doc (character), 112,
    116, 118
Zuckerman, Nathan (character), 47,
    111, 114, 117, 119, 122
Zuckerman, Sidney, 113
Zusya, 69, 71